Stephen Joseph

Paul Elsam trained at Manchester Polytechnic School of Theatre, and works variously as a teacher, writer, director and actor. He has taught widely, including at the universities of Teesside and Hull, at the Savannah College of Art and Design and at the Academy of Live and Recorded Arts. He holds a doctorate in Drama from the University of Hull and is author of *Acting Characters* (Bloomsbury Methuen Drama, 2006).

Also available from Bloomsbury Methuen Drama

Bertolt Brecht: A Literary Life
Stephen Parker

Ten Ways of Thinking about Samuel Beckett: The Falsetto of Reason
Enoch Brater

John Gielgud: Matinee Idol to Movie Star
Jonathan Croall

Keith Johnstone: A Critical Biography
Theresa Dudeck

Played in Britain: Modern Theatre in 100 Plays
Kate Dorney and Frances Gray

Tales of the Tricycle Theatre
Terry Stoller

Modern British Playwriting: The 1950s
David Pattie

Modern British Playwriting: The 1960s
Steve Nicholson

Modern British Playwriting: The 1970s
Chris Megson

Modern British Playwriting: The 1980s
Jane Milling

Modern British Playwriting: The 1990s
Aleks Sierz

Modern British Playwriting: 2000–2009
Edited by Dan Rebellato

Stephen Joseph

Theatre Pioneer and Provocateur

Paul Elsam

B L O O M S B U R Y

LONDON • NEW DELHI • NEW YORK • SYDNEY

Bloomsbury Methuen Drama

An imprint of Bloomsbury Publishing Plc

50 Bedford Square	1385 Broadway
London	New York
WC1B 3DP	NY 10018
UK	USA

www.bloomsbury.com

Bloomsbury is a registered trade mark of Bloomsbury Publishing Plc

First published 2013, paperback edition published 2014

© Paul Elsam, 2014

British Library Cataloguing-in-Publication Data
A catalogue record for this book is available from the British Library.

ISBN: HB: 978-1-4081-8567-4
PB: 978-1-4725-8671-1
ePDF: 978-1-4725-1550-6
ePUB: 978-1-4081-8537-7

Library of Congress Cataloging-in-Publication Data
Elsam, Paul.
Stephen Joseph: theatre pioneer and provocateur/Paul Elsam.
pages cm
ISBN 978-1-4081-8567-4 (hardback) – ISBN 978-1-4081-8537-7 –
ISBN 978-1-4725-1550-6 1. Joseph, Stephen, 1921–1967–Criticism and interpretation.
2. Arena theater–Great Britain–History–20th century. I. Title.
PN2081.A7E47 2013
792.02'33092–dc23
[B]

2013024814

Typeset by Deanta Global Publishing Services, Chennai, India
Printed and bound in Great Britain

Contents

Foreword

I have in my time given a number of interviews when I've often been asked to comment on and explain the reasons I took this or that choice of action, why I decided to do this rather than that.

Faced with such questions, I have generally taken the easy way out, glibly justifying my decision as being based on shrewd judgement or cool appraisal of the circumstances at that particular stage of my life.

If truth be told though, I suspect like many others that my so-called ordered life has really been comprised of a series of unexpected, unplanned, unforeseen events to which I responded with snap judgements based on nothing more than instinctive gut reaction.

In the midst of all the usual being in the right place at the right time, just occasionally people stepped into my path unannounced, whose help and advice I subsequently gratefully accepted.

These people I have come to think of as my 'guardian aunts and uncles'. Although there was an element of luck in our meeting in the first place, I like to think that at least I had the youthful wit to accept the guidance of these wise interlopers into my life.

One of whom was Stephen Joseph. From our first chaotic meeting (for details of that, please see Chapter Two of this excellent book), over the next 10 years, we were to become close friends. His enthusiasm and vision, combined with an almost scornful disrespect for the theatrical establishment, his anarchic attitude to conventional thinking, and his sheer *dangerousness* made him an irresistible figure to this 17-year old.

There's something deeply exciting at that age to feel you've joined the forefront of a revolution. Though he remained self-contradictory to the end, being neither a playwright (judging from the appalling bits of suggested dialogue he appended to my early scripts) nor a director (rarely in rehearsal and when he was busily involved in rebuilding the auditorium around us) and certainly never an actor (my own experience appearing alongside him in David Campton's *Frankenstein* can endorse that), he could talk lucidly and sensibly about all three, writing, directing and acting better than anyone I have ever known.

I suppose he could be best described as a teacher, but a teacher who threatened at any moment to blow up the classroom. A sentimental cynic or should that read a cynical sentimentalist? A romantic who would never allow anyone too close. A public man with a private heart. I hope that this book will capture for others a little of the charisma and magic of a man for whom I still retain great affection and eternal gratitude.

Sir Alan Ayckbourn, August 2012

Acknowledgements

Thanks to: Richard Boon; Keith Peacock; Stuart Andrews; Tony Meech; Philip Roberts; Simon Murgatroyd; the University of Manchester; the Society for Theatre Research; the British Library; Sir Alan Ayckbourn; Peter Cheeseman; Clive Goodhead; Trevor Griffiths; Walter Hall; David Harris; Ian Hogg; Neville Hunnings; Shirley Jaffe; Sir Ben Kingsley; Harry Landis; Alan Plater; Mark Ravenhill; Heather Stoney; Peter Thomson; Stacey Morley; Jimmy James; Steph Sims; Michael Weller; Faynia Williams; Rodney Wood; Jonathon Petherbridge; Fiona Bannon; Duncan Holt; Martin Dove; Christopher Baugh; Rachel Carroll; Gerda Roper; Ronan Paterson; Sarah O'Brien; Mark Dudgeon; Nick Stafford.

Thanks also to the Scarborough Theatre Trust for permission to use the photographs included in this book.

List of Illustrations

(All photographs – photographer unknown. All are published courtesy of the Scarborough Theatre Trust)

Figure 1 Alan Ayckbourn's *'The Sparrow'*, staged above the library in Scarborough (1967). Courtesy of Scarborough Theatre Trust

Introduction

The Stephen Joseph Theatre is a producing theatre in Scarborough, North Yorkshire, on the northeast coast of England. It's set within the elegant former Odeon cinema, opposite the end-of-the-line railway station, and next to the hotel (now public house) where former Hollywood star Charles Laughton was born in 1899. Yorkshire locals refer to the big theatre building as either 'the SJT' ('Ess Jer Tee') or 'the Ayckbourn theatre'. To a confused few, it is the 'Saint Joseph Theatre'.

Sir Alan Ayckbourn was artistic director there for many years, although he hasn't run the venue since 2009. Stephen Joseph never did run it; his work in Scarborough began and ended decades earlier in rented rooms above the main public library. That first theatre space – long re-established as a concert room – is just a short walk away from the SJT, past the small shops, the bigger pub and the little cafes. A third former adapted professional theatre, the Stephen Joseph Theatre-in-the-Round – long ago returned to use as a college venue – completes a neat triangle which can be walked briskly in 10 minutes. But who is, or was, Stephen Joseph? And why should his name mean anything to students, educators, theatre makers and audiences around the world, in the twenty-first century?

The short answer is that Joseph was a theatre all-rounder who, dying young, left behind him twin gifts: a radical legacy – still there, but now obscured; and a print record of experimentation and provocation – still there, but now little-read. This book offers then illumination: a fresh and deep reappraisal of Joseph's work, and a thorough re-examination of his discoveries. It's my keen hope that ideas examined in this book might provide fresh impetus to the democratization of theatre making – perhaps even helping theatre and performance artists a little further along the road towards a place within the centre of society.

Stephen Joseph's interest in theatre was eclectic, and international. Like few English theatre radicals besides contemporaries Peter Brook and Joan Littlewood, Joseph was quite strongly outward-looking – to the United States, to continental Europe, to the former Soviet Union. He visited all with a practitioner-researcher's eye. Yet not so much like Brook or Littlewood he also took time to record, examine and value theatrical innovation within England.

Beyond Scarborough's 10-minute walking triangle and the SJT website, Stephen Joseph's name is now all but unknown. There are brief entries in some

current theatre encyclopaedias. Theatre historians still sometimes offer a page
or less on a specific Joseph achievement – typically either introducing round
and adaptable theatre to Britain (e.g. Shellard 1999: 129–30), or supplying Sir
Alan Ayckbourn with his first writing commission (e.g. Billington 2007: 201).
So what? The proscenium stage still dominates in London and throughout
the West; and although Ayckbourn became and remains internationally
successful, a generation of British critics and historians has lived and died
branding him merely a populist writer for the middle-classes. Stephen
Joseph's relative absence from modern historical narratives might therefore
seem at least explainable.

Yet there's profound inconsistency in the historical record. As early
as August 1956 – just one year after the Scarborough launch of Studio
Theatre – Michael Barry, the BBC's London-based Head of Drama, was
telling Joseph how '. . . many of us have been conscious, with interest, of
the plucky work you have been doing' (Barry 1956) within fringe theatre.
Eleven years later, a 1967 obituary in London's *The Times* newspaper offered
up Joseph as 'the most successful missionary to work in the English theatre
since the Second World War' (*The Times* 1967). These two intriguing
quotations – and the status of each source – combine to provoke simple
questions. What was Joseph's mission? How did his plucky work change
English theatre, roughly half a century ago? Who are his inheritors, and
what was bequeathed?

The 1950s and 1960s are now regarded as intensely fertile decades for
theatrical innovation; and Joseph's *The Times* obituary clearly locates him as a
key agent for change. Yet the modern historical record only names others as
England's most important innovators and provocateurs. Littlewood, Devine,
Brook, Hall, Osborne, Pinter, Tynan: these, and a disputed few other giants of
mid-to-late-twentieth-century theatre, command recognition with surname
alone. Crucially, these 'giants' each enjoy multiple advocates – within academia,
within theatre criticism, or indeed, within both fields. Stephen Joseph's
constant torchbearer has long been Sir Alan Ayckbourn, a practitioner. More
than half a century after Joseph first employed him as an acting stage manager,
Ayckbourn possesses Olivier, Molière and Tony awards, and a knighthood.
Joseph's protégé mentions him in lectures, workshops, interviews, programme
notes; a 1981 book *Conversations with Ayckbourn* includes a chapter, *The
Joseph Years* (Watson 1981: 35–60), which records in detail Ayckbourn's debt.
Yet he struggles in vain to keep Joseph 'on the map'.

A single recent spark within academia hints at some new thinking.
Simon Shepherd's important 2009 Cambridge text *Modern British Theatre*
opens with a stand-alone photograph of Stephen Joseph's (and Britain's)
first theatre-in-the-round in that room above Scarborough's public library

(Ibid.: xv.). Noting Joseph's 'radical experiment' (Ibid.: 27) in theatre space, Shepherd raises the provocative assertion that 'Joseph's staging initiative may have had a deeper impact on the artistic development of modern theatre than the experiments at the Royal Court' (Ibid.).

So what did Stephen Joseph do that has impacted so hard on modern theatre in the decades since his death? Lots. He launched Studio Theatre Company Limited – better-known at the time as 'Theatre-in-the-Round', based in northern England but also touring to London and beyond. The group is considered by international theatre maker and BBC producer Faynia Williams – a former Studio Theatre member – to be Britain's first community theatre company (Williams 2008). Joseph rescued young playwright Harold Pinter after his critical humiliation in 1958: Pinter agreed to personally redirect _The Birthday Party_, and Joseph later brokered the play's career-saving transfer to television. Royal Shakespeare Company (RSC) director Clifford Williams, whose early RSC productions 'define[d] what became known as a classic RSC style' (Shorter 2005), became a more experimental and design-minimalist director-playwright under Joseph. Joseph hand-picked proscenium theatre director Peter Cheeseman and placed him 'in-the-round' in charge of a radical ensemble theatre group: soon after Cheeseman would invent verbatim theatre and the community-based musical documentary. In fact Joseph's company debuted and supported a spectrum of provocative playwrights, including James Saunders, Alan Plater, David Campton and Alan Ayckbourn. Joseph even helped trigger experimental new writing in the United States through his teaching of New York City-based playwright Michael Weller.

And more. Joseph's tireless advocacy of open stages directly influenced spatial design within radical new theatre building in Britain. The University of Manchester's Stephen Joseph Papers archive records numerous examples of Joseph's generally unpaid design consultancy work, which frequently saw him encouraging people new to theatre. Radical playwright and director Trevor Griffiths was employed as a young college lecturer when he worked briefly with Joseph to adapt a college theatre space: although the two men never met again, Joseph remained one of 'the two most important people in my life, as far as theatre's concerned' (Griffiths 2008). Joseph was also an active designer of theatres: the giant adaptable Nuffield Theatre at Lancaster University – now central to performance experimentation – was designed by him as a 'logical extension' (Taylor 1998: 12) of the black box space he created inside the German Church at the University of Manchester. Joseph's work on theatre space would seem to have paved the way for thrust and adaptable spaces nationwide; in 1996 Alan Ayckbourn stated that 'There are open stages across the country as a result of this extraordinary man' (Ayckbourn 1996).

Joseph's design for the Nuffield space (Joseph 1965) sets a new standard for adaptability: it includes plans for a trapped area, a two-level basement, and four staging options – Elizabethan public playhouse, Globe variant, Proscenium stage and a variant with an orchestra pit. There was even, in the final, realized design, a central rotating stage driven by electricity (Sims 2013). I have included a summary in the Appendix which clarifies what was in the original design, and how and why the space has since been altered.

More still. Joseph co-founded the influential Association of British Theatre Technicians (ABTT) and the Society for Theatre Consultants, and sought links abroad through the Association Internationale de Techniciens de Theatre (AITT). He helped to provoke a seismic expansion and philosophical shift within university drama education in Britain. And he remained a career-long provocateur to the British theatre establishment: his was after all 'the first theatre in England not to play the National Anthem' (Ayckbourn 2007).

At the heart of Stephen Joseph's career-long missionary work was a longstanding, previously unbreachable conundrum: How do you popularize theatregoing when it has been so unpopular for so long? More specifically, how might you attract and keep a new audience for live theatre, when modern English theatre is a minority art form that has been structurally elitist for as long as anyone alive can remember?

Joseph's preferred solution was characteristically simple and direct: start afresh. Find new playwrights who can write entertainingly for the very many who would happily attend a live football match or go to the cinema, but who somehow 'know' theatre is not for them. Build new theatres in a style welcoming to everyone – so, strip away all trappings of hierarchy, from preferential seating, to having to dress up, to forcing audiences into silence for *God Save the Queen*. Banish, in short, the 'old-fashioned bullshit' (Cheeseman 1998: 9–10) within English theatre – onstage, front-of-house and backstage too. Build first, and build fast, in those many places where England's theatrical 'tradition' had yet to divide communities.

English theatre staging in the mid-1950s was startlingly homogeneous. There were no permanent indoor round, thrust or transverse stages; neither were there custom-designed adaptable theatres or 'black box' spaces, either in London or in the regions. Indeed virtually all British theatre – experimental, as well as commercial – was staged proscenium-style – included the work of Joan Littlewood's Theatre Workshop at Stratford East and, from 1956, the English Stage Company at the Royal Court. Both companies embraced a traditional method of staging featuring, in the words of Jerzy Grotowski, 'the stage in one place and the audience in another' (Grotowski 1969). Joseph's missionary campaign was therefore fought on two fronts: first, persuading proscenium theatre traditionalists (on both sides of the arch) to try something genuinely egalitarian and fresh; and second, simultaneously, fighting for a new audience drawn mainly from the lower social classes. At a point when regional theatre was 'taking a beating' (Joseph 1959n: 46) and 'many of our largest cities [were] without a resident professional repertory company' (Ibid.), Joseph's central weapon was a portable theatre: a theatre-in-the-round, with rostra for raked seating, which he toured mainly to theatreless towns across the country. Each visit to a new town would see Joseph reveal a customized model for public display – the 'Penny Theatre' – a miniature building which he claimed could be made real if the local council charged each resident just one penny extra on the council rates. In time, Joseph hoped, there would be a network of self-sustaining theatres-in-the-round; new audiences would join established theatregoers to experience immersive, even transformative live theatre in an intimate setting. Popular theatre would at last reclaim the central place in society that had been lost decades earlier.

This is the tale, then, of a tireless yet conflicted egalitarian who came to realize that his radical yet common-sense ideas might just help democratize Western theatre. It 's the story of the 'half-genius, half-madman' (Yaldren 2005: 41) whose often magnesium-white-flash experiments and provocations – ignited mostly in remote, jerry-built 'garden sheds' far from England's capital – came to bequeath to us a series of free-thinking, practical, yet thoroughly researched texts on excellent theatre making. That Joseph's strangely solitary mission met with such resistance – humiliation, even – that he was driven to despair and an early death; and that his legacy has been so nearly forgotten – are Joseph's twin tragedies. That we should continue to ignore the great depth and startling currency of his discoveries – this, I believe, would be our continuing folly. This book attempts, then, to offer modern theatre makers a way forward: new, yet old.

Stephen Joseph: Timeline

13 June 1921	Michael Stephen Lionel Joseph is born in London to publisher Michael Joseph and entertainer Hermione Gingold
Autumn 1935	sent to Clayesmore School, a rural school with a strong arts curriculum
Autumn 1937	aged 16, begins the acting course at the Central School of Speech and Drama ('Central') as the school's youngest-ever recruit
4 June 1941	joins the British Royal Navy – initially as an Ordinary Seaman
November 1944	engaged in a successful action against German destroyers: awarded the Distinguished Service Cross
January 1946	teaching at Heatherdown School
early 1947	begins English degree at Jesus College, Cambridge; writes and directs for 1947–48 'Footlights' reviews
December 1948	witnesses an amateur touring in-the-round production in Lowestoft
1948–9	directing, acting, and working backstage in repertory theatre – mainly in coastal Lowestoft and Frinton, northeast of London
1949–51	teaching and directing at Central
1951–2	studying playwriting at the University of Iowa; visits theatres across northeastern United States
1952–5	further teaching and directing at Central: students include a young Harold Pinter
1953	leads a student visit to the fourth communist World Festival of Youth and Students in Bucharest, Romania. Begins playwriting evening classes in London
1954	Playwriting workshops continue around the country

1955   leaves Central to launch Studio Theatre. Designs and
                       builds Britain's first professional theatre-in-the-round,
                       in Scarborough

1957   recruits Alan Ayckbourn to a stage management role
                       with Studio Theatre

Autumn 1958   commissions Harold Pinter to direct *The Birthday
                       Party* – a late addition to Studio Theatre's winter tour

1960   increasingly involved in design and consultancy for
                       open stage spaces – including (over several years) at
                       Hampstead, Manchester, Stoke and Lancaster (the
                       Nuffield Theatre)

1961   co-founds the ABTT. Recruits Peter Cheeseman to
                       help develop theatre-in-the-round in the Potteries.
                       Appointed a Fellow at the University of Manchester

1962   opens Stoke's Vic, Britain's first permanent theatre-in-
                       the-round – a cinema conversion built without state
                       funding

1963   publishes *The Story of the Playhouse in England*

1964   publishes *Scene Painting and Stage Design* and (as
                       Editor) *Actor and Architect*. The Society for Theatre
                       Consultants (first proposed by Joseph) is founded

1965   final Joseph-led Scarborough summer season: com-
                       missions and directs the play that becomes *Relatively
                       Speaking*, Alan Ayckbourn's first major West End suc-
                       cess

1967   publishes *Theatre in the Round*

5 October 1967   dies from cancer at home in Scarborough

1968   Joseph's important *New Theatre Forms* is published
                       posthumously

1

Mission

At sea during World War II, the **Captain** *of a British warship stands beside one of his ship's heavy guns. Also with him are* **Stephen Joseph** *and a* **Gunner**. *They watch as an enemy vessel – a suspected German warship – approaches, still some distance away but moving quickly. The British ship's heavy gun is primed for firing.*

Stephen Joseph: Do you want to get the ship or don't you?
Captain *(warily)*: Well of course I want to.
Stephen Joseph: Well, in that case, fire! *(To the* **Gunner***)* FIRE!
(The **Gunner** *fires the gun.)*
Captain *(pulling out his revolver and holding it straight at* **Stephen Joseph***)*: Mutiny, sir!
*(***Stephen Joseph** *is restrained. They watch as the shell lands – a direct hit. The enemy warship starts to sink.)*

Former Studio Theatre employee Terry Lane records this incident, apparently reported by Joseph's step-sister Shirley, which brought him Britain's Distinguished Service Cross (DSC) – awarded despite his ignoring the authority of his own commander. Lane concludes: 'It was mutiny, strictly speaking. Stephen had given orders without permission' (Lane 2006: 57).

Rodney Wood, another former Joseph employee, cites a second, more modest award received for wartime service: Joseph 'jumped into a wintry sea off Scotland to save a puppy, the ship's mascot from drowning' (Wood 1979: 4). Joseph's mother wrote later that he was 'Almost as proud of this as he was of the DSC' (Gingold 1988: 71).

For me, these two incidents highlight three important and recurring themes with Joseph: a keen, at times reckless appetite for risk; a strong and active disrespect for formal authority; and huge confidence in his own plans and ideas.

Alan Ayckbourn, a young acting stage manager, joined Studio Theatre in Scarborough 12 years after the end of the war. Ayckbourn remembers Joseph, the theatre's sole founder, to be

a complete revolutionary, and not loved much by the Establishment –
which for a seventeen-year-old, always made for an interesting guy. –
"Do you want to join up with a bloke so unpopular?" – because perhaps
you'd joined the Revolution (Ayckbourn 2009).

During a 2008 interview with director and verbatim theatre pioneer Peter
Cheeseman, Peter played to me a recording of Stephen Joseph's voice
(Cheeseman 2008). What I heard was a distinct upper-class English accent:
low, clear, expressive and 'posh'. Joseph was to become, in adulthood, an
Establishment outsider; yet a glimpse at his parentage and education suggests
he might actually have claimed lifelong membership. The second son of
successful London publisher Michael Joseph and Hollywood entertainer
Hermione Gingold, Joseph was educated privately before joining the fee-
paying acting course at the Central School of Speech and Drama. After
graduation, and before joining the British Navy in 1941, he was allowed time
to experiment: working for a theatre company, training as an engineer and
teaching at a challenging private school. There were lengthy leisure breaks
too, staying with the wealthy David family in Wales (David 2004).

What can we truly know about someone who is long deceased? Bind
together fragments of a life and we can assert all sorts of things. Stephen
Joseph was a spy. More accurately, a selective appraisal of bits of material
relating to him suggests that Stephen Joseph may have been a spy – perhaps
a James Bond-style secret agent operating internationally. Or even a double
agent, working for Soviet paymasters.

The evidence? Like infamous double agents Guy Burgess and Anthony Blunt,
while at Cambridge University Joseph was a member of the socially exclusive
Pitt Club (Lane 2006: 69). Joseph attended university on a special armed
forces scholarship (Lane 2006: 62). As the Cold War intensified, Joseph led a
trip behind the Iron Curtain to an aggressively pro-Communist international
festival in Bucharest, where anti-Western Korean War veterans were honoured:
high-level pressure in Britain failed to cancel the enterprise (Landis 2007)
and Joseph went on to stage a play – his own – featuring a highly charged
monologue attacking the British government's military intervention abroad
(Joseph 1953). During peacetime Joseph was apparently arrested in France on
suspicion of committing murder: on production of his British passport he was
instantly released (Lane 2006: 67–8). In 1956 Michael Barry – a senior figure
in the stated-owned and intelligence-led British Broadcasting Corporation
(BBC) – noted in a letter that he had heard that Joseph was 'no longer going to
Baghdad' (Barry 1956a). Barry's letter is dated 28 August 1956 – the very day
Egypt expelled two British envoys for spying, during the most dangerous year
of the Suez crisis. Three years earlier Joseph had directed an Egyptian tour of

Seagulls Over Sorrento – a play with a central theme of secret military research (Lane 2006: 103). Joseph's own surviving copy of the play contains a two-sided sheet insert describing strict rules for conduct while 'in the Canal Zone'. Even when running his Scarborough theatre company Joseph was notorious for his sudden disappearances – supposedly to take up hard-to-confirm casual manual work digging roads, or delivering coal. All in all, this is surely an intriguing patchwork of circumstances.

So, was Stephen Joseph a British spy? Or a double-agent working for Soviet paymasters?

Frankly I've no idea. The evidence isn't there – or at least I haven't found it – to convincingly support either case. Instead there's a mix of reported memory, supposition and partial information. The reported arrest by French police, if it happened at all, may simply have been a case of mistaken identity during a walking holiday. Troops abroad need entertainment – especially in potential war zones (though Joseph's planned 1956 trip was to Baghdad, not Egypt; and it was *cancelled*). The Soviet Union did at times seek understanding from foreigners – especially traditionally more left-wing students; and Burgess's and Blunt's membership of the Pitt Club – a society whose members have also, incidentally, included Sir David Frost and two former British kings – predated Joseph's by many years.

When there are few reliable fragments, it's surely unwise for a writer to claim a secure dramatic history for a subject. 'History' – the historical record of what and why things happened in the past – is ever-shifting as new information emerges, and as earlier historians' allegiances are interrogated. A useful word here is 'historiography'. Ironically, there's more than one dictionary definition of the word; here, I use it to mean the active questioning of history. It's surely a useful starting point for scholars and other readers to know that 'history' is an inherently unstable thing. If I'm smart I can persuasively claim at least two versions of Stephen Joseph: Joseph was a spy; Joseph was not a spy. Even oral history – the recording of versions of events offered by people who were there – must be treated with caution: different people who knew Stephen Joseph told me (without prompting) that he was probably homosexual; or heterosexual; or asexual.

It's possible to provide a different narrative on Joseph's work and personality. As a child he was the victim of one of the most high-profile marriage collapses in literary and theatrical London. Both parents were known around the world: stern father Michael Joseph was a major figure in publishing; his eponymous imprint survives to this day. Mother Hermione Gingold was a lifelong performer and Hollywood star, perhaps now remembered most of all for *I Remember It Well*, her bitter-sweet 1958 screen duet with Maurice Chevalier in the MGM musical *Gigi*. We might picture the maturing young

Joseph, darkened by the scale and nature of these mighty twin parental shadows, seeking to find or create his own light. We can surmise much trauma on the way. Gingold admitted to 'no love for my babies' (Gingold 1988: 43), and threw her energy into her career instead. During a family holiday on the Isle of Wight, Michael is said to have reacted to Hermione's affair with a work colleague by beating her 'black and blue with a wooden curtain rod' (Ibid.: 46) before threatening to murder her with a razor (Ibid.). Asked later by her divorcing husband if she wanted custody of their children, Hermione 'said no, he was welcome to them, but I'd like my cat' (Ibid.: 49). A difficult new family adaptation followed: Joseph and his sporty elder brother Leslie joined their father and stepmother in a new home where, Hermione claimed, Joseph 'was not allowed to mention my name at home' (Gingold 1988: 70). Early dispatch to boarding school preceded self-discovery for a 16-year-old acting student at London's Central School of Speech and Drama: young Joseph, feeling perhaps unloved yet entitled, wrote and directed emotionally charged plays and revues that sought to create that personal light and space, but inevitably pulled him back to the dramatic public and private worlds of a mother whom he 'worshipped' (Landis 2008). The final words of Joseph's book *Theatre in the Round* – published in 1967, the year he died aged just 46 – record that 'as the son of Hermione Gingold and the late Michael Joseph, both the theatre and literature are [my] natural heritage' (Joseph 1967: rear dust jacket sleeve note).

So: was Joseph a tailor-made theatrical and literary *enfant terrible* – a 'chip off the old block' launched into theatrical space? Flung northwards by the slingshot effect of disastrous parenting from the famous, and clutching a golden ticket to play? Perhaps. How can we be sure what motivates someone? Harold Pinter characteristically said much in few words in a 2008 interview at the British Library. Prompted to explain an unsolicited invitation from Stephen Joseph to personally direct the career-changing second production of his own play *The Birthday Party*, Pinter paused at length before growling: 'You'd better ask him. But you can't, because he's dead . . . I don't know' (Burton 2008).

Once again the narrative starts to crumble. The popular view that Hermione was a comedy entertainer who 'never played what you might call a real, real part' (Landis 2008) is challenged within her own record: in her pre-Hollywood years she was 'something of a regular' (Gingold 1988: 53) as an actor working within BBC radio drama, often playing 'straight dramatic roles' (Ibid.). She was even part of extreme artistic experiment – a planned radio recording of Jean Cocteau's *Les mariés de la Tour Eiffel*, 'a play scored for two whips, a washboard, and an iron' (Ibid.: 55): rehearsals reached an advanced stage before BBC founder Sir John Reith intervened to cancel the entire project (Ibid.). Perhaps then Hermione was instead a serious artist who led Joseph towards continental experimentation and the avant-garde? Although this sounds unlikely, Gingold did also write 'several plays for the BBC' (Ibid.) including *Tickets, Please*, 'about a theatrical company . . . stranded on tour' (Ibid.).

The strands are intriguing; some match, some don't. I'd like very much to test the detail by returning to each of the key participants and asking them. But I can't, because many are dead – Pinter too, now.

Herewith, then, what I *can* offer: a first scholarly examination – drawing on many cautiously trusted sources, including a series of new interviews – of a radical, influential yet almost entirely forgotten man who, although never entirely a mainstream figure, may one day prove to be Britain's most important post-war theatre maker.

A missionary context: Britain's post-war fringe theatre scene

When Stephen Joseph began his theatre-in-the-round experiment in Scarborough, he was operating firmly within a professional fringe theatre tradition; essentially, 'the fringe' is where he remained until his death in 1967. In Britain, then as now, the fringe theatre movement was active and influential both within and beyond London. During Joseph's lifetime the movement was young and unnamed, important but non-mainstream, constantly evolving. Never especially coherent, its key figures included Joan Littlewood, Ewan MacColl, Terence Gray, John English, Bernard Miles, Faynia Williams and John McGrath.

For fringe theatre makers, experimentation mattered more than commercial success. Small audience sizes were accepted – expected, even. Separated perhaps by as much as united it, this early alternative theatre scene possessed a range of general features that continue today:

- budgets were small
- radical work was staged that was either new, or new to the British stage
- new ways to create new plays were explored
- non-proscenium staging was attempted, typically within adapted non-theatre buildings
- controversial or traditionally non-commercial subjects were tackled

- contrasting styles of acting were investigated
- company models challenged the established hierarchical model

The work of non-mainstream practitioners frequently contained some, occasionally all of these characteristics. The developing fringe tradition could also see companies refresh the work of classical writers including Shakespeare, reshaping meaning for contemporary audiences: Theatre Workshop's 1955 production of Shakespeare's *Richard II* was noted (though broadly disliked) by national critics for its radical divergence from the traditional manner of Shakespeare production seen in a production staged in parallel at London's more mainstream Old Vic Theatre (Shellard 1999: 65–6).

The established narrative within British fringe theatre history broadly dismisses experimental activity in the 1940s and early 1950s, and almost always locates London's Royal Court Theatre as pivotal within Britain's post-1955, post-*Look Back in Anger* theatre revolution. Selective memorializing was taking place almost as quickly as experimentation was occurring. In 1959 Stephen Joseph was goaded into a direct challenge to *Daily Telegraph* critic W. A. Darlington's labelling of the Court as 'the only nursery of national importance' (Darlington 1959a); Darlington's statement ignored Joseph's own radical five-seasons-long touring of in-the-round productions of new plays to the capital. At risk too, it seems, was the very definition of 'experimental': Joseph claimed in 1967 that the term had already 'deteriorated . . . to mean nothing more than the staging of a new play' (Joseph 1968: 71). It's perhaps worth remembering that during this period commercial producers were at times gambling on radical new work: the critically excoriated 1958 debut production of Harold Pinter's *The Birthday Party*, part-funded by Michael Codron, stands as one example.

We might therefore view new work for the English theatre as a spectrum. At one extreme a 'tried and tested' universal subject is revisited by a popular playwright, whose work is staged in a proscenium theatre in central London, in a production featuring famous actors in lead roles. At the other end we might see unknown (though still) professional actors working collaboratively to create material targeted at a specific community, perhaps in a region far from London, in a production given a non-proscenium presentation in an adapted building. The earlier, northern-based ensemble work of Joan Littlewood and Ewan MacColl which preceded the northern-based ensemble work of Stephen Joseph, locates the work of all three theatre figures very much towards the latter end of the spectrum; such activity also prefigures the work of a new wave of fringe experimentalists working beyond the capital, including John McGrath, Faynia Williams, Peter Cheeseman – and Alan Ayckbourn. All were to become known for taking risks with theatre space.

The heart of the mission: Theatre-in-the-round

'Ooh – it's in colour!' – audience member at Scarborough's Library Theatre
(Ayckbourn 2007)

In-the-round staging represents a significant innovation within theatre. Unlike within proscenium theatre, actors and audience are brought together in a single room. Typically there is a central, square-shaped stage. Seats are placed around the stage, sharply raked to ensure good visibility, and there are three or four voms (short for 'vomitoria') which launch the actors onto the stage from between or below the seating. The action takes place mainly on the central stage but can easily spread around the auditorium and also, using sound and lighting, behind and even beneath the seating. In a tall auditorium actors and properties can be lowered from above; in one with under-stage space things and people can snap into view and vanish without warning, sometimes inches from an audience member. While there's no single fourth wall to imagine, actors and audience may collaborate to visualize up to four walls simultaneously. With no hard backdrop there's little scope for projection of still or moving images, although the rear walls of the auditorium (behind the audience) can facilitate limited screening. The main stage can be used for striking or subtle lighting effects; carefully chosen colours and simple gobo effects (such as moonlight through a shaped window) can be especially evocative. Theatre-in-the-round is a communal experience: audience members sit facing the actors onstage, but beyond the stage they can clearly see and sense other audience members and can observe their responses to the performance. Actors too can clearly see and hear audience responses: sudden sharp breaths, sniffing, tutting, small nods and head shakes, gains and losses in concentration, all take place within close proximity to the performer.

Richard Courtney's 1967 book *The Drama Studio* (Courtney 1967), published in the year Stephen Joseph died, offers one pithy summary of the historical development of round theatre outside Britain:

> In Russia early this century, after Meyerhold had experimented with placing scenery in front of the proscenium and arranging exits and entrances through the audience (at about the same time that Pirandello, in Italy, was writing his anti-proscenium trilogy), Okhlopkov staged a May Day spectacle in the square of Irkutsk in 1924. It was on this experience that Okhlopkov based his later Arena and flexible stagings at the Realistic Theatre, Moscow. Then Meyerhold's pupil, Eisenstein, turned the Protecult Theatre into a circus ring to achieve more active audience participation. In the United States, after an initial Arena

performance at the Teachers' College, New York, in 1914, T. Earl Pardoe created a theatre-in-the-round at Brigham Young University in 1922. Later Glenn Hughes' Arena theatre was built at the University of Washington in 1932, Margo Jones's version at Dallas came in 1947, and there were various others (Courtney 1967: 7).

Courtney notes understatedly that 'The English professional theatre realized the possibilities of Arena staging a little later' (Ibid.). He continues:

> After Robert Atkins' Arena productions at the Ring, Blackfriars, before the Second World War, it was not until the late 1950s that further constructive experiments were carried out – by Ann Jellicoe at the Cockpit Theatre Club, by Clement Scott Gilbert at Croydon, and by Stephen Joseph who toured Scarborough and elsewhere with Arena productions and later established a permanent theatre-in-the-round at Stoke-on-Trent (Courtney 1967: 7–8).

In fact Stephen Joseph's own discussion of Ann Jellicoe's Cockpit experiment (Joseph 1968: 40) clarifies that her work was taking place in a thrust format; while Alan Ayckbourn reports that Croydon's short-lived in-the-round Pembroke Theatre was offered first to Joseph, who declined to take it on (Ayckbourn 2007).

Stephen Joseph's own in-the-round work, explored initially in Scarborough, grew quickly to include tours to London and to mainly theatreless towns; in time, a second base was indeed created in Stoke-on-Trent. When Joseph died in 1967, protégés Alan Ayckbourn and Peter Cheeseman became Britain's – indeed Europe's – foremost round theatre experts. Ayckbourn would continue his round theatre work on the Yorkshire coast while 'moonlighting' alongside his full-time post as a Leeds-based BBC radio producer; in 1972 he became Artistic Director in Scarborough. Cheeseman meanwhile established himself at the helm of Staffordshire's increasingly versatile and respected Victoria Theatre.

New building-based in-the-round theatres were emerging in northern England at a rate of roughly one per decade: Bolton Octagon in 1967; Manchester Royal Exchange in 1976; Cheeseman's New Vic Theatre in 1986; Scarborough's third round theatre, the Stephen Joseph Theatre, in 1996. In London in 1991 the new version of Richmond's Orange Tree Theatre opened, with seating for 172. The capital also retains the for-hire Cockpit, adaptable to the round; while the English Lake District has the similarly adaptable Old Laundry touring house in Bowness-on-Windemere. In fact adaptable spaces – especially studio theatre spaces – now proliferate; 'borrowed' spaces are common too. These include Yorkshire's 300-seat in-the-round Mart Theatre, usually a working cattle market but also part of the touring circuit for Halifax-based Northern Broadsides.

Though adaptable spaces can be found throughout mainland Europe, fixed intimate theatres-in-the-round barely exist there. The closest are perhaps the Piccolo Teatro, in Milan – a city that once hosted the tiny transverse Teatro Sant'Erasmo, a space known to Joseph; and the adaptable Andrej Bagar theatre in Nitra, Slovakia which, like London's Young Vic Theatre, features a balcony on all sides. More widespread in northern Europe are permanent large 'circus ring' spaces – used chiefly as winter circus venues, often seating more than a thousand spectators. Similar large adapted round-stage spaces include Sweden's Gaswerk and the Westergasfabriek in Amsterdam. Like London's Roundhouse, such venues are often used for spectacular events including live music concerts; however, these are not spaces within which audience members can connect with ease across an intimate central space.

Promenade theatre remains an experimental form throughout both mainland Europe and the United Kingdom. There is at least one dedicated promenade venue – a theatre in Sibiu, Romania, 'which is completely adaptable for performances such as Purcarete's *Faust*, where the audience moves around the venue over two hours' (Witts 2012). Some years ago London's shape-shifting Bubble Theatre made the bold transition to promenade staging under Artistic Director Jonathon Petherbridge, who had taken over a company which typically staged work endstage, in a round tent. Petherbridge's own early exploration of different styles of staging taught him that the tent 'amplified the difficulty . . . and hid the beauty of nature' (Petherbridge 2010): there were distractions from passing traffic, the cold and rain falling on (and leaking through) the tent roof, while the natural features of landscape and sky remained unseen. Petherbridge 'got rid of the tent' (Ibid.) and replaced it with promenade work 'which allows you to stage a scene in the shape that best stages [it]' (Ibid.): so the company's audience-selected 2010 production of *The Odyssey* moved between endstage, in-the-round and traverse settings. The company's educational work – inspired by the ideas of the American teacher Vivian Gussin Paley – is similarly spatially flexible. Petherbridge cites theatrical influence from his witnessing of in-the-round work staged by both Peter Cheeseman in Stoke-on-Trent and David Thacker (now running Bolton's flexible Octagon Theatre) at the Dukes Playhouse in Lancaster. Incidentally the modern Dukes actually comprises no fewer than three different theatres: a 240-seat in-the-round space, a 313-seat endstage space and a 112-seat traverse space.

Though Stephen Joseph designed large adaptable spaces such as Lancaster's Nuffield Theatre, his greatest enthusiasm was reserved for intimate, fixed-seating theatre-in-the-round spaces intended for an audience of no more than a few hundred people. Here, actor-audience proximity is of central significance; audience hierarchy also. A typical intimate in-the-round auditorium is less hierarchical than a traditional proscenium theatre since, with the audience seated on all four sides, a large number of seats can be fitted in close to the stage. Indeed at the original Studio Theatre base in Scarborough all tickets were priced the same, and no specific seat could be pre-booked. In most round theatres there is no audience circle, and virtually never an upper circle; at the SJT in Scarborough six rows of seating on one level in a single 'room' accommodate as many as 406 people.

The close proximity of actors and audience in an intimate theatre-in-the-round allows for a nuanced, quite naturalistic style of performance. While vocal projection must be maintained, little physical or emotional projection is required. In fact Stephen Joseph's programming rarely included naturalistic work; his preference was for 'more or less epic treatment' (Joseph 1967: 155–6). Joseph's choice of a mainly non-realist repertoire proved that heightened theatricality and stylized performance also works well in-the-round.

Theatre-in-the-round presents unique challenges for designers. Since there is no vertical backdrop, the now-frequent use of giant cinematic projection located against one wall has no place in round theatre. Further, stage furniture has to be limited in scale and quantity to allow the actors free movement around the stage. Award-winning designer Alison Chitty, apprenticed under Peter Cheeseman in Stoke-on-Trent, developed her passion for design minimalism while working in-the-round:

> The potency of a cup of tea in the middle of the stage is phenomenal. You put a pair of specs next to it on the floor – I'm not talking about anything else – and you're beginning to tell a story. (Williams 2005)

It is even possible, when working in-the-round, to entirely remove stage features that might seem crucial in a proscenium theatre. Alan Plater, first commissioned as a playwright by Joseph and Cheeseman, has recalled a 1965 Stoke production of Norman Smithson's new play *The Three Lodgers* in which the action was set simultaneously in neighbouring rooms. The floor of the stage 'was the ground plan of the house . . . there were no walls . . . (yet) it worked like a dream' (Plater 2008).

As pioneers, Stephen Joseph and his company needed to discover the features and the potential of the round stage by trial and error. Joseph first saw live theatre staged in the new format in a December 1948 touring production performed by amateur actors; director Jack Mitchley remembers meeting Joseph for a 'long talk afterwards' (Mitchley 1976). Joseph then went on to visit professional and campus theatres-in-the-round in the United States – including the theatres in Dallas and in Washington, D.C. – before launching his own professional version in the United Kingdom in 1955.

One of Joseph's immediate challenges in 1955 was to help actors and directors discover the differences between acting on a proscenium stage, and acting on an in-the-round stage. He labelled the typical proscenium actor's approach *linear projection* – pushing a performance and characterization outwards in a single broad direction; round theatre acting required *organic projection* – reflecting, Joseph wrote, 'an acceptance by actors that they are three-dimensional figures, occupying three-dimensional space' (Joseph 1968: 40). Joseph's work on acting dynamics is examined in more detail later in this chapter.

Joseph's mission: Early role models

Although much of Joseph's theatre experimentation took place in an empty space, he never claimed to be working in a vacuum. In *New Theatre Forms* (1968) Joseph recalls the work of a range of influential, mainly British innovators. Among these is theatre manager Terence Gray at the Festival Theatre in Cambridge, England. Gray's work, starting in 1926, epitomized 'producer's theatre' (Joseph 1968: 68) – an idea 'rooted in anti-realism [that] resulted in such measures as the abolition of properties in addition to the abolition of the proscenium arch' (Ibid.). Gray's inter-war work at the Festival brought

> a completely fresh approach to the whole business of theatre . . . he invented programmes that could be read in the darkened auditorium, devised new ideas for setting and for lighting, he chose a fantastically wide range of plays, he produced with outrageous originality, and he employed people whose talents soon made them famous (Ibid.).

In *New Theatre Forms* Joseph identifies a second role model. John English's touring Arena Theatre company – exploring thrust, not round theatre – launched in Birmingham shortly after the World War II at a time when 'radio, film and television had all affected the drama, and . . . our concept of the playhouse needed bringing up to date' (Ibid.: 41). The seating tiers from an old circus provided English with the means for a travelling playhouse, which then toured to mainly theatreless towns.

English had 'argued that the theatre of our day had become a minority entertainment, and that we should do something to improve on this' (Ibid.).

English is quoted articulating the view – held also by Joseph – that, after 1956, though

> ... the Royal Court and Theatre Workshop had done valuable work with playwrights ... this work had perforce been carried out in nineteenth-century playhouses which had blunted the effect of the plays. [English] concluded that radical rethinking and replanning were necessary to find a valid theatre form, which would match the fresh work of writers, actors, and directors (Ibid.).

Joseph next summarizes English's philosophy on the actor-audience dynamic. It too matches closely Joseph's own view:

> The reasoning behind the design of the Arena Theatre ran as follows: actors and audience come together to share an occasion. Each group has a contribution to make, so they must be put under a single roof, in the same room; they come together to concentrate on the drama to be recreated, and the drama will therefore be placed in the centre of the room (Joseph 1968: 41).

In fact Joseph only really disagreed with English on the role and status of scenery. English's 'insistence on the importance of the scenic world [led him to devise] a curtain to wrap around the [thrust] stage' (Ibid.: 41). In contrast Joseph was a minimalist: working fully in-the-round, he preferred to retain only essential representational items of setting – all of which were placed onstage in full view of the whole audience.

Though English's Arena Theatre 'had to face all the problems that beset a new venture launched with enthusiasm and too little money' (Ibid.), his initiative achieved some real success:

> [English's theatre] won audiences, and it was exciting for actors and directors to work in. It gradually found a style of its own, characterised by a directness and clarity in interpretation, by visual freshness, simplicity and vigour, and by vocal and physical assurance in the actors. Here was a playhouse that gave everyone an inescapable sense of belonging to the occasion, a playhouse that could take a very wide range of drama and where actors could be at the same time more subtle and more "theatrical". No mean achievement (Ibid.: 41).

And yet. Both Terence Gray and John English conducted their experiments some distance from the London 'scene': Gray in Cambridge, English in Birmingham. Neither would achieve success in the capital; and their continuing efforts drew little interest from the important critics there.

Joseph concluded that 'for the most part the Festival Theatre was ignored and its influence has been slight, perhaps because so many of Gray's ideas were so iconoclastic' (Ibid.: 70). Joseph's posthumously published words carry a degree of introspection: he too felt he had achieved less than hoped. Certainly ABTT co-founder Percy Corry's Foreword in *New Theatre Forms* supports such a view: Corry offered the ailing Joseph the reassurance that his 'innate modesty occasionally misleads him to under-estimate the influence of his liberal casting of pearls' (Joseph 1968: v).

Two other important theatre makers influential for Joseph were to achieve marked success in London. One is all but forgotten. Neither have been previously noted for their influence on Joseph; both were identified to me by Joseph protégé Peter Cheeseman.

The first – writer, broadcaster and social commentator J. B. Priestley – produced 'one of the most important instruments for Stephen' (Cheeseman 2008) in the shape of his 'very important book' (Ibid.) *Theatre Outlook* (Priestley 1947). Published during the year Joseph began study at Cambridge University, Priestley's short 1947 work identified a cultural crisis – what he called '*Now or Never* for the English Theatre' (Ibid.: 14). Priestley's book is a curious hybrid – both a warm-toned and photograph-rich beginner's guide to English theatre and a forum for railing against perceived 'Enemies of the Theatre' (Ibid.: 16). For Priestley there were many enemies: a landed gentry who regarded theatre as simply 'a show of pretty women' (Ibid.: 17); the 'new rich manufacturing class of the Midlands and the North' with its 'puritanical prejudices' (Ibid.); disinterested Westminster politicians; commercial managers who 'insist on moulding the Theatre to their own dreary taste and outlook' (Ibid.); and an ignorant and disingenuous press:

> At least two-thirds of our attempts at dramatic criticism are no longer even honest reporting, show no signs of taste, sensitiveness, or technical knowledge, and are well below the level of the average member of the audience (Ibid.: 18).

Further blame was allocated to a film industry which 'contribute[s] little or nothing, but take[s] away a good deal' (Ibid.: 19). Finally, even playgoers were criticized – for sustaining a culture in which 'half-witted mobs . . . visit theatres only to see film stars in the flesh' (Ibid.: 20).

Theatre Outlook outlines Priestley's radical manifesto on the future of theatre within English society. For him, theatre must 'not be something existing precariously on the edge of the community, but . . . set squarely inside it, in an honoured position' (Ibid.: 53). Priestley's theatre would be 'a place where serious professional men and women, properly trained and equipped, go to work, as surgeons and physicians go to work in a hospital'

(Ibid.) Work 'start[s] with a clean bare stage, solidly set in the community and linked with hundreds of similar sensible organizations, a stage on which something good and true and glowing can be created' (Ibid.). He urges readers to 'Bring order into chaos, remove the obstacles' – stating a conviction that 'we could astonish the world' (Ibid.). In this brave new theatre world, '. . . the artists on the high level will help those below . . . experienced theatre-workers will deliberately move down, to give a lift to the less experienced' (Ibid.: 54). Priestley provocatively notes that such a model is what 'gives the Soviet Union its strength' (Ibid.).

The publication of Priestley's call-to-arms predates by some 8 years Joseph's 1955 launch of Studio Theatre in Scarborough. However it's worth noting that this 1947 battle cry came not from a practicing theatre manager or artistic director, but from a playwright, novelist and social commentator. A dozen years later Joseph entirely failed to persuade Priestley to accept a playwright mentoring position with Studio Theatre: Priestley claimed simply to be 'too much out of the Theatre to appeal to writers' (Priestley 1959).

A second major unrecorded influence on Joseph comes from theatre maker Peter Cotes. Cotes is now only dimly remembered for directing the original 1952 production of *The Mousetrap*, the world's longest-running commercial theatre production. As such, if Cotes retains any sort of theatrical reputation, it is connected with tradition, even conservatism.

Cotes is absent from all modern accounts of English fringe theatre; however, a 1998 obituary in Britain's *Independent* newspaper provokes a rethink. In 1949 Cotes published his ideas on group theatre, after he had created and briefly run his own London fringe company. Cotes is remembered in the carefully worded obituary as 'a kind of pathfinder in what are considered by people who did not live through them to have been the darkest days of British theatre, the 1940s and 1950s' (Benedick 1998). Here was a man who 'struggled hard, and to some extent successfully, to establish in the 1940s and 1950s a group theatre company along the democratic lines of Harold Clurman's famous pre-war American model' (Ibid.). The obituarist further notes – and here we might reflect on Cotes's subsequent near-invisibility – that during Cotes's fringe campaign he 'defied the two most powerful men in the British theatre, the Lord Chamberlain as censor of plays, and Hugh ("Binkie") Beaumont who controlled the fortunes of the West End theatre and the lives of most people who worked for it' (Ibid.).

Cotes's 1949 book *No Star Nonsense* (Cotes 1949) arrived shortly after Stephen Joseph had first experienced theatre-in-the-round (Mitchley 1976), and during the year in which Joseph began teaching at the Central School of Speech and Drama (Wood 1979: 10). As a potential influence it therefore predates by several years the London theatre work of George Devine at the

Royal Court, Peter Hall at the Arts Theatre and Joan Littlewood in London's East End. In fact several of the areas of interest to Cotes would also receive keen attention in Joseph's own subsequent work, including experimentation with group theatre methods, the staging of new writing (for Cotes, at the New Lindsey Theatre Club) and the touring of challenging drama to working-class communities in theatreless towns. Cotes even managed a provocative and turbulent relationship with members of the theatre establishment. Cotes's book – subtitled *A Challenging Declaration of Faith in the Essentials of Tomorrow's Theatre* – offered three related elements: a record of his attempts to change non-commercial theatre making in Britain, a personal manifesto for reshaping English theatre and a template medium for disseminating such ideas.

Cotes's group theatre company seems to have achieved real impact during its brief work in London. The rear dustsheet cover of his book lists a series of reviews by national theatre critics under the title 'Postscript on Teamwork' (Cotes 1949: rear cover): labelled 'excellent' by Harold Hobson (Ibid.), the Peter Cotes Players were described as 'well-balanced and beautifully together' (Ibid.) by W. A. Darlington. Alan Dent from the *News Chronicle* recorded that 'The team-work of the Peter Cotes Players is excellent judged by any standards' (Ibid.).

So what were the ideas that helped to shape Joseph's own vision? Cotes argues in his book that an English group theatre company should sidestep the lure of a possible West End transfer. He focuses on a range of areas, including the role and status of actors (Cotes 1949: 13–27) and directors (Ibid.: 79–95); the 'Group Idea' (Ibid.: 28–38), in which Cotes discusses group theatre initiatives – chiefly ones developed abroad; issues around 'The Audience' (Ibid.: 96); and the role and responsibilities of theatre critics (Ibid.: 106–21). Cotes also reports on his own company's work, including what was then his most celebrated success – a first British production of the provocative American issue-based play *Pick-up Girl* which, despite cuts demanded by the Lord Chamberlain's Office, transferred from a small club theatre to the West End with both cast and script intact (Ibid.: 50–61). Each chapter provides a simple yet provocative analysis of group theatre approaches to creating work within a small, permanent ensemble.

Like northern-based contemporary theatre makers Ewan MacColl and Joan Littlewood, Cotes was involved in taking small-scale work to theatreless communities. Cotes describes in some detail an Arts Council-inspired tour of Wales – 'part of a scheme for taking the classics to the coalfields' (Ibid.: 64) – which saw his company tour to non-theatre spaces with minimal theatre technology: the repertoire comprised Eugene O'Neill's *Anna Christie*, and also J. B. Priestley's *An Inspector Calls*, which Cotes labelled 'propagandist fare' (Ibid.: 70).

Cotes's book contains a number of proposals unfamiliar within a city that, in 1949, had yet to host the move south of Joan Littlewood's Theatre Workshop. In essence Cotes was advocating a group theatre approach, with key features which included:

- privileging the playwright above actors and directors
- encouraging actors to play a range of character types and role sizes, as part of a long-term commitment to company working
- providing a longer rehearsal period (up to 5 weeks) to enable deeper exploration of a script
- holding interviews with actors, rather than 'dog show' (Cotes 1949: 84) auditions which required actors to 'do their party pieces' (Ibid.)
- widening the audience demographic by removing traditions that might alienate first-time theatregoers (Ibid.)

Joseph's mission: A developing manifesto for experimentation

Cotes's model intrigued and inspired Joseph; however, his adoption of it was far from slavish. Peter Thomson, Joseph's former colleague at the University of Manchester, notes that '[Joseph's] ideas were interesting, but they were more interesting because they were his' (Thomson 1977: 2). Importantly, Cotes and Joseph appear to have drawn on very different historical influences: Cotes would have his group theatre members study 'Hazlitt and George Henry Lewes [along with] Kean, Garrick and Mrs. Siddons' (Cotes 1949: 21); Joseph's informal syllabus looked instead to Louis Jouvet, Jacques Copeau, Vsevolod Meyerhold and Max Reinhardt. With regard to theatre space, Peter Cotes was to remain a traditionalist – steadfastly rejecting non-proscenium methods of production, which in his view 'embarrass the playgoer, who is never really carried away, as the actors are too self-conscious to be convincing' (Cotes 1949: 101). Cotes's widely shared belief that 'The magic of make-believe is dispelled the moment the actor steps out of the fourth wall' (Ibid.: 101), led him to conclude that 'Actors and audience, to my way of thinking, should be kept in water-tight compartments' (Ibid.).

The field was left clear, then, for Stephen Joseph to begin experimenting with the dynamics of theatre-in-the-round. Over time, his exploration of the role and experience of those with a presence in four key areas within live theatre – actors, directors, playwrights and audiences – would lead to a series of valuable discoveries.

Experimental area 1: Acting technique

The 'star nonsense' of Cotes's book title – the distorting feature of large-scale theatre which frequently turned plays into star 'vehicles' – was not something that would ever personally trouble Stephen Joseph, since Studio Theatre could almost never afford to employ stars. Despite this – likely, perhaps, because of it – Joseph considered the actor to be the key figure within live theatre. For him, theatre was 'a passionate affair between actor and audience' (Joseph 1967: 124) in which, in open staging, the audience 'wraps itself around the acting area in a metaphorical embrace' (Ibid.).

Joseph's developing views on the centrality of the actor would grow more radical over time. His incomplete 1965 'Prolegomena to a New Dramaturgical Theory' (Wood 1979: 82) even formally advanced the view that 'the play is not, in the theatre, primary creative material but is secondary to the actor' (Ibid.). Joseph was not here advocating a return to star nonsense; rather, at a time when playwrights and directors were the new stars of the English theatre, he was reminding critics that the hundreds of non-famous actors seen nightly on English stages were creators in their own right. Such countercultural thinking could be said to acknowledge – nurture, even – two emerging and important areas of contemporary innovation: the actor as collaborator, including (initially under Peter Cheeseman) as community-focused documentarist and co-author; and the anti-authoritarian Performance movement.

In essence, Stephen Joseph's role within Britain's theatrical landscape was as a practitioner-researcher. His writing on, for example, the skill of acting shows how experimentation – combined with close attention, and with careful reflection over a long period – can lead to insightful, accessible and generally applicable results. Joseph's evolving theory on acting delineates two discrete modes of performance projection used by actors in response to their surroundings. 'Linear' (Joseph 1968: 40) projection – initially dubbed by Joseph 'forced' (Joseph 1959k: 1) acting, and later described by Peter Cheeseman as 'mono-directional theatre' (Giannachi and Luckhurst 1999: 13) – describes the performer-to-audience dynamic that is typically present within productions in proscenium or endstage theatres, where the audience is gathered beyond the imaginary fourth wall of the proscenium arch or stage edge. Joseph noted that linear projection is 'possible even on a small thrust stage' (Joseph 1968: 38–9) – adding dryly that 'however inappropriate it may be, it is what actors and critics recognise as "acting"' (Ibid.).

The second mode of performance – 'organic' (Ibid.: 40) projection – requires actors to recognize and accept that they are three-dimensional figures working within three-dimensional space – 'and it expects the audience to subscribe to this notion' (Ibid.: 65). Organic projection is experienced at its most natural and effective in an intimate theatre-in-the-round, where it would be unhelpful for two or more actors to project their performances in a single direction.

For actors experienced only in proscenium or endstage performance – which meant almost all British professionals working during Stephen Joseph's lifetime – the shift from linear to organic projection could be both challenging and highly rewarding. A new approach was required. Former Studio Theatre actor David Harris recalls Joseph's advice to 'start at a level which is quite low, in terms of the acting dynamic, so that the audience will almost imperceptibly lean forward [as if to say] "What was that?"' (Harris 2007). Actor Walter Hall recalls that 'you were so close to your audience that you didn't need to project . . . therefore you could act, as it were, as you would in television or film' (Hall 2007). Actor Heather Stoney had accompanied Peter Cheeseman from a proscenium theatre at Derby to an in-the-round theatre at Stoke-on-Trent, and recalls the transition as 'alarming – [though] it was funny how quickly you got used to it' (Stoney 2007). Stoney remembers realizing that 'you were concentrated and you were "in the moment", and I really rather liked this . . . I started to work in a completely different way' (Stoney 2007). Ben Kingsley, 'learning basic skills in that classic Stephen Joseph arena of theatre in-the-round' (Kingsley 2008), has stressed how 'we didn't cheat the audience – there was no hiding place' (Ibid.). Kingsley also recalls that, in-the-round,

> There were no ghastly tricks – like trying to upstage your fellow actor, or fiddling around with a prop to get the audience's attention. I discovered all this appalling behaviour [later] in the proscenium arch days (Ibid.).

Joseph was to make an important discovery in relation to a longstanding twin theatrical conundrum. Within proscenium, endstage and thrust formats there had always been an ineluctable imbalance of status between onstage actors; further, it had always proved impossible for actors performing in these staging formats to sustain persuasively authentic onstage naturalism. Joseph realized that such problems existed only when organic projection was impossible: place skilful, responsive actors on an intimate in-the-round stage, and the problems vanish. The key, Joseph realized, was simply to nurture in actors a commitment to organic projection as a feature of ensemble performance:

> At times the reactions of one character will illuminate the intentions of another. Such playing is valued on any stage, but it is particularly useful on the centre [i.e. theatre-in-the-round] stage. It even gives a special responsibility to those confidants, usually considered such dreary parts, in French classical tragedy. Action and reaction, the free

use of the whole acting area for the actors to create three-dimensional images, this is the beginning of organic projection (Joseph 1968: 37).

Joseph's earliest professional in-the-round experimentation provoked con-demnation from national theatre critics. The first production in Studio Theatre's 1955 debut season – Eleanor D. Glaser's *Circle of Love* – prompted John Shrapnel in The *Guardian* to dismiss the '"realistic" triviality . . . likely to lead to a flatness unequalled even in the ordinary theatre of our time' (Shrapnel 1955). Interestingly, despite Shrapnel's cynicism towards in-the-round staging, he recorded too an 'embarrassing feeling that we were eavesdropping on actuality' (Ibid.) – a sign, perhaps, that as a theatregoer he was experiencing for the first time moments of authentic psychological immersion.

Shrapnel's words were not however meant to flatter; and soon other, bigger critics joined in. Kenneth Tynan lambasted the 'extremely dubious . . . aesthetic advantages' (Tynan 1956) of Joseph's chosen staging method – demanding to know 'what conceivable purpose' (Ibid.) could justify a form in which audiences were obliged to surround the actors. In fact the public argument was to remain at a frustratingly basic level: Joseph pleads in his final book for a simple acknowledgement 'that actors, like the rest of us, have backs; and, incidentally, what goes on behind a person's back may be fascinating to watch' (Joseph 1968: 65). He offers the counter-argument that, surely, an audience member new to proscenium theatre needs some preparation 'to meet an ocean of heads between him and the actors' (Ibid.: 66).

Despite critical opprobrium, Joseph was to persevere in his experimen-tation, and he and his team would learn much about the subtleties of acting in-the-round: this despite Joseph's own professed disinterest in onstage realism. Joseph began to examine ways in which characters' shifting psychological states might be expressed realistically through actors' movement onstage. Alan Ayckbourn remembers Joseph saying in rehearsal, ' "Look, if you feel uncertain about this person, don't present to them full on. Go slightly sideways. If you don't like them at all, try [turning] the back" ' (Ayckbourn 2007).

After more than a decade of professional experimentation, Joseph came to the radical conclusion that 'a central stage does not necessitate a single meaningless move from any actor' (Joseph 1967: 125). Writing in his 1967 book *Theatre in the Round*, he further asserted that in the new format

The actor has at his command what is almost a new vocabulary of subtle gestures. His least expression is crystal clear to the audience. His motives and intentions are transparent even through his very back (Ibid.).

Joseph concludes that 'There is nothing new here, merely the omission of any thought of a linear projection' (Ibid.: 126). Thus, for the first time in any medium – theatre, film, television, even radio – the actor was freed from the psychological and practical need to turn their performance in one particular direction.

The dynamics of interpersonal movement for actors are discussed further, and in some detail, in Joseph's *Theatre in the Round* (Ibid.: 123–9).

Experimental area 2: A new approach to directing

Peter Cotes claimed somewhat bafflingly that 'Even though the group system, in direct opposition to the star system, is tantamount to democracy in the theatre, it still has a place for a dictator' (Cotes 1949: 34). Cotes's benign dictator was the director – someone who 'commences [rehearsals] with a complete knowledge of the play as a whole' (Ibid.), guiding actors to performances 'of which they would be incapable if left to their own devices' (Ibid.: 87). Simon Shepherd notes that such potentially infantilizing approaches that 'did not share the work of creation with the actor' (Shepherd 2009: 105) were common even among experimental directors: Michel Saint Denis 'arrived for rehearsals for Obey's *Noah* with all the positions and moves worked out' (Ibid.); George Devine habitually 'prepared an "annotated prompt copy" before rehearsals' (Ibid.).

A director working with actors on a proscenium, end- or thrust stage will eventually settle on a blocking arrangement that optimizes 'linear' actor-audience communication. The director functions at least in part as a stand-in for the audience; sightline and technology choices must privilege the audience's view of the stage. Even a theatre collective such as Joint Stock, which from its beginnings in 1974 engaged performers in a partial devising process, needed to 'choose to allocate power to a director' (Ibid.: 74). As a consequence 'not very confident' (Walter 2003: 49) actor-members who disagreed with the direction of a project, might still simply 'let things ride' (Ibid.). There is an inherent and unavoidable inequality here: Alan Ayckbourn has noted that non-round staging will always need 'the grand figure at the back of the stalls going, "don't do that!"' (Ayckbourn 2007).

By contrast, Stephen Joseph quickly discovered the near-redundancy of the in-the-round director's role in relation to blocking actors' movements. Quite simply, if you build a stage picture that works for just one section of a theatre-in-the-round audience, you have simultaneously damaged the scene for those sat opposite, or to one side. Joseph advised Peter Cheeseman that round theatre 'is structured like life, and that consequently movement organises itself like it does in real life' (Giannachi and Luckhurst 1999: 14).

Joseph quickly became known among Studio Theatre actors for a non-directive and, at its best, a highly collaborative approach to rehearsal. However at times Joseph's non-interventionism could be extreme; indeed Peter Cheeseman considers that Joseph 'used to get really bored in rehearsal, it was a joke' (Cheeseman 1998: 2). Faynia Williams concluded that 'You couldn't rely on him doing the work for you' (Williams 2008); indeed 'a whole rehearsal could go and [Joseph] wouldn't look up from his magazine' (Ibid.). Williams adds however that 'if you gave him something, he was with you for twenty four hours or however long was needed, and he would really then give you so much . . . it gradually gave me an awareness, actually, which wasn't about me. You know, it was about the work' (Ibid.).

Joseph's unstructured approach to direction extended to his preparation before rehearsal. An unreferenced Joseph quotation from his period at the University of Manchester suggests a radical approach to the role of director:

1. Open mind. Don't read the play. Listen to and watch the actors.
2. Independent exercises in physical range control, imaginative expression.
3. Never tell the actor how to say a line, where or how to move. Advise when asked, enlarge don't limit, say it five different ways.
4. Seven full dress rehearsals. (Lane 2006: 187)

Joseph was an experienced director; yet his conceptualizing of organic acting seems to have led him to downgrade the status of the director to that of a type of support worker for the actors who, given the right circumstances, would instinctively provide the responses needed to bring a script to life. Joseph (using here the older term 'producer' to describe a role that is now referred to as 'director') summarized that

> The producer's main task is to feel his [sic] way into a fresh relationship with his actors. If he makes a success of this, he will get good performances from them. Between this and conventional production it is a question of balances, slight shifts of emphasis, some of which are obvious and some so subtle as to defy cold print (Joseph 1967: 124).

Above all, then, the director should be skilled in working with people. Alan Ayckbourn has recalled Joseph 'saying to me, "Directing is very, very easy. It's the art of creating an atmosphere in which an actor can feel free to create"' (Ayckbourn 2007).

How is all this significant? Joseph was working as a professional director – often with new plays and new playwrights – at a time when 'directing was itself a mode of writing' (Shepherd 2009: 104). The Royal Court Theatre was hosting the emergence of 'defined teams of directors and [new] writers'

(Ibid.): John Dexter and Arnold Wesker, Lindsay Anderson and David Storey, William Gaskill and Edward Bond. Yet Stephen Joseph's delineation of the responsibilities of a director in rehearsal falls very far short of the image of an envisioning, interventionist insider-figure who could set free the work of an individual playwright:

> The producer's job, then, is to pay attention to all the many technical matters that help the actor in his performance. He should co-ordinate the diverse elements of costume and stage lighting, of publicity and work schedules, and above all should promote this team-work and this special relationship between actors and audience (Joseph 1967: 124).

For Joseph, then, the director – a figure increasingly omnipotent within English theatre – essentially needed to facilitate: to get out of the way of the actors and to help others do the same.

Over time the 'somewhat older method' (Shepherd 2009: 105) employed by directors including Michel Saint Denis and George Devine has given way to a more playful, less interventionist approach. Joseph's profound redefinition of the director's role may actually have contributed to the emergence of a very different type of contemporary British director, such as Complicité's Simon McBurney, who creates a 'playground' (Ibid.) from which ideas 'emerge organically' (Ibid.). Indeed even in the field of devised theatre, Joseph may have been an early influence. As early as 1959 Joseph was actively seeking to create plays which were unscripted; in January that year he wrote to the office of the Lord Chamberlain, Britain's theatre censor, sharing the thought that 'we have been feeling our way towards a more creative form of presentation. The next step we wish to take is this – improvisation from a synopsis . . . there will never be any fixed script' (Joseph 1959o). The response was unequivocal – Joseph was told that, Commedia dell'Arte traditions notwithstanding, 'unless you produce your improvisations in circumstances where the Theatres Act 1843 does not apply, you will be breaking the law' (Lord Chamberlain 1959); nevertheless Joseph's 1959 enquiry highlights that just 4 years after creating Studio Theatre, he was beginning to think quite differently about the role of the director – and about writing for the stage.

Experimental area 3: Playwrights and playwriting

Peter Cotes and Stephen Joseph disagreed on the relative status of each of the three indispensable non-audience figures within live theatre – actor, director and playwright. Cotes – curiously attracted to hierarchy throughout his personal vision of group theatre – dubbed the playwright 'the king [sic] in the theatre . . . he is the artistic creator before whom we should all bow' (Cotes 1949: 31). Cotes's belief was motivated by a desire to overturn a star system which, at its most extreme, saw audiences 'pay to see a star personality performing her [sic] tricks in a play made to measure by a dramatist who had been commissioned to write a suitable vehicle' (Ibid.). Cotes's director would be 'the author's high priest [whose] sole aim is to serve the playwright by interpreting his work to playgoers by means of the players at his disposal' (Ibid.: 33).

Cotes was responding here to the plight of 'The poor playwright . . . barred from the theatre during rehearsals' (Ibid.: 32) before being admitted 'to the dress rehearsal, when his protests are soon silenced by the inevitable fact that it is too late to do anything about them' (Ibid.). Alan Ayckbourn remembers witnessing such hostility towards a writer when he was stage managing at the Oxford Playhouse in 1957: the management 'conspired to keep the bugger out – kept misinforming him as to when it was going on. There was a sort of place for writers, and it wasn't in the rehearsal room' (Ayckbourn 2007).

Ayckbourn had a comparable experience as a playwright when his comic play *Mr Whatnot* transferred, in radically altered form, from the Victoria Theatre at Stoke-on-Trent to the West End, with a new (commercial) producer, new director, new designer and a mostly new cast. The transformed production was a piece that had 'grow[n] out of a small regional concept' (Ayckbourn 2010); the West End version remains with Ayckbourn as 'like a grossly-overdressed Christmas tree that fell over' (Ibid.). For Ayckbourn, the production's 'critical drubbing' (Ayckbourn *in* Watson 1981: 73) was 'cushioned by the fact that I sort of knew it was going to happen' (Ibid.): even so the experience – which occurred beyond the reach of mentor Stephen Joseph – 'was enough to stop me writing for quite a long time' (Ayckbourn *in* Watson 1981: 73).

Joseph's interest in plays, and his support for playwrights, is examined in some detail later in this book.

Experimental area 4: Reaching new audiences

The drive to bring in new audiences was a central concern for both Peter Cotes and Stephen Joseph. In *No Star Nonsense* Cotes summarizes the plight of poorer theatregoing audiences before 1949:

> When they are finally admitted they are hardly *welcomed* into the theatre. Their money is snatched from them at the box-office and after

toiling up endless stairs to their uncomfortable perch in the gallery they are relieved of sixpence by the programme girl for the privilege of learning the names of the characters, the actors who play them and the synopsis of scenery (Cotes 1949: 97).

Much of Studio Theatre's work was a response to the unchanging nature of the situation described by Cotes. There was an ongoing need 'to break down the formality of the boundaries' (Ayckbourn 2007) – between actors and audience, but also between different audience members. Alan Ayckbourn recalls that in Scarborough there were 'no reserved seats' (Ibid.), and that each fixed-price ticket entitled the customer to a free programme, free coffee and cake, plus a nightly post-show 'chance to meet the actors' (Ibid.). During the summer of 1959 Joseph even successfully lobbied the Arts Council to provide a small travel subsidy to allow poorer theatregoers to use public transport to reach the theatre (Joseph 1959m).

Yet audience apartheid remained – indeed, remains – a central feature within England's ubiquitous large proscenium theatres. Stephen Joseph notes in *New Theatre Forms* how proscenium theatres typically

present a quite different performance to people in the front rows and to people in the back. . . . Even the small court theatres of eighteenth-century Europe do not provide an equally good view to all spectators. Indeed they were positively intended for the opposite purpose: to provide one seat and one seat only with a perfect viewpoint (*New Theatre Forms* 1968: 64).

Such sightline problems were also present within the emerging thrust stage auditoria. Joseph makes the obvious yet still-valid point that 'if the thrust stage is to make any sense at all, there must be no feeling that the seats at either side are not so good as those centrally placed' (Ibid.: 56). Although auditorium design can play a vital role in democratizing theatre-going, Joseph observes that 'theatre directors are as liable to be casual about sightlines as theatre architects: certainly in England you could support the thesis that only a few privileged people are meant to see and hear a play properly' (Ibid.: 64).

Joseph revisits the theme of hierarchy in a discussion on Elizabethan playhouses. Such spaces were now being dismissed, he noted, as epitomizing socially stratified seating – despite the close-up exposure of 'less educated playgoers [to] the full impact of the actor's performance' (Joseph 1968: 115). Yet designers' modern response to Elizabethan playhouses often simply increased the sense of hierarchy:

. . . mid-century democratic feeling abhors circles and galleries which it takes to be the signs of social stratification. Trust mid-century democracy to worry about removing signs while taking little trouble to remove the abhorrent thing itself, and to misunderstand the signs anyhow! (Ibid.)

Bite the bullet, Joseph seems to be urging, and start building genuinely egalitarian spaces that locate audiences equally around a central stage. Joseph next lambasts the inequality of ticket pricing policies within proscenium theatres – including those run by radical theatre makers who long for a non-hierarchical theatre:

> Their tendency is to have the smartest seats in the stalls, and the cheapest accommodation in the farthest reaches of the gallery. Students and working people get a diluted impression of the play, which may help to account for the fact that they mostly watch television rather than go to the theatre. The efforts of a Joan Littlewood or an Arnold Wesker to take drama to the people might be reinforced by allowing such people to get a good look at the drama for a change (Ibid.).

In fact the need for clear communication between actors and audience, and the importance of audience comfort, were to become key features within Joseph's fresh vision for theatre. Since everyone was welcome, audiences would include people unfamiliar with even the basic unwritten rules of behaviour in the theatre; some television viewers and cinema-goers, for example. Joseph muses on this in a 1959 article for *Theatre World*:

> Have you ever asked yourself what the theatre can do that the cinema and the TV cannot? Worry it out. In the end you'll remember that the theatre has live actors who are responsive to a live audience and vice versa. You can eat fish and chips through a TV show. You can switch off. They go on acting just the same. You can cuddle your girl friend at the flicks. They go on acting just the same. In the theatre, actors feel the response of the audience. Every performance is a unique work of creation, a work of art made by the audience and those actors at this moment in time. So to hell with the scenery that the films can do so much better! To hell with the frame that protects the cathode ray tube! Let's have the actors in the same room as the audience, let's have four front rows, let's get really excited about this acting business! (Joseph 1959n: 46–50).

Writing years later in *New Theatre Forms*, and adopting the now-familiar role of iconoclast, Joseph would challenge the English theatre establishment's sticking-plaster responses to class division – proposing instead that 'subsidies spent on sending out touring units from, say, the Royal Shakespeare Theatre to factories might be better spent on putting your factory-hand where he can properly see a play in the theatre itself' (Joseph 1968: 115). He added caustically: 'Even in twentieth-century democratic England, such a procedure might upset the privileged stallholder' (Ibid.).

Experimental area 5: The problem of subsidy

The privileged status of Joseph's proscenium stallholders – and the increasing use of government subsidy to keep them there – was something that bothered him throughout his career. He came to believe that subsidy was

> being used to fossilise out-of-date notions of theatre and to ensure that what happens on stage can never be more than a nostalgic, harmless, and indulgent ceremony to attract the middle-class, middle-aged and middle-brow sector of a sleepy society (Ibid.: 124).

The complaint was in part personal, since Arts Council funding for Studio Theatre's experimental work began low and would remain so. While Joan Littlewood's Theatre Workshop received just £500 for their 1955–56 season, and the Royal Court garnered £9,500 (Billington 2007: 76), Studio Theatre's combined 1956 summer season and national touring schedule (including to London) received a mere £250 (Lane 2006: 143). In 1959, 4 years on from Studio Theatre's launch, Joseph had to make a personal payment of £776 to keep the company solvent (Baker 1960). He was not, though, the sole donor that year: £1,291 was forthcoming from regional local authorities, £750 from Independent Television (Arts Council 1959) and £900 from the Pilgrim Trust Fund (Baker 1960).

Joseph may have felt that his lack of reliance on Arts Council funding empowered him to openly criticize those who controlled government theatre budgets. It's hard, in truth, to believe that such criticism did him anything but harm. His 1961 attack on the 'absolute idiocy . . . of the Government's fiscal policy' (Joseph 1961a: 70) sealed the collapse of state funding for his proposed custom-built theatre-in-the-round in the Potteries; astonishingly, the building of Joseph's Plan B venue – Stoke's 'Vic', Britain's first-ever permanent adapted theatre-in-the-round – received no national publicity, and not one penny of state funding. (Issues around this are explored in Chapter Five of this book). The funding gap was filled instead by individuals and organizations, including Granada TV and Merseyside Unity Theatre, Margaret Rawlings and William Elmhirst, and local amateurs (Lane 2006: 171).

Yet once again, Joseph's 'outsider' status seems to have provided him with a unique perspective. Writing in *New Theatre Forms* at the end of his career, he records:

> I am shocked by the dependence of so many theatres in England on subsidy. For the most part, subsidy as at present distributed does not support artistic endeavour so much as underwrite extravagance, waste and indolence in our theatre: the vices, one might have thought, of the commercial theatre. I might even tolerate extravagance if there were any indication that it has a byproduct of creativity, or waste if it were a necessary part of originality, or indolence if it were essential to the dramatic temperament. But no such thing. Our standards of presentation and performance are too low to give much sign of having been helped by subsidy (Joseph 1968: 123).

From a twenty-first-century perspective, Joseph's views on public funding might seem problematical – in tune, arguably, with the type of aggressive right-wing policymaking applied years later in Britain. The three-pronged work of the Thatcher administration – cutting state subsidy for theatres, demanding business efficiency 'improvements' and insisting on a shift to private sponsorship – led quickly to the extinction of numerous companies, many of which were experimental and politically left-wing (Shellard 1999: 188). It's worth remembering however that Joseph's warning to 'aggressive' (Joseph 1968: 71) theatre makers to 'plan without [state subsidy]' (ibid.: 124) was something he had broadly managed to do – including, most spectacularly, when creating Stoke's Vic Theatre. He wanted more, not less, live theatre – believing that 'every town with a population of 50,000 or more ought to have its own professional theatre [that] should be able to prosper . . . without subsidy' (Ibid.: 123). Nevertheless Joseph – arguably predicting the explosion in community and agitprop theatre in the years following his death – urged that 'when public money must be accounted for and when there is comparatively little money to give away for the purpose of promoting drama, the most deserving companies are the smaller ones, the pioneering ones and the experimental ones' (Ibid.). The larger public theatre venues – including, implicitly, the National Theatre and the Royal Shakespeare Company (RSC), already garnering between them a substantial slice of the Arts Council's budget – were now targets. Joseph suggested that 'If a long-established, big company, in a major city, cannot pay its way, then it probably does not deserve subsidy, and should be the first candidate for closure in any rational scheme' (Joseph 1968: 123). A little under two decades after Joseph wrote this, Arts Council theatre funding had reached a point at which the National Theatre and the RSC were together 'devour[ing] 47 per cent of the budget' (Shellard 1999: 189).

In the mid-1950s, however, so much of this was still to come. Joseph was on a mission; to that end he had created the experimental Studio Theatre company and was busy teaching, writing, consulting, designing. Increasingly aware that his work was unique – and aware, too, that no important critic had yet come forward to support his missionary cause – he began to ponder how his discoveries might be taken forward.

Publishing the research: The Joseph books

What's the best way for a missionary theatre maker to spread their message? For many years Joseph favoured demonstration. He toured new plays to makeshift theatres-in-the-round in theatreless towns, mounting in each location a photographic and model display of a possible low-cost theatre-in-the-round. He provided workshop demonstrations to a wide variety of community groups, including the Women's Institute. He also lobbied – writing articles, letters, reviews and copy for free programmes; and he taught – including through frequent evening classes and summer residential courses.

During the last 5 years of Joseph's life, his evangelizing became increasingly channelled into formal book-length publications. Such work served both to record his personal vision for the future of Western theatre, and to archive his own ongoing praxis.

Figure 2 Studio Theatre demonstration rehearsal for the Women's Institute. Courtesy of Scarborough Theatre Trust

Joseph's general writing style is conversational, and also forthright – especially in his criticism of authority. Each new book expands his survey of professional theatre. The posthumously published *New Theatre Forms* (1968) completes an uncompromising manifesto for change, drawing on two decades of experimentation.

Joseph's missionary ambitions can be glimpsed in his first full-length offering, *The Story of the Playhouse in England* (Joseph 1963a). Here he seeks explicitly to 'show how rich and various a past our theatre has had, in the hope that we can get ideas for restoring vitality to it in the future' (Ibid.: 2). Aimed mainly at younger readers, Joseph's analysis contains provocative assertions and revisions, including a discussion of why theatre-in-the-round is 'particularly important' (Ibid.: 143). Joseph also attempts to re-insert playwright John Whiting into the narrative of British theatre; Whiting's play *Saint's Day* is identified as 'anticipating' (Ibid.: 131) the emergence of 'the new dramatists [through] *Look Back in Anger*' (Ibid.). Joseph even labels Whiting's play 'more original in its technique and more typical of the new style' (Ibid.: 131) than Osborne's play. Despite such provocation, the more openly confrontational style that peppers Joseph's later published works is almost entirely absent from this first book.

The next publication was the Joseph-edited *Actor and Architect* (Joseph 1964e), a 1964 text summarizing a Manchester University conference with the same title. Contributors – all innovative theatre makers, many working outside the proscenium theatre frame – included: internationally renowned director Tyrone Guthrie, whose Minneapolis thrust space would open the following year; Sean Kenny, known for his high-profile work in exploring ways of 'making the transformation of the scenes part of the [theatre] spectacle' (Hunter 2002); Christopher Stevens, 'responsible for designing the Chichester Festival Theatre' (Joseph 1964e: viii) with its auditorium 'embracing three-quarters of the stage in the Elizabethan style' (Joseph 1963a: 141); and Joseph's role model John English, a 'pioneer of the open stage in this country' (Joseph 1964e: vii) and director of Birmingham's Arena Theatre Company. A final chapter transcribes a 'Brains Trust' discussion chaired by Professor Hugh Hunt which includes contributions from former Theatre Workshop member David Scase. The book thus serves to preserve and disseminate some of the thinking and collective expertise of a range of important theatre innovators whose work was mainly taking place away from London; perhaps for this reason, longstanding London-based *Daily Telegraph* critic W. A. Darlington was invited along too. The 'Brain's Trust' discussion records a somewhat incendiary Joseph provocation aimed squarely at national government:

The question of the distribution of public money is a very vexed one.
Don't build the next bomb (and I'm sure no one particularly wants to)
and with the money saved you could build 500 theatres in this country
and run them without anyone paying for a single ticket for the next
fifty years (Ibid.: 93).

Actor and Architect is followed by an intensive sharing in print of Joseph's
own research, observations and suggestions, offered in three volumes.
Curiously, the first, *Scene Painting and Design* (Joseph 1964a), is most of
all a design, construction and painting handbook for readers working in
either proscenium or endstage theatre. Not that Joseph acknowledged a
contradiction: he later wrote that 'I am myself both an advocate of theatre in
the round and a scene painter. . . . One can love theatre in the round without
having to hate everything else' (Joseph 1968: 38).

Offered within Pitman's *Theatre and Stage* series, *Scene Painting and
Design* is essentially a practical handbook containing relatively little reflection
and analysis. Joseph does though offer brief case studies of Studio Theatre
productions staged in-the-round, including the Harold Pinter-directed
second professional production of *The Birthday Party* (Joseph 1964a:
105–6). Joseph also guides the reader through a bizarre and surely ironic
re-imagining of David Campton's absurdist 1957 piece, *The Lunatic View.*
This play quartet – first directed by Joseph, and commissioned specifically
for staging in-the-round – is examined for re-staging in a proscenium
format, behind a giant mock-up of a television screen (Ibid.: 94–105).

Scene Painting and Design is written mainly to educate, with a secondary
aim to promote round theatre to those future theatre makers – students
and amateurs in particular – who seem to represent the book's intended
readership. Intriguingly, the sharply critical tone in this book belongs only to
stage designer Sean Kenny, writer of the book's Foreword. Kenny rails against
the 'useless hobby' (Kenny *in* Joseph 1964a: v) theatre has become, and issues
a call-to-arms:

Forget all *Art and Culture* labels attached to the theatre and try to
see how we can make this one form of art a live, real, exciting voice!
Forget all habits and old-fashioned ways of presenting theatre and
begin again to think: how can one best tell a story to a group of people?
(Ibid.)

Kenny continues:

The theatre at the moment is full of wishy-washy people. . . . It is
people like Mr. Stephen Joseph who give the theatre its lifeblood and

vitality. They ask questions – even about the Emperor's new clothes. The energy and excitement we are looking for will come from them (Ibid.: vi).

Theatre in the Round (Joseph 1967), the second in a trilogy of provocative handbooks, picks up on Kenny's tone. Published in 1967 as a response to the 'controversy . . . over-enthusiasm or prejudice' (Joseph 1967: front dust jacket sleeve note) that had surrounded the use of the round theatre form in Britain, this is a book 'that until now no-one has acquired the knowledge to write' (Ibid.). Joseph – 'the best known authority in the country' (Ibid.) –

dissects all the elements which go into this form of theatre, dealing with new buildings, conversion of old ones, "fit-ups" in existing halls, play selection, acting, production, lighting, sound, decor and costume, and he leavens the whole with the accounts of his own experiences in Britain and America (Ibid.).

Theatre in the Round circumscribes, then, much of Joseph's legacy as a theatre innovator. Published during the year in which he died, it represents a detailed and confidence-boosting guide for those willing to experiment with round theatre. Parts of the book are autobiographical. Two early chapters (Ibid.: 34–59) report on and discuss the work of Studio Theatre. Joseph includes lighter memories, such as when 'During one of our matinee performances [in a church hall] a clergyman walked right through the hall, past the actors, and announced in the foyer that some people were rehearsing in the dark' (Ibid.: 50).

Joseph's final book, the wide-ranging *New Theatre Forms* (Joseph 1968), was inspired by 'a visit to America with a camera [to] record the new theatre buildings I found there' (Joseph 1968: vii). Theatre lighting expert Percy Corry's single-page introduction offers a poignant sketch of Joseph at the bitter end of his missionary campaign: he is 'a vigorous iconoclast with the courage of his convictions [and also] an enthusiastic prophet crying in the wilderness' (Ibid.: v).

Mainly, *New Theatre Forms* surveys and discusses non-proscenium forms of theatre throughout the West – noting *en route* historical precedents for each form. Joseph's openly stated purpose is 'to present arguments against the proscenium and in favour of other forms, with the intention of encouraging the building of more of them' (Joseph 1968: 17) – a strategy which, crucially, he hopes might 'enlarge the scope of drama [in order to] increase its significance and popularity' (Ibid.: 18). As part of this process Joseph notes that 'at the time of writing this, there is in England only one theatre in the round; a converted cinema in Stoke-on-Trent' (Ibid.: 23). Joseph – by now estranged from Peter Cheeseman, and therefore exiled from a theatre he, Cheeseman and Ayckbourn had built entirely without public funding – offers: 'It is, I hope (having designed it), an interesting theatre, and a creditable achievement in view of the small amount of money spent on it' (Ibid.).

Joseph died before *New Theatre Forms* reached publication. He probably anticipated this; his Introduction records how 'In the later stages of preparation. . . . I fell seriously ill, and was given substantial help by David Campton with the text and by Percy Corry with the illustrations' (Ibid.: ix). Knowing this to be his final book, in it, he rails Lear-like against poor practice and harmful thinking in the English theatre. Joseph's targets are many and varied; each criticism highlights a career-long preoccupation, while hinting at what his posthumous legacy might be. Joseph's language is that of a provocateur – a warrior, even. Highlighting the ever-present threat of competition from cinema and television, Joseph characterizes liveness and intimacy as key factors in ensuring the survival of theatre:

> Real actors, acting in the presence of a real audience: this is the essence of theatre. In designing a theatre this meeting can be seized upon and developed so that the presence of the actor is more strongly felt and the contribution of the audience is increased (Joseph 1968: 19).

Joseph's ambition in writing *New Theatre Forms* was plainly to provoke action. After more than a decade of touring round theatre productions of new plays by writers including Ayckbourn, Pinter, David Campton and James Saunders – and with the prospect of personal success in London now gone – Joseph's missionary work was far from complete:

> Here is the theatre, even with all its limitations, as it is because our society is conservative and lazy. There is nothing I can do about it; nor you. But such a view is utterly inappropriate within the realm of theatre. From its beginnings drama has been concerned with action, it has been driven along by the idea of will; and, faced with disaster or with success, the chief figures of dramatic literature have been manufactured to persuade us that human endeavour, no matter what the opposition, is worthwhile (Ibid.: 21).

For Joseph, writing in 1967, there was a need for urgent action – especially in relation to theatre-in-the-round. Yet the few supporters to be found beyond Joseph's own company remained nervous of the reach and potential of round theatre. An impatient Joseph wrote that 'To argue that the new forms of theatre must wait for special plays is simply a gesture of cowardice in the face of a call to adventure' (Joseph 1968: 19).

The central challenge was to increase audience attendance. After a 12-year-long campaign of evangelizing, Joseph was now wearily feigning ignorance at ways 'to win an audience into the theatre. It is a subject that fascinates me and I wish I could find a few enthusiasts to discuss it with . . . [however] my friends are either successful and complacent, or subsidised and above such concerns' (Ibid.: 128).

Within *New Theatre Forms*, Joseph discusses the experimental theatre work of others – including designs never built, such as the 'highly original and grandiose theatres' (Joseph 1968: 82) of Norman Bel Geddes, 'a genius rejected' (Ibid.). Bel Geddes is quoted writing as early as 1932 that 'The release of dramatists, directors, actors and audiences from the limitations of the present-day conventional type of theatre would be a tremendous stimulus for the drama' (Ibid.). In fact Joseph's radical theatres are nearly all abroad, since 'we in England understand money better than we understand aesthetics' (Ibid.: 17); besides which

England [is] a fundamentally conservative nation, [where] above all in the arts we move very slowly from one idea to the next . . . we do not examine the new idea thoroughly, and we certainly will not wish to give it a fair trial or a reasonable test (Ibid.: 15).

Praise goes to James Hull Miller's work in the United States, where 'the battle was won in the educational field and not in professional theatre. But it was a real battle and each of the new [open-stage] theatres . . . has called for hard campaigning' (Ibid.: 83). There is praise too for Tyrone Guthrie, whose non-proscenium theatres in Stratford, Ontario and in Minnesota could only be built after Guthrie 'went to work in America' (Joseph 1968: 44) – and for fellow self-exile Charles Laughton, whose remarkable Turnabout Theatre in Los Angeles had 'each seat swivel, like so many executive chairs' (Ibid.: 89).

In England, by contrast,

as the examples of the theatre in the round at Stoke and the Arena theatre both show, the climate of opinion is unsympathetic if not actively hostile. A board of directors can hardly be found to take such ventures seriously, and, if found, the board will be hamstrung by lack of money, resulting in poor buildings, inadequate staff and administration, and by prospects so gloomy that only a blind enthusiast could carry on (Ibid.: 44).

Joseph heavily criticizes the one major new English non-proscenium theatre to have garnered wide praise:

The thrust stage at Chichester managed to materialise and earn fame, thanks to the persistence of Leslie Evershed-Martin, whose brain-child it was, and of Sir Laurence Olivier, who directed the first seasons. But neither of them knew very well what he was doing, and when the building opened it suffered from bad sightlines, bad acoustics, and inadequate technical facilities, while the first plays directed there proved to be awful examples of open-stage production, full of meaningless gyration, restless movement and irrelevant trickery (Joseph 1968: 44).

Joseph follows up with a characteristic surveyor-style report on the theatre's design faults – including seating levels, where 'an error can creep into your design if you have a lateral gangway and forget that the slope must allow for it' (Ibid.: 111). Readers are invited to visit Chichester to '[test] this mistake' (Ibid.) as a warning not to allow 'motives of economy drive you to accepting lower standards: unless, that is, you really want to wreck the theatre' (Ibid.).

For Joseph, the battleground within English theatre was complex. There were issues around, variously: theatre architecture – including the design of the actor-audience dynamic, and the treatment of audiences on arrival at a theatre building; government policy – including towards ongoing subsidy, and funding for the building of new theatres; technical skills training – including attitudes towards its status; and the role, status and skill of actors – including the need for non-realist interventions. Binding these issues together was an urgent need to engage a much wider audience. For Joseph, even the language of alternative theatre had become problematical. Demonstrating an early awareness of the 'politics in the naming' (Shepherd 2009: 223), Joseph considered that the term 'experimental'

> has been cheapened. The activity has been enfeebled. . . . It may become necessary even to invent new words. The important work done by the Vieux-Colombier and the Cambridge Festival, called experimental, must be carried on by theatres that may have to resort to calling themselves aggressive, pioneering, way-out, or whatever best carries implications of assault, onslaught, iconoclasm, radical exploration, and huge entertainment (Joseph 1968: 71).

Joseph returns to the theme of radical intervention towards the end of the book. Adopting a comradely, persuasive tone, he first offers:

> I hope you are attracted to new theatre forms because you enjoy watching actors who bring their full creative talents to the moment of performance, because you trust that drama can help in the process

of enlarging our humanity, and because you want to face today's ideas in art as well as in life, since the one is a reflection of the other (Ibid.: 124).

Next he cajoles:

I hope you like the thought of an aggressive theatre, arising from fresh imaginative concepts, and that you are not content with second-hand goods (Ibid.).

Finally – with a backward glance, no doubt, at his own experience – he counsels dryly:

Well, an aggressive theatre is not likely to get subsidy, so plan without it (Ibid.).

At the heart of Joseph's ambition to democratize live theatre, was the need for new – preferably small, round – theatres designed to improve the audience experience. Not that Joseph was advocating close-up realism; indeed he delivers in his final book a parodic Strindbergian attack on the lack of realistic set and props within realist theatre:

In a production of *The Cherry Orchard* or *The Three Sisters* by the Moscow Art Theatre, from Stanislavsky's time to the present day, the interiors are wonderfully credible, but the exteriors are absurd, with their inadequate tree-trunks, the overhead foliage trying to pretend it isn't a border, the dense forestation of the wings, and comic humps trying to disguise the flatness of the floor. It is all so obviously canvas and a bit of chicken-wire, fine for pantomime, but quite out of key with the interior settings (Joseph 1968: 134).

Earlier in the book Joseph offers a dramatic reframing of the long-settled battle between the populist non-realist theatre in Britain and the emergent realist movement:

As theatres got bigger and bigger to cope with increasing spectacle, acting perforce became less and less "real". A conflict between the delights of visual gluttony and the pleasures of realistic imitation broke out with the attack of Ibsen and the disciples of a literary theatre on the absurdity of melodrama. The battle, as commonly reported, resulted in a victory for the realists. But, not so often noted in this connection, there were full theatres, large theatres, numerous theatres for melodrama, and the literary drama after the conquest could command only decimated audiences, small theatres, and few theatres, which were soon all crying out like spoiled children for subsidy (Ibid.: 60–61).

Developing his argument – that elitist theatrical realism should no longer be allowed to dominate the English stage – Joseph reminds readers that

> The literary realists did not have it all their own way. In the name of "literature" they may have banished melodrama; which promptly returned (with music) as opera and ballet. Side by side with the realists and their tendency to explore the sordid aspects of life and to present it in drab colours, the exponents of ballet revelled in brilliant colour, richness and exoticism (Joseph 1968: 61).

Joseph's citing of opera and ballet as the natural inheritors of the characteristics of popular melodrama, rather sidesteps an awkward truth, at least in Britain: that the tone of sophistication inherent within the two forms also served to alienate many of the working-class theatregoers who had patronized melodrama in such great numbers. Although Joseph's last book is about theatre spaces and theatre buildings, and not about playwriting, it's surprising that Peter Cheeseman's ground-breaking community-based musical documentaries in Stoke receive no commendation. Here, surely, could be found a genuine and current example of the type of non-realist yet popular theatre Joseph espouses.

Joseph's deep yearning for a return to popular theatre is evident within all his books. His proposal for an in-the-round 'Fish and Chip Theatre' (Joseph 1967: 117) – seen in design form in *Theatre in the Round* (Joseph 1967), and discussed in more detail in the concluding section of this book – would seem to respond to the contemporaneous shared longing of Joan Littlewood, Arnold Wesker, Peter Cheeseman, John McGrath and others for a theatre space built for a potential new audience drawn most of all from Britain's working class. In *New Theatre Forms* Joseph builds in some detail the case for a popular revolution within English theatre. Joseph first identifies the broad nature and scale of the problem:

> . . . theatre is potentially a popular art, yet at present it only entertains a small proportion of the population; most people enjoy watching sport, or staying at home in front of the television set. . . . All sorts of theatres can exist side by side. We should have large theatres for popular entertainments, and small ones to cater for special interests (Joseph 1968: 17).

Next he summarizes his own wish that

> some fresh thinking about the theatre may lead to activity within the theatre that will in turn lead to a wider, beneficial activity in society.

As the theatre reflects society, so does society catch something back
from the theatre. The opportunity is there. We can choose to pursue
it, or not (Ibid.: 21).

For Joseph, English theatre had become, and remained, class-prejudiced.
There was even a problem within the ranks of theatre professionals. Alluding
perhaps most of all to the 'university men' (Shepherd 2009: 13) increasingly
running English theatres, Joseph observes how:

To many Englishmen there is something foreign about technical
competence. The Germans put lights in the right places, and the
Americans perhaps. But in England artistic endeavour is a privilege
of the middle classes and it can only escape the scorn of the upper
classes (who may occasionally want to dabble) by being rigorously
unpractical. To know how to focus a spotlight belongs to the lower
orders, who really could not be consulted when building a theatre
(Joseph 1968: 76).

In *New Theatre Forms* Joseph challenges head-on the motivation of those who
run theatres – implying that inequality within English theatre is protected –
cherished, even. He can see 'little sign, in England, that anyone cares much
about promotion or does anything vigorous to bring the public into the
theatre. Perhaps we are all convinced that theatre is a privilege for those
in-the-know?' (Ibid.: 126). Joseph next offers a poignant and specific example
of how theatre in England casually alienates first-time audience members:

At the Opera House in Manchester there is a sign in the auditorium
announcing "Gentlemen and Buffet", but initiates know that the buffet
has been long closed; only beginners are fooled and their blushes are a
guarantee that they won't be troubling the theatre again. Theatregoing
has become too stupid a ritual to allow of new audiences (Ibid.: 127).

Joseph ends with a series of specific suggestions – all of which had become
established practice for Studio Theatre – that might help to democratize
theatre. He suggests active engagement with the community through 'door
to door salesmen' (Joseph 1968: 127), who might offer 'a trial sample' (Ibid.)
and then be present as hosts, welcoming 'the tentative spectator arriving at
the theatre' (Ibid.: 127). He urges that 'the design of the theatre should be
such that all seats give an equally good opportunity for full enjoyment of the
play' (Ibid.: 128); and he proposes that 'The price of tickets should be reduced
for bulk bookings by parties and for students, pensioners and other hard-up
people' (Ibid.). He counsels: 'never charge for programmes' (Ibid.). As part

of a drive to locate the theatre at the heart of a community, he suggests too that the theatre should be used 'as much as possible for talks, trade shows, conferences, and concerts' (Ibid.) to ensure that a wide range of visitors to the building 'will want to come again' (Ibid.).

Joseph's now modest-sounding wish list serves to remind us that such a level of service was actually rare within English theatre in the 1960s. Here then may be found another clear glimpse of Stephen Joseph's legacy within Western theatre.

The launch of Studio Theatre in 1955 meant that Joseph was providing an ongoing working model of a different way to 'do' theatre. Anyone interested in learning about a new way to reach new audiences could come to Scarborough, or Stoke-on-Trent, or simply visit the company on tour. In Joseph's final book, he offers a concise summary of what it was that made theatre-in-the-round different in 1967:

> . . . it is the most radically different form of theatre, in terms of acting style, from the enclosed stage; it presents the most extreme extent of audience embrace, i.e. the audience is all round the stage: it thus allows the maximum number of people in the audience to be close to the actors; it is the cheapest of all theatre forms; it breaks the greatest number of today's conventions of presentation and thus collects more than its fair share of fanaticism from its supporters and from its detractors; it is as old as the hills (and, in some respects, a good deal older). If you want to explore it, go to the United States (or stay in England and have patience with the Library Theatre at Scarborough and the Victoria Theatre at Stoke-on-Trent) (Joseph 1968: 38).

Joseph had already gone to considerable lengths in *Theatre in the Round* to highlight the benefits of the form. Although his final book was supposed to examine the full range of non-proscenium staging formats, evidence of his strong personal preference for round theatre peppers the text. Within a 19-page exploration of thrust staging, Joseph asserts that 'plays less terrific than [Shakespeare's] tend to look a bit thin when presented on a thrust stage' (Joseph 1968: 55). In a 14-page analysis of endstage theatre (Ibid.: 58–71) Joseph characterizes the format 'as makeshift proscenium [theatre] acceptable to hard-up Englishmen who are afraid to make artistic experiments' (Ibid.: 66), concluding that 'nothing original has come out of our own theatres with end stages except a West End transfer or two' (Joseph 1968: 67). Later in the book, Joseph offers a nod to his proposed Fish and Chip Theatre in a section on medieval promenade staging, noting how 'I have often wished that I were not imprisoned in a seat and could escape without being noticed, as those medieval spectators were able to' (Ibid.: 91).

However Joseph's greatest ire within *New Theatre Forms* is reserved for theatre design that inhibits clear communication between actors and audience:

> I would not recommend you deliberately to design a theatre with bad sightlines if only because I myself do complain about them, and I believe that, where people do not complain, it is either because they are so used to awful theatres that they don't know sightlines can be good, or because the entertainment is so awful that it is not worth seeing anyhow. To build theatres with bad sightlines is common practice, and is a major factor in determining the relative lack of interest shown by people towards drama in England; if you have a puritanical aversion to theatre, or an academic interest in dramatic literature, you may welcome bad sightlines. Then put twenty rows of seats on floor level and most of the audience will not see the action of the play properly (which will help to prove that you get more pleasure from reading a play at home than from going to a theatre to watch it.) (Ibid.: 108–9).

Elsewhere in his final book, Joseph openly and enthusiastically condemns particular groups of decision-makers. He reports that 'Only too often local councillors, and others who find themselves in control of the money available for theatre building, know very little indeed about the theatre' (Joseph 1968: 22). Ignorant school managers – who failed to realize that 'to put the audience in a theatre on a flat floor is to utterly destroy the possibilities of drama' (Ibid.: 12) – were guilty of a range of other 'destructive conditions' (Ibid.):

> . . . money is wasted on putting a series of bars over the stage in imitation of Renaissance scenic techniques; lighting is put on such bars in memorial of the time when gas had to be fed through pipes; drab curtains are hung to commemorate classical wings and borders; and money is wasted on elaborate and irrelevant control boards to enable a so-called technician to vary the degree of badness with which the actors are lit (Ibid.).

No holds barred, it seems. Indeed Joseph's wide experience of 'the stultifying effect of so many truly awful . . . imitation theatres' (Ibid.: 13) left him questioning how anyone could retain an interest in drama:

> . . . a disgraceful imitation [of a theatre] will convince most ordinary, sensible people that the theatre is a waste of time, better spent by audiences in the cinema or in front of the television set, better spent by actors doing a different and more useful job, and a waste of money which, no matter what permissive legislation may allow in the

expenditure of rates, will be better not spent at all (a notion that is common all over England) (Ibid.).

In truth, of course, Joseph was much more than merely a sniper at the frayed edges of theatre, including educational theatre. He had long been available for consultation – free-of-charge, usually. It was a smart strategy for a missionary: schools, colleges and universities could save money on architectural design costs, while Joseph could penetrate deeply into areas where radical future theatre makers, hungry for ideas and inspiration, might be lurking. Educators rejecting Joseph's proposed round theatre designs would frequently be offered instead a rotating stage: this now little-seen feature – identified by Joseph as a 'pictorial open stage' (Ibid.: 83) – could be examined with reference to Joseph's published photographs of Frank Lloyd Wright's Kalita Humphreys Theatre in Dallas, Texas (Joseph 1968: 83–6). Foreign referencing was necessary since, for Joseph, 'The revolving stages at, for instance, the Nottingham Playhouse and the Guildford Yvonne Arnaud theatre offer very limited opportunities. In my opinion, both have been a waste of money and will be a hindrance to many designers' (Ibid.: 88). Characteristically, Joseph followed up his dismissal of contemporary English examples with a fresh design of his own (Ibid.: 87), 'suitable for a college where stagecraft extends to building scenery, but where the emphasis remains, in performance, on the actor' (Ibid.: 85).

Audience comfort should be of paramount concern. Joseph, much taller than average height, noted that 'Too many theatres have seating rows closer than is comfortable for people who are tall' (Ibid.: 112–3). Access for late-coming audiences mattered too – although Joseph confessed to managing in Scarborough 'the worst possible arrangement... [with] only one entrance for audience and to have actors use the same entrance: latecomers can too easily find themselves following an actor onstage' (Ibid.: 114). This idiosyncratic design feature – partially echoed in Alan Ayckbourn's later Scarborough auditorium at Westwood – was excused dryly on the grounds that 'no-one really designed the Library Theatre; it just happened' (Ibid.: 114). There was more: dressing rooms could be gender-mixed, like the one in Scarborough (where in fact they had no choice) which 'did much to make the standards of performance higher than one might expect from a young company, overworked, underpaid, and, many of them, inexperienced' (Joseph 1968: 138).

There, then, is the missionary landscape that mattered to theatre maker Stephen Joseph: new discoveries and perspectives to be shared in relation to acting, directing, playwriting, funding and reaching new audiences. But, looking back more than half a century after Joseph's death, how might we describe his overarching vision?

In fact it's frustratingly difficult to pin down a clear Joseph philosophy that unites his ideas. His love for sentimentality in the theatre would have been anathema to his better-known contemporaries, while his passion for epic storytelling led him directly away from the burgeoning English social realist revolution. He staged first work and new work by a huge range of playwrights, including non-British writers; three of the four playwrights debuted in his first Scarborough season in 1955 season were female. Yet only David Campton and Alan Ayckbourn enjoyed Joseph's secure patronage over a period of years. Joseph's programming was rarely overtly political; indeed entertainment was valued above all else. A 1959 Joseph programme note for Alan Ayckbourn's co-written play *Love After All* (Allen 1959) teases:

> Having been labelled an experimental theatre, we are not surprised that people expect us to act like one . . . it is not usually considered proper . . . to stage farcical entertainments designed to make the audience enjoy themselves with unsophisticated laughter . . . [yet] we have been able to provoke laughter without provoking too much high-brow disapproval (Joseph 1959f).

My own view is that Stephen Joseph resolved early on to be something of an intellectual and stylistic moving target – actively subverting his own potential status as a Peter Brook-style visionary. There's an interesting sketch that brings the two men together during the Granada Northern Lectures series that led to Brook's iconic text *The Empty Space*. Former University of Manchester teaching colleague Peter Thomson considers that Joseph, who 'always saw the feet of clay beneath the "great" names of theatre' (Thomson 2008c), may have been provoked by 'Brook's aura of grandeur, and by the sycophantic responses to his presence'. Terry Lane offers a report of Joseph's student-led question-and-answer session with a man whose family wealth derived from Brooklax laxative products:

> [Joseph had briefed] two students to ask irritating questions. . . . Mike Weller on one side interjected and giggled, while Mike Stott opposite asked about the purgative qualities of Greek tragedy, and how tragedy had declined with the invention of chemical purgatives (Lane 2006: 181).

To his credit, Peter Brook seems to have enjoyed the joke. He enjoyed too an early encounter with Studio Theatre's then unique permanent 'empty space', the intimate and design-minimalist Vic Theatre, an adapted cinema in Stoke-on-Trent. There he saw what was probably his first professional in-the-round production. After his visit – likely hosted by Joseph, during the visit to

Manchester – Brook recorded his impressions. He wrote in *The Empty Space*: 'The combination of lively actors, lively building, lively audience, brought out the most sparkling elements of the play' (Brook 1968: 144). Although Brook was dismissive of presentational aspects including make-up, he concluded that 'it is unlikely that anywhere in London that evening the theatrical temperature was nearly so high as in Stoke' (Ibid.).

Despite this report, Brook does not seem to have ever mentioned Joseph as an influence; certainly, Joseph never claimed that status for himself. Harold Pinter did briefly acknowledge Joseph's importance to his early career; however, such influence was never really discussed, least of all by Joseph. Indeed Joseph declines throughout his five books to claim credit for shaping the work of numerous other theatre makers. So: did the energetically iconoclastic Joseph actively and consistently subvert his own potential status as a theatre icon?

It's a nuanced idea – a clever one too, perhaps, if I want to argue that Joseph's invisibility derives from much more than a general lack of interest. So where might we uncover secure evidence of Joseph's role in provoking innovation and risk-taking by important theatre makers?

2

Ayckbourn and Cheeseman –
Twin Protégés

Here we can turn to two Stephen Joseph protégés whose experimental work has had a major impact on Western theatre: Sir Alan Ayckbourn (1939–) and Peter Cheeseman (1932–2010).

Although there's quite a lot of published material on both men, much of it is out of print – and anyway, there's little detail anywhere on Joseph's influence. Books on Ayckbourn include a 2001 full-length popular biography (Allen 2001) and an earlier pocket-book-length analysis of his plays (Billington 1983). There are numerous newspaper profiles and press articles discussing Ayckbourn and his theatre work. There's also www.alanayckbourn.net – a free online resource which provides interview transcripts, programme notes, photographs, news items, lists and production reviews. The physical archive of Ayckbourn's career is held nearby, at the Borthwick Institute for Archives at the University of York.

Peter Cheeseman's pioneering musical documentary and verbatim theatre work has been quite widely acknowledged in print. Sources include Derek Paget's 1990 text *True Stories?* (Paget 1990: 70–3), which identifies Cheeseman as leader of 'The most significant and influential development for the True Story in mainstream British theatre' (Ibid.: 70). Gary Fisher Dawson's 1999 study of the 'Stoke-method of documentary theatre' (Fisher Dawson 1999: 16) considers Cheeseman, who produced 'a working-outline for the process of creating a documentary play' (Ibid.), to be 'a major contributor to the precise use of oral history in the form of transcribed interview material' (Ibid.). Further sources include Gillette Elvgren and Attilio Favorini's 1992 text *Steel/City* (Elvgren and Favorini 1992). The physical archive of much of Cheeseman's work is now held at Staffordshire University within the Victoria Theatre Cheeseman Archive. Staffordshire academic Paul Jones has noted how 'Joseph's influence extended into Cheeseman's core programming policy' (Jones 2009a). The programme was always highly eclectic; actor Sir Ben Kingsley remembers that alongside the new and devised plays 'We did Ibsen, we did Shakespeare, we did classical theatre' (Kingsley 2008).

Both theatre makers enjoy the advocacy of high-profile practitioners. Ayckbourn – early on dismissed by John Osborne as a 'right-wing boulevadier' (Watson 1981: 113) – has been noted by Kevin Spacey among others for his 'Chekovian quality' (Spacey 2009), while Mark Ravenhill considers Ayckbourn's *A Small Family Business* (1978) to be one of Britain's most important political plays. Ravenhill has spoken of how in the play Ayckbourn

> . . . remorselessly shows how this "business" stifles all the people involved, and how "the family" stifles all the people involved, so by the end it's turned into a kind of mafia family . . . both "family" and "business" seem to be things that just completely destroy those people and kind of trap them . . . until they can't breathe. And that final image of the family, closed together as a kind of mafia outfit, and meanwhile there's the daughter who's upstairs in the toilet, jacking up (Ravenhill 2010).

A 2010 obituary on Peter Cheeseman contains deep praise from playwright and film director Mike Leigh, a former member of the Stoke company. Leigh recalls 'a special and creative time. The spirit in which we worked, to be political and truthful, was down to [Cheeseman]. He was a genius, a vagabond, a facilitator. What he achieved is colossal' (Leigh 2010).

Alan Ayckbourn had 'never heard of' (Ayckbourn 2007) Joseph's Studio Theatre when he applied for a 1957 vacancy as an assistant stage manager (ASM) with the Scarborough company. Prior to this Ayckbourn had been an acting ASM (involving some acting responsibilities) in the south of England, and, earlier, with Sir Donald Wolfit's company at the Edinburgh Festival. Ayckbourn remembers being persuaded by Rodney Wood, Stage Manager at the Thorndike Theatre in Leatherhead,

> to give up one of my weekly rep valuable Sundays to go and have a look at a show at the Mahatma Gandhi Hall in Fitzroy Square in London – to see a Sunday night one-night-only performance of Sarte's *Huis Clos*, which was my first experience of theatre-in-the-round, let alone Stephen's company. And it was of quite a high standard, because he was then using actors who were perhaps not playing plum roles in long-running West End shows, but that were good supporting working actors. I mean, the quality was very good. And it was an eye opener for me (Ayckbourn 2007).

Part of the surprise and the excitement for Ayckbourn was the audience proximity to the actors. At this time the sort of theatre I'd seen . . . was always – you know, a hundred feet away, at the back of the circle. And you only had their word for it that it was Laurence Olivier! I mean, his voice was relayed through a speaker and you had a pair of binoculars . . . (Ibid.)

Watching Joseph's intimate production, he remembers thinking

I'd never been so close to actors before. I mean, it was quite a big space – but nonetheless, for a student, with very little money, to be three or four rows back . . . to be that close to real acting was certainly . . . . I thought, yeah, this guy has something. (Ibid.)

Peter Cheeseman, whose 'own background . . . was entirely proscenium' (Cheeseman 2007), had been watching the Studio Theatre company for some time before he joined the group on a permanent basis in the early 1960s. He 'knew of' (Ibid.) Joseph

because he used to write on occasion these dotty letters about the importance of theatre-in-the-round, against all the people who thought it was ridiculous, you know. He used to write these letters, and I thought, "what's that?" All this "theatre-in-the-round" stuff (Ibid.).

In November 1959 Cheeseman wrote a long letter to Joseph offering his services as a potential assistant director, stage manager or manager who had 'no ambitions whatsoever' to act (Cheeseman 1959). Cheeseman, a qualified teacher, had 'no professional theatrical experience' (Ibid.) but could offer a comprehensive practical knowledge of theatre from his years as an amateur with the Workers' Educational Association in Liverpool, with Sheffield University and from National Service with the Royal Air Force (RAF). While in the RAF he had designed and lit settings – and had even built 'a new stage with a cyclorama and a 20-way interlocking switchboard' (Ibid.). Cheeseman and Joseph began corresponding; soon after, Cheeseman was in his first professional job, helping to direct productions at the 'old-fashioned' (Ibid.) proscenium Derby Playhouse. Cheeseman remembers feeling

terminally disappointed when I got there and found out the intercourse in that level of theatre was so hollow, so empty – it was a joke . . . [the] play programme seemed to be, "West End comedy – Week 1". "West End thriller – Week 2". "West End comedy again – Week 3". And Week 4 – "one for the Arts Council". And that was exactly what was going on! It was depressing, and I thought "no – is this what I dreamed about?" (Ibid.)

Cheeseman found himself running a traditional 'weekly rep' model at Derby; there was 'no proper rehearsal' (Ibid.), resulting in 'terrible' (Ibid.) productions. Newly appointed as Manager, he achieved a somewhat pyrrhic victory when he moved to staging shows fortnightly, allowing for two-week rehearsal periods. Production standards improved; audience attendance rose sharply and stayed high. However afternoon rehearsals were suddenly needed – and the extra workload was received as a 'revolution in the company' (Ibid.) by certain older actors who had, Cheeseman felt, been enjoying a 'very cushy time' (Ibid.). The theatre's Board responded by banning afternoon rehearsals. Cheeseman, his experiment now frozen, found himself 'thinking of contacting the Arts Council to see if there was anything I could do' (Ibid.).

Ayckbourn and Cheeseman each recall dramatic first encounters with Stephen Joseph. Ayckbourn had already joined the Studio Theatre Company before he met his employer; the brief unplanned meeting happened during a live performance at the temporary theatre-in-the-round above Scarborough library:

> I was running the show, and we had an old slider dimmer board which [was] . . . terribly stiff. And sparks came out. To do a fade to blackout – they were all set at different levels – you put your arm across them all and dragged them all down, but sometimes missed one . . . [as] I was doing one of these fades I was suddenly aware of this big man standing next to me and he said, "There's a better way to do that, you know." So I said, "Yeah, sorry, do you mind? I'm running a show and I've brought up the lights for the next scene." He said, "Well, if you get a bit of wood," and he found a piece lying in this corner, and he said, "you just put it across these and you just pull that down, you see, and that's a blackout. Absolutely surefire one." I said, "You've just put the scene into darkness!" He went "Oh Jesus!" and he ran out. And people came offstage – "What's happened? We blacked out in the middle of the scene, I was in the middle of my big speech!" I said, "Well I'm sorry – a great big man came in here and just took the lights out." Somebody said, "Ah yeah, that was Stephen" (Ayckbourn 2007).

Peter Cheeseman first encountered Joseph during a London meeting of the Council of Repertory Theatres (CORT). Cheeseman, there representing Derby Playhouse, remembers disliking the formality of the event:

> in the traditional way of British conferences you don't talk to each other, you talk to a grand person who's grown a plinth and never noticed . . . [theatre director] Philip Hedley and I used to, when we reached the

first coffee break, we used to change all the chairs so that we were in a circle (Cheeseman 2008).

During the second day of the conference, CORT group members were locked in a heated discussion with West End promoters over regional production rights for recent stage hit *Roar Like A Dove* – a comedy drama that was also a 'real star piece' (Ibid.). Cheeseman remembers that at one point Stephen Joseph interjected. Joseph

> didn't know what the fuss was about – *Roar Like A Dove* was "sexual bosh". – It was like farting at the Queen! That was his view – what were we doing worrying about this damned stuff? That was "Enter Stephen". (Ibid.)

Cheeseman, disillusioned at Derby, filled in a letter of application to join the Studio Theatre Company and soon found himself working as 'a new member of staff to help [Joseph] build the new theatre. This was what he wanted from me' (Ibid.). After Derby he found Joseph 'like a shot in the arm' (Cheeseman 1959). Since it was off-season and there was as yet no theatre building, Cheeseman mostly worked 'setting up two or three tours of one-offs', which meant 'long car rides with Stephen in which he told me his whole life' (Ibid.). Cheeseman remembers Joseph describing his own unsettled upbringing, before offering a telling piece of self-analysis: 'he said – "in adult life you try and create around yourself the atmosphere of your childhood, and mine was insecurity" ' (Ibid.). Politically, Cheeseman found Joseph to be 'an egalitarian. He was a democrat. His worldview was Left' (Ibid.). On a personal level, Cheeseman 'was always impressed by his manners, by what he thought about people' (Ibid.).

Cheeseman's first season as a Studio Theatre employee saw him direct a touring production of Ibsen's *A Doll's House*. He also had a hand in staging a slimmed-down production of Shakespeare's *Hamlet*, although a review in *The Stage* (*The Stage* n.d.), names Stephen Joseph as director. It's likely that Joseph was helping to train Cheeseman to direct in-the-round – a mentoring role Joseph shared with Alan Ayckbourn (Watson 1981: 70). Curiously, all three men appeared onstage in the production: Cheeseman and Joseph 'were Voltimand and Cornelius, it must have looked ludicrous as he was about six feet six and I'm about five feet five' (Cheeseman 1998: 1). It was during the run of *Hamlet* that Joseph heard news of the withdrawal of public funding to build his new theatre-in-the-round in Newcastle-under-Lyme; the context of this will be examined later in the book.

Alan Ayckbourn's initial recruitment to Joseph's 1957 company was temporary. At its launch in 1955 the Studio Theatre group had been largely a summer-only Scarborough enterprise; as funding increased, activity quickly expanded to include brief visits to London and off-season touring to a growing roster of theatreless English towns. Ayckbourn's role evolved too, and within months he was a regular leading actor with the company. Although Ayckbourn has long been dismissive of his own acting skill, he received strong review notices for some of the dozens of plays in which he performed; he seems to have been a playful, versatile actor who understood the value of stillness.

Ayckbourn's commitment to acting led directly to his first playwriting commission, after he complained to Stephen Joseph about his role in a new play. He recalls:

> [Joseph] said to me: "If you want a better part, you'd better write one for yourself. Write a play, I'll do it. If it's any good." And I said: "Fine." And he said: "Write yourself a main part" – which was actually a very shrewd remark, because presumably, if the play had not worked at all, there was no way I as an actor was going to risk my neck in it (Watson 1981: 48).

Working with his then wife Christine Roland, and writing as 'Roland Allen', Ayckbourn produced the farcical play *The Square Cat* (1959) which premiered on 30 July 1959. The piece was a hit with audiences, and Joseph granted it an extended run. Some 6 months later it enjoyed a second production in Newcastle-under-Lyme; this time Ayckbourn was absent from the cast due to very brief National Service commitments.

One reason for the brevity of Ayckbourn's National Service was that his theatrical employer Joseph – a decorated British Navy veteran – successfully lobbied Royal Air Force (RAF) authorities to exempt Ayckbourn from service. Joseph's letter – arguing that Ayckbourn had an important contribution to make to British theatre – received a curt formal response from the RAF; yet it does seem strings were pulled. Ayckbourn remembers:

> The medical officer from whom I eventually got my exit visa, as it were, was very sympathetic, and he said, "Do you wanna do this job?" And I said, "No." He said, "Oh look at this. Oh yes. You've got a knee injury, I think." I said, "Oh, that's from cricket. It tends to twist a bit." He said, "Could you just walk to that wall, and then come back again?" . . . . So I walked to the wall. He said, "I don't like the look of that leg at all. I've got some very bad news for you – we're going to have to turn you

down." And I said, "Oh – oh. What a shame." . . . He said, "I expect my cheque in the morning" (Ayckbourn 2008).

It seems curious that Stephen Joseph should lobby the RAF on Ayckbourn's significance as a playwright: at this point only one Ayckbourn play had seen production, performed in a small temporary theatre far from London. In fact Ayckbourn had been writing plays – generally one-act pieces – for some time before *The Square Cat* premiered in 1959; such pieces were typically either upbeat and entertaining, or were effortful tributes to the work of a famous playwright whom the young Ayckbourn admired.

After just a couple of days of National Service, Ayckbourn was summoned to rejoin the Studio Theatre company in the Potteries. Ayckbourn was soon writing again, producing the popular pieces *Love After All* (Allen 1959) and *Dad's Tale* (Allen 1960). The former – again written with Christine Roland – is an Edwardian farce based on *The Barber of Seville*; the latter is a curious hybrid, in that Ayckbourn's own writing needed to dovetail with choreographed dance sequences staged by members of the British Dance Drama Theatre.

Early on, Joseph seems to have attempted to mould Ayckbourn into the type of entertaining yet experimental political satirist company regular David Campton had become. In 1960 Ayckbourn was persuaded to write a play based on an idea by Joseph: the result, *Standing Room Only* (1961), turned out not to be the Venus-located science-fiction meditation on overpopulation in the twenty-third century requested by Joseph, but rather a humanist comedy set in 1997 on board a permanently traffic-jammed London bus. Here was a London in which, in Ayckbourn's words, 'children [were] no longer smiled upon and there'd be very complicated exams in order to have them' (Murgatroyd 2008).

Joseph actively nurtured Ayckbourn's sense of company loyalty. In the build-up to the 1961 Scarborough summer season Joseph wrote to praise 'the way your talent as an actor is developing and also the increasing sense of responsibility you seem to have towards the whole company' (Joseph 1961j: 1), before adding prophetically:

> You may well tuck into the back of your mind a nice ambition to be actor/author/manager one day in the good old tradition! (Joseph 1961j: 1)

Ayckbourn responded instantly, offering his services 'as a foundation stone of permanence' (Ayckbourn 1961: 1). Months later Ayckbourn was granted his first opportunity to direct when he took on a production of Patrick

Hamilton's *Gaslight*; the production received critical praise for its in-the-round 'claustrophobic immediacy' (*The Stage* 1961a).

Ayckbourn turned madcap political satirist with his next play, *Christmas v Mastermind* (1962), which opened on Boxing Day 1962. This odd, funny children's play, with its evil-plot-to-cancel-Christmas storyline, is dimly reminiscent of Dario Fo's yet-to-come comic agitprop work – and was to be a rare box office failure for Ayckbourn. Co-directed by Ayckbourn and Peter Cheeseman, it was staged in Stoke's newly adapted and virtually unheated Victoria theatre-in-the-round with a cast including Ayckbourn and his future wife Heather Stoney, plus (cast as A Gnome) actor-playwright David Halliwell. Although reviewed locally as a 'wonderfully wholesome entertainment for anyone aged from nine to 90' (*Evening Sentinel* 1963), Ayckbourn considers the piece a disaster; he was, he felt, 'learning what I can't do' (Watson 1981: 60). More than a quarter of a century passed before Ayckbourn wrote again for children.

The perceived failure of *Christmas v Mastermind* was surely a blow too for co-director Peter Cheeseman. Lured from a secure leadership post in Derby, recruited to co-run a custom-designed in-the-round theatre that was never built, and new to the heavily industrial Potteries district, his eventual first season directing in the round had produced something of a Christmas turkey. Yet he respected and trusted Stephen Joseph. Throughout my interview with Cheeseman he was at almost constant pains to articulate his deep admiration for the man; asked to recall his recruitment interview, he replied instead:

> [Joseph] struck me to be brilliant – he was the nearest to a genius, very practical, very extraordinary. His analysis of what theatre was, was so illuminating I couldn't get over it – I thought, "oh – I've not seen this before." When Stephen would talk about theatre you'd think, "Yes, that's it." He talked, and something about it just moved these dusty, crusty, cobweb-covered ideas that weren't real, they were just imaginings (Cheeseman 2008).

Cheeseman recalled his feelings on first working with Joseph:

> Stephen was such an extraordinary man – and such a different person. All the other people that I'd met – he was just brilliant. I thought, it'd be an honour to be with, it'd be wonderful to work with him – [he] had something that was really – he was a huge man. He was, in every way (Ibid.).

While accompanying Joseph, Cheeseman 'saw him lecture – brilliant. Absolutely hilarious' (Ibid.). Joseph was 'amazingly efficient . . . terribly

Figure 3 Alan Ayckbourn's *Christmas v Mastermind* (1962). Courtesy of Scarborough Theatre Trust

organised, his organisational skills were extraordinary' (Ibid.). Cheeseman remembered how a company member had 'fallen in love' (Ibid.) with Joseph: Cheeseman felt that 'anyone could be, very easily' (Ibid.).

Alan Ayckbourn shares much of Cheeseman's awe at his mentor's insight into live theatre:

> I thought he was wonderful, I mean, he just embodied all alternative ideas in theatre. . . . He just questioned everything. He threw up questions like there was no tomorrow – "Why do it that way? Why not do it that way?". . . . He upset a few people, I mean, namely for the first theatre in England not to play the National Anthem (Ibid.).

Characteristically, Ayckbourn's 'take' on Joseph is nuanced. As an experimenter Joseph

> was always for the – either the new, or certainly – the original. His choice of work was, to say the least, variable, but then he always knew that as you accepted risk, if you do it, everything's new and a lot of it falls off the edge of the cliff, – but a lot of it is significantly valuable enough to pursue (Ibid.).

For Cheeseman too, his mentor was not entirely without flaws:

> [Joseph] could never see that you wouldn't get any progress in the long run unless you stuck at it. He used to, every year for five years, to come [to Stoke and build] an audience, and then it would just fall off . . . he'd have to start again next year. All the things to do with box office depended on constant attention. You couldn't play about with it (Cheeseman 2007).

Cheeseman felt he had a solution:

> I believed very strongly in continuity and in keeping at it, but it's so difficult to get audiences to the theatre that you needed to stick at it . . . to stay here, and work at it, and build an audience. [But] that had no interest for Stephen. He was quite content to let me do it (Ibid.).

Here then was a key feature of Cheeseman's own evolving vision: a permanent theatrical presence at the heart of a community, built around an ensemble of actors contracted long enough for them to become integrated. Did Stephen Joseph share this vision? It would seem not. Soon after Stoke's Victoria Theatre was operational under Peter Cheeseman, Joseph left to take up a Fellowship at the University of Manchester.

Around the time of Joseph's withdrawal from the daily running of The Vic, a disagreement began to develop between him and Cheeseman, which would become a long-running, attritional and at times quite a public dispute. Opinions differ regarding the reasons behind the schism; former company member Rodney Wood considers that

> The problem with Stoke was that both Stephen and Peter felt it was their theatre. Stephen had the resources to set up a permanent theatre in the round but I think Peter found the premises and pushed it through. There was a battle between them, over finances as much as anything (Wood 2009).

Joseph began plotting to unseat Cheeseman, who had become, he told Ayckbourn, 'an absolute liability' (Ayckbourn 2007). For Cheeseman, Joseph's plot was at least partly motivated by 'jealousy' (Cheeseman 2008) at his growing success in running The Vic. There was also Joseph's developing sense of being an outsider in Stoke: in Rodney Wood's recollection, 'I don't think Stephen got much of a say in policy' (Wood 2009). Yet as Ayckbourn recalls, Joseph's approach was hardly diplomatic:

> We opened with a play called *The Birds and the Well-wishers* in Stoke, and then Stephen came into the building on the first night . . . and he marched round it, looking for things that weren't right. He said, "Should have put 'Exit' on this door," and Peter was saying, "Right. Yes. We've only just got open." And we'd all been working all damn night, so I must say I sympathised with Peter at that point. [Joseph] was just spoiling for a row. But, you know, psychologically, all that work he'd put in – and then here was a building that was custom designed . . . as [an] adaptation, which was permanently there fifty-two weeks of the year. After all his schlepping around and, you know, setting up in church halls and . . . school halls and everything. I mean . . . it must have felt curious for him, to put it mildly. And there was a sort of celebratory air of which he was not really part – although, I think at that point, we all acknowledged that he was instrumental in making that happen (Ayckbourn 2007).

Ayckbourn goes on to recall a fundamental Joseph philosophy that must have seemed under threat with the creation of a permanent theatre:

> His quote about "All theatre should be designed to self-destruct in seven years," – not a joke – I mean, for most of us, we took that with the spirit, rather than the letter of the law. But I think Stephen would have just smashed it down and started again (Ibid.).

At a key point, Joseph sacked Cheeseman. Alan Ayckbourn remembers that the two men 'came absolutely nearly to blows . . . the correspondence was so acrimonious' (Ayckbourn 2007). In the end, representatives of the Arts Council sided with Cheeseman. According to Rodney Wood, 'Somebody leaked to the Arts Council that Stephen was terminally ill and they changed to Peter's side' (Wood 2009). Cheeseman was reinstalled as manager; Joseph, privately sick and now publicly humiliated, could only watch as Studio Theatre's entire Arts Council budget was guided away from him into a new Trust.

Years later Peter Cheeseman asserted that 'all people know about me and Stephen was that we quarreled, but it wasn't a quarrel about anything important' (Ibid.): in fact Cheeseman recalls that 'one of the things [Stephen Joseph] said to me before this all fell to pieces was, "I was right to give you the freedom that I have always enjoyed"' (Cheeseman 2008).

The quarrel arose, then, in response to a variety of factors. Early on, as the company struggled to find a regular audience in the Potteries, Joseph increasingly questioned Cheeseman's ability to manage company finances. There was too a level of jealousy at Cheeseman's success in forging new work, building on Joseph's own work. Joseph – employed full-time away from Stoke, and increasingly unwell – was feeling ostracized by the company. A complex situation was made more complex because there were not two but three potential leaders of Studio Theatre: Joseph, Cheeseman and Alan Ayckbourn. Although Ayckbourn appears to have been the company's Associate Director (Allen 2001: 88), in 1970 Peter Cheeseman – recalling opening the Vic 'under my direction' (Cheeseman 1970: ix) – named Ayckbourn merely as an actor, playwright and 'member of the new permanent company of four men and two women' (Ibid.). Ayckbourn has highlighted some of the confusion with regard to company leadership, after a relocation from Scarborough in which 'the whole [Arts Council] grant went with the Stoke operation' (Ayckbourn 1997):

> Peter Cheeseman, who was in fact my sort of – Stephen was notionally the Artistic Director of the Company – Peter was the General Manager who did direct a bit, and I did most of the directing – so when we arrived there Peter was the Manager, and I was both leading actor and director, and I used to alternate with shows – quite exhausting . . . (Ayckbourn 1999).

Against this confused backdrop, around a year or so after the 1962 opening of the Vic, the company began to lose its regulars – including its actor-writers. Ayckbourn had become preoccupied with his first West End transfer, the 'silent farce' (Ayckbourn 2008) *Mr Whatnot*. Ayckbourn's quirky play, opening on 12 November 1963, became the first Ayckbourn piece to be directed solely by its author (Murgatroyd n.d., a) at a time when playwrights' direction of their own work was 'not considered the done thing' (Ayckbourn 2010). Ayckbourn resigned from Studio Theatre to accompany fellow actor-playwright Peter King, who had been retained in a lead role, for what was to be a critically savaged 1964 West End restaging. King would return to act in Cheeseman's company, appearing in the premiere of the musical documentary *The Knotty* (Cheeseman 1970: v); Ayckbourn stayed away, giving final acting performances in Cardiff and Rotherham (Murgatroyd n.d., b), before accepting a post as BBC radio producer in Leeds.

In fact Ayckbourn's departure from Studio Theatre had been driven by more than just a wish to follow *Mr Whatnot* to London. Alongside the emerging confusion around company hierarchy, there were deepening philosophical differences between Ayckbourn and Cheeseman. For Ayckbourn, the 'rift was there early' (Ayckbourn *in* Watson 1981: 71). Cheeseman's direction of *Christmas v Mastermind* had revealed that the two men 'had very different views on what children's theatre should be about' (Ayckbourn *in* Watson 1981: 58); but there was more. Ayckbourn recalls that 'As [Cheeseman] developed – and he developed very fast – he got very strong ideas about what he wanted to do with that theatre, which didn't necessarily chime with mine' (Ibid.: 71). Ayckbourn remembers a 'row we had at Stoke' (Ayckbourn 2008) after news broke of the assassination of John F. Kennedy:

> Peter Cheeseman came to me, and he said, "I think we should have two minutes silence just before [*Mr Whatnot*] starts," and I said, "No!" I mean, if these people decided to come see *Mr Whatnot* on the day the President of the United States [was assassinated], they are the ones that don't give a stuff. I mean if they really wanted to mourn him, they can stay at home. And so we didn't [have silence] (Ibid.).

It seems though that the core of the disagreement lay in each man's view of the role and status of the actor. Ayckbourn – 'a little bit more show-biz than Peter' (Watson 1981: 73) – regards actors as outsiders who provide a touch of glamour. He asks, 'Are actors as other men, or are they not?. . . . The public, I suspect, prefer them not to be. . . . I'm sure that most of the public would love [actors] to jump into the Rolls and steam off' (Ayckbourn *in* Watson 1981: 73). For Cheeseman, actors were insiders – fellow workers embedded within the local community. Theatregoer Mona Mason, who ran a newsagents' shop close to the Stoke theatre, has recalled how

> these people who were in the plays would come past. They'd always . . . stand and have a chat with you and [then] you'd see them doing the warm up in the foyer, you know. . . . I'd stand there in, by my shop window, you know, looking across and thinking "what are they doing?", you know, "I wonder what they're doing that for?" You don't realise what goes into a play (Mason 2003).

Ayckbourn considers that Cheeseman – 'graduating rapidly towards the documentary' (Ayckbourn *in* Watson 1981: 73) – was increasingly privileging the authentic voice as central to theatre. Cheeseman 'found it dramatic for real shop stewards to stand up and tell you about their day-to-day plight; which became dramatic because they were real shop stewards' (Ibid.: 73). Ayckbourn – 'moving rapidly in another direction' (Ibid.) – has summarized the perceived difference between his and Cheeseman's approach to working with actors, as being that while 'Peter believed essentially (and this is to put it a bit crudely) that no actor could do anything unless he fully understood the concept . . . [I] insisted that there was such a thing as an actor's instinct, which must be allowed to flourish' (Ibid.: 72). In fact Ayckbourn's characterization of Cheeseman's view – that 'no actor could play a nuclear scientist unless he had read all the books about nuclear science' (Ibid.) – could be said to highlight two key features of Cheeseman's theatre making: he was favouring the type of research-based approach to role creation developed by Bertolt Brecht and Joan Littlewood; and he was beginning to involve actors as collaborators. A solution to the exodus of company playwrights was emerging.

Cheeseman's introduction to *The Knotty* (Cheeseman 1970) places in context Stephen Joseph's influence on the development of Cheeseman's musical documentaries. He begins:

> THE KNOTTY and all our documentary work at Stoke-on-Trent have quite particular and deliberately local motives and quite particular characteristics. The principal motive derives from the basic policy of the Victoria Theatre. This was opened in October 1962 by Stephen Joseph as the permanent home of the Studio Theatre Company founded in 1955 by Stephen Joseph to do new plays and explore the possibilities of theatre in the round. Stephen's policy inevitably and deliberately led to the presence of writers in the company, which lived by touring theatreless towns from 1955 to 1962 (Ibid.: viii–ix).

For Cheeseman, 'The presence of a writer working in the company seemed to me to provide an essential factor in the creative potency of the group' (Ibid.: ix). Years later he identified the sudden absence of writers within his own ensemble, after Alan Ayckbourn had left the company in 1964, as 'terribly dangerous' (Giannachi and Luckhurst 1999: 15). Cheeseman recalls that 'Though we were dedicated to the idea of giving expression to the life of our new home community we had found no local writer and had no means of using local subject matter' (Cheeseman 1970: x). Since Cheeseman wanted to continue to produce new work – preferably community-focused work that would allow the community 'to be onstage at some point' (Giannachi and Luckhurst 1999: 15) – he needed people to create it. In 1964 Peter Terson – a playwright, although not also an actor – was taken on 'as resident dramatist with a year's salary . . . from the Arts Council' (Cheeseman 2004); Terson's mainly single-authored plays were to form a key part of the provision of new work in the Potteries under Cheeseman's leadership. Around this time radio documentarist Charles Parker introduced Cheeseman to the idea of 'using contemporary material by recording it' (Giannachi and Luckhurst 1999: 15). Cheeseman – now working with a company of actors, not actor-playwrights – devised and implemented a new formula. The start of the process was simple although radical: 'If we had no writer amongst us, we must assume the function collectively, as a group, shape our own material out of documentary research into the history of this community' (Cheeseman 1970: x).

Such an approach could yield only raw recorded material, which would then need to be shaped. Cheeseman identified a potential source of inspiration for such shaping:

> Years of working in the exciting freedom of theatre in the round under Stephen Joseph's intelligent and imaginative leadership had already enabled David Campton and Alan Ayckbourn to develop racy theatrical narratives (Ibid.).

Cheeseman was drawn too to Ayckbourn's sound-effects-led, almost prop-free comic piece *Mr Whatnot* – written in part as a response to being 'Cursed with the currency of psychological realism' (Cheeseman 1970: x) – which Cheeseman considered to be 'a true and uncompromising piece of self-expression by a group of young artists' (Ibid.). When placing older characters onstage, directors were too often required, Cheeseman noted, to 'prod on youngsters drenched in white powder and with painted faces, pretending to a maturity that disappears in the cloud of white dust which every violent encounter provokes' (Ibid.). Ayckbourn's play and production 'took a fair and square look at all our [company's] limitations' (Ibid.), and made imaginative use of limited resources: 'Various locations [were] indicated by props rather than use of set' (Murgatroyd n.d., c) – 'a steering wheel, for instance, represented a car' (Cheeseman 1970: x). Ayckbourn, directing, 'threw naturalistic casting to the winds' (Ibid.). Notwithstanding differences between the two men, it seems likely then that Ayckbourn's writing and direction helped to provoke Cheeseman's dramatic shift in style of presentation. On 14 July 1964 Cheeseman opened *The Jolly Potters*, his first musical documentary: pieced together from research and from actors' interviews with members of the local community, the production featured non-naturalistic multi-role casting, representative props and costume, and ubiquitous recorded sound.

While Ayckbourn seems to have influenced Cheeseman's style of production, there is no suggestion that the content of the musical documentaries owed a debt either to Ayckbourn or indeed, to any significant degree, to Stephen Joseph. In his 1970 introduction to *The Knotty*, Cheeseman labels Ayckbourn 'an ingenious and whimsical comedian' (Cheeseman 1970: xi) – regarding himself, by contrast, as 'A bit serious and guiltily academic' (Ibid.). Cheeseman has instead identified 'film and television, especially during the war' (Giannachi and Luckhurst 1999: 14) as key influences on the content of his musical documentaries, along with the work of Brecht, Piscator and Living Newspaper performances staged by the Unity Theatre group in Liverpool (Ibid.).

By 1970, then, Stephen Joseph's twin inheritors were already some distance apart as theatre makers. Cheeseman – established as artistic director of Britain's only permanent round theatre, located in a previously theatreless community in an industrial northern English heartland – was chief collaborator on a series of innovative, politically provocative and verbatim speech-based musical documentaries. Meanwhile Ayckbourn continued to combine occasional playwriting and guest directing in Scarborough with the Leeds-based BBC radio production work he had taken on in 1964. His 1965 play *Meet My Father* (later retitled *Relatively Speaking*) had, in 1967, finally brought Ayckbourn serious playwriting success in London's West End; his 1969 comedy *How The Other Half Loves* secured his reputation. In 1970, 3 years after Stephen Joseph's death, Joseph's increasingly successful twin protégés were each headed in important, innovative yet very different career directions.

Peter Cheeseman died in 2010. Eleven years earlier, asked to describe his status within a European theatrical landscape, he offered that he was an 'unknown British regional theatre director' (Giannachi and Luckhurst 1999: 18) – an over-modest assessment, surely, considering the attention intermittently given to his work in the Potteries. Cheeseman's posthumous reputation is now evolving independently of the man; and it's interesting for me, writing a book on Stephen Joseph, to observe how the edges are blurring between the work and achievements of Joseph and Cheeseman. Obituaries on Cheeseman appeared quite widely in 2010 – including within Britain's The *Guardian* and *The Times* newspapers, both of which offered significant profiles. The *Guardian* obituarist mistakenly credits Cheeseman with 'developing [Ayckbourn] as [a] new talent' (Thornber 2010), while *The Times* characterizes the fierce and complicated power struggle between Joseph and Cheeseman as simply a disagreement within which 'the ageing Joseph tried to persuade the trustees to sack [Cheeseman]' *(The Times* 2010).

It's been said that 'history is written by the victors'. Leaving aside the neat irony that no one seems certain who first said this, there are interesting historiographical issues that arise when someone loses – including their life, and thus their right to reply. Stephen Joseph and Peter Cheeseman are now both deceased. So who did what, who thought what, who was and is the more influential? The death of a noted figure can instigate a 'land grab' between eminent advocates: the most important archive, the most popular monograph, the most funding-worthy research project, will probably be the one claiming the deepest influence on others.

An unpublished 1998 interview with Peter Cheeseman would seem to summarize a key feature of what was Joseph's philosophical influence on his late protégé. Cheeseman reflects that Joseph had

> a kind of radical spirit – questioning, intelligent, imaginative radicalism. There's so much humbug and old-fashioned bullshit in the theatre . . . it's full of this rubbish, sort of toffee-nosed nonsense . . . Stephen, I suppose, taught me to cut through the humbug, to see things from a fundamental viewpoint, – like the act of theatre – "actor and audience" (Cheeseman 1998: 9–10).

Both Cheeseman and Ayckbourn have described how, after Joseph's early death, they felt obliged to maintain his missionary work. Peter Cheeseman recalls that

> when Stephen died, I think both Alan and I felt we had to carry on, you know not as a sense of filial duty as it were – although he was very much a father figure, particularly to Alan . . . but both of us out of sheer excitement of what Stephen had taught us, and wanting to carry that out and bring about his ideas (Cheeseman 1998: 3).

Alan Ayckbourn, still living and working, although no longer running the Scarborough company, continues to highlight his debt to Stephen Joseph – including, of course, within the Foreword for this book. In 2005 he went as far as to state that 'Without [Stephen Joseph] a lot of my life would never have happened' (Ayckbourn 2005: 25'37"). In the same interview Ayckbourn implicitly highlighted the extent to which Peter Cheeseman had begun forging his own path away from Joseph. Ayckbourn recalled how

> . . . in the early 1970's I took up the challenge [of running the Scarborough theatre] mainly because I didn't want to see Stephen's good idea die – and it looked like it would, because – I thought I knew

him better than most people, and I thought I knew where he wanted to go with it (Ayckbourn 2005: 26'15").

What then was the legacy that the protégés felt obliged to sustain? The thread of Joseph's continuing influence existed throughout Ayckbourn and Cheeseman's parallel work in leading internationally recognized in-the-round theatres in the north of England. Both men sought to use the role of artistic director to programme a bold repertoire of provocative live work that spanned a range of genres. Although Joseph's work was independent of any specific philosophical or political ideology, a left-leaning bias has been ever-present in the work of all three figures. Work staged drew heavily on the sense of audience-performer intimacy that is an inherent feature of small-scale, in-the-round theatre. Further, despite national and international success, both Joseph protégés made an early commitment to a single regional location: Ayckbourn still lives in Scarborough, a short stroll from the location of Stephen Joseph's first, temporary round theatre; Cheeseman lived for decades within stone-throwing distance of the permanent round theatre he went on to establish in Newcastle-under-Lyme. In fact each man signalled early on his intention to stay 'local' by buying a home. Both men orchestrated moves to consolidate the presence of round theatre in their respective adopted towns: Ayckbourn supervised the round theatre adaptation of, first, a former boys' school, and later a cinema – both theatres bearing Joseph's name; while in 1986 Cheeseman opened the New Victoria Theatre, Britain's first entirely new professional, non-adaptable in-the-round theatre building, in a complex which incorporates the small Stephen Joseph Studio.

Predictably, Joseph's posthumous influence can be seen in the auditorium design of the in-the-round theatres still standing in Scarborough and in the Potteries. Neither the New Vic nor the two Scarborough theatres incorporate any sort of upper circle; indeed both Scarborough spaces feature just one level of deeply raked seating incorporated into a single volume, shaped around a broadly rectangular stage – echoing the configuration of the original Studio Theatre space in the Concert Room at Scarborough's main public library. By contrast Manchester's Royal Exchange Theatre – built after Joseph's death, and without consulting either Ayckbourn or Cheeseman – features triple-level hierarchical seating redolent of a traditional proscenium theatre: modestly raked stalls seating, a deeply raked circle and precipitous upper circle seating.

Joseph also bequeathed to Ayckbourn and Cheeseman a socially diverse local theatregoing community which remains to this day unafraid of either theatre-in-the-round, or (within limits) new writing. This long-term feature has provided each protégé with something of a bespoke laboratory in which to examine, with a high degree of community participation, prevailing conditions within society. Mark Ravenhill has noted how the current Scarborough theatre applies Stephen Joseph's 'strong sense of what theatre, and how theatre, could be within a town, and the impact – the importance it could have for a community' (Ravenhill 2010); the same can certainly be said to apply in the Potteries.

Yet the laboratory conditions have been very different for each theatre maker. Peter Cheeseman, working in the heavily industrial Potteries region, would provoke the creation of highly collaborative musical documentaries located textually, narratively and physically within the heart of his local community. Alongside this, audiences helped to nurture the developing work of new theatre makers, including Alan Plater, Peter Terson, Bob Eaton and Ken Campbell. Challenging classical work was staged too: actor Ben Kingsley recalls that the Stoke company worked hard 'to [bring] the audience up to a level at which they comprehended, and were thrilled by, beautiful dramatic poetry and language. So nothing was diluted. Nothing was compromised' (Kingsley 2008). In 1970 Cheeseman – by now something of a reluctant role model for those who sought to destroy the perceived hegemony of playwrights – felt obliged to disassociate himself from 'the intolerance of writers' plays that some of my professional theatre colleagues have expressed' (Cheeseman 1970: vii). Actor-collaborators mattered; but then so too did playwrights: Cheeseman pointed out that in Stoke-on-Trent 'In any one year we present about fourteen new productions, of which only one is likely to be a documentary' (Ibid.).

Alan Ayckbourn's most recent laboratory is the Stephen Joseph Theatre (SJT) in Scarborough – a town reliant, not on heavy industry, but on regional tourism. Local theatregoers' pride has long been derived from twin sources: from their 'guinea pig' status as the first to appraise Ayckbourn's latest work (and that of others, including *Woman In Black* dramatist Stephen Mallatratt and *Calendar Girls* author Tim Firth) and from the sense that Ayckbourn's fictional characters are drawn from observation by a playwright who has adopted, and lives in the heart of, their town. Ayckbourn's own sense of community is built into SJT design features away from the auditorium: a viewing gallery built into the main rehearsal room allows actors and directors to glimpse audience reaction, even before first preview; while the theatre's green room features a central, sofa-filled 'hang-out' space containing a wall full of mugs and the building's only kettle, a large water heater. Thus everyone from artistic director to intern is encouraged to mix socially, reducing barriers and enhancing communication.

For many years, Peter Cheeseman and Alan Ayckbourn each led theatres offering an unusually wide repertoire of plays: new and established work, classical drama, alternative and popular fare. Thus a clear link can be made to the highly eclectic repertoire of Joseph's Studio Theatre group. Indeed it seems apposite that Peter Brook's 1965 visit to Stoke's 'lively' (Brook 1968: 129) Vic Theatre saw him witness a production of *Pygmalion* – Bernard Shaw's comic-romantic anatomizing of class barriers in English society – rather than Cheeseman's still-noted production of *The Staffordshire Rebels*, the second of his radical political musical documentaries (which had closed just days before Brook's visit). Brook's reporting of a powerful and memorable theatre event, that was superficially just another revival of a well-established and decades-old play, suggests much about Cheeseman's success in wanting 'to be relevant to the people of Stoke-on-Trent' (Kingsley 2008). Although Stephen Joseph did not live to read Brook's published description of that evening, he would perhaps have enjoyed praise from a theatrical icon for a small yet important regional event in which, tellingly, 'The audience participated fully' (Brook 1968: 129).

3

Joseph's Seven Routes to the Unknown

Beyond Ayckbourn and Cheeseman, how did Stephen Joseph influence new writing for the theatre? Joseph's search for new writing began early on in his theatre career – and followed as many as seven different routes for uncovering new plays and playwrights. Even before the 1955 launch of his theatre company, he was running courses in which potential playwrights 'had their work criticised and discussed in seminars' (Wood 1979: 50). The emerging need for a low-cost forum for the professional staging of such new work (Ibid.) provoked, it seems, the founding of Joseph's Studio Theatre Company Limited.

The company's inaugural 1955 Scarborough summer season featured four plays – all of them new, all written by unknown authors. The staging of David Campton's *Dragons Are Dangerous* marked the start of a working relationship with Stephen Joseph that was to outlast the company. The three other playwrights debuted in that first season – Jurneman Winch, Eleanor D. Glaser and Ruth Dixon – were all female. Thus at a point when women were virtually unrepresented within professional playwriting, three-quarters of Joseph's 1955 repertoire comprised new plays written by female authors. Joseph re-commissioned all three, giving full productions in Scarborough to Eleanor D. Glaser's *Call the Selkie Home* in 1956 and Ruth Dixon's *Honey in the Stone* in 1957. Joseph also sent copies of the playwrights' work to George Devine at the Royal Court Theatre – even offering to resubmit work by Dixon and proposing a further play, *We Are For The Dark*, by unknown playwright Margaret Turner (Joseph 1958e: 1). Devine rejected all submissions; and each of the four female playwrights appears to have subsequently faded from view.

The 1969 edition of John Russell Taylor's *Anger and After* discusses Joseph's support for James Saunders, and notes that David Campton was 'discovered' by Joseph (Russell Taylor 1969: 144–5). Former Studio Theatre member Terry Lane identifies seven successful writers whose theatre work was debuted by Stephen Joseph: Robert Bolt, James Saunders, Joan Macalpine, Richard Gill, Mike Stott, Alan Ayckbourn and David Campton (Lane 2006: 220–1) – a not unimpressive group of playwrights. Lane reports too Joseph's commitment to staging non-British work at his temporary London base in Fitzroy Square:

> Apart from new plays, he was putting on the world's avant-garde classics. From the States, Steinbeck and Saroyan; from France Adamov, Giraudoux (which the Royal Court mounted the following year) and Tardieu; German expressionism and Spanish eroticism, Dostoevski and a new Brazilian author. Eleven new writers had one or more of their works performed, and there were provoking classics from Priestley, Chekov [sic], Pirandello, Henry James and of course the *Phèdre* of Racine (Ibid.: 133).

The translation of Adamov's *Professor Taranne* was, incidentally, Stephen Joseph's own. Joseph's own books do little to highlight his profile as a champion of new playwriting. Indeed Joseph tends not to claim direct credit for the discovery of new writers: for example reference to his work with James Saunders is limited, in *Theatre In The Round*, to a brief comment on the minimalist staging of Saunders's play *The Ark* (Joseph 1967: 148). Eight pages later Joseph discusses the work of four playwrights, yet he omits to mention his own role in bringing their first work to the professional stage (Joseph 1967: 156). One of the four, Joseph's former University of Manchester student Mike Stott, had already gone on to co-script Peter Brook's controversial Royal Shakespeare Company production *US*; Joseph simply names Stott as someone whose debut piece *The Play of Mata Hari* was 'great fun to do' (Ibid.).

Curiously, new playwriting staged in Scarborough and Stoke-on-Trent drew in audiences far more successfully than new work (often the same work) staged in London. The broad failure of the poorly attended Mahatma Gandhi Hall showcases for new writing may in part have been a consequence of the need to hastily construct a temporary round theatre – without raked seating – in the venue in London's Fitzroy Square. Joseph wrote down what he would like to have said publicly, in a private letter to a theatre supporter:

> Look hear, you lousey [sic] Londoners, we've been giving you a good deal of fascinating experimental theatre and you won't come to it; and without a paying audience we cannot survive, so we'll go where there is a paying audience – for instance, Scarborough (Joseph 1958o: 1).

Scarborough's location – some 250 miles from London, beyond easy reach of the capital – created its own problems. Joseph recalls in *Theatre in the Round* that

> a critic who had given a series of very harsh reviews to our new plays was asked if he really thought they were all that bad; and he replied that

they couldn't be any good as they hadn't been done in London (Joseph 1967: 159).

The conditions that encourage such a view warrant attention. Even today, historians – who are uniquely well placed to rebalance things – can inadvertently obscure and distort them. The seminal 1999 text *British Theatre Since The War* – which opens with a statement that 'London has been *the* site of theatrical activity throughout the [post-WW2] period' (Shellard 1999) – sees the author urge a 'debate about the advisability of such centralisation' (Ibid.). Such unswerving confidence naturally compounds the idea that centralization actually exists. The late Alan Plater observed in 2008 that 'The history of British theatre so much is the history of London theatre, and it disregards the whole of the English regions, the whole of Scotland, most of Ireland' (Plater 2008). Writer and director Trevor Griffiths has spoken of 'another axis' (Griffiths 2008):

> There is London and the south-east, then there's the rest of the country ... historically, you can see different oppositions, between the capital – "capital culture" – and these other [regions] (Ibid.).

Yet perhaps a debate on centralization is precisely what is now needed. Trevor Griffiths claims that capital culture can 'single people out and smash them' (Ibid.). Mark Ravenhill holds up the London location of the national theatre critics as a key distorting factor:

> a play that's going to play in a theatre like [London's Theatre] 503 with, what, seventy seats or something, is going to probably get two, three, four national critics – open it in the main house in Birmingham and [you'd] get one or two national critics (Ravenhill 2010).

In fact Ravenhill's historical and geographical insights on 'the most capital-centric country in the world' (Ibid.) merit attention. He adds:

> We've gone backwards. France made that massive effort to devolve theatre and send the arts out, and they did quite successfully do that – push things out from Paris. And Germany's always been very regional because that's the history of Germany – it's always been based around those Principalities. There really isn't any centre, a "capital" of theatre in Germany – every city more or less has its own. They're all competing – it's much more like football teams, they're all competing to be the best theatre, there isn't one central place. England's become more focused – the critics and casting people – become more looking into London. Which is a weird thing (Ibid.).

Ravenhill sees regional touring as part of the solution:

> I started working with touring companies, so *Shopping and Fucking*
> was produced by Out Of Joint and was taken around the country. I did
> think that was really important. There were lots of new plays produced
> at the time . . . but not many of them actually went and played lots of
> different venues around the country. I've always tried, when I've done
> a play, to get it to tour as well. So I got the National to tour *Mother
> Clapp's Molly House* and I got the Donmar to tour *The Cut*. Because
> I just think – I don't like the idea of writing a play that's for London. I
> want to see how it reads with different audiences in different parts of
> the country (Ibid.).

Ravenhill believes that the process of touring a new play 'is good for having
a perspective on your work, and getting criticism, and seeing your work in
context' (Ibid.). Stephen Joseph's writers' company was launched at a time
when falling audiences were leading to the mass closure of theatres. Between
1950 and 1954 the number of commercial theatres with permanent repertory
companies dropped from 94 to 60 (Jackson and Rowell 1984: 87); surviving
theatres adopted a conservative policy of scheduling proven West End
successes. And the choice of such plays was narrow: in 1956 – the year *Look
Back In Anger* first opened in London – the popular plays were by Bagnold,
Ustinov, Coward and Douglas Home – 'none of them exactly harbingers of
revolution' (Billington 2007a: 4).

Stephen Joseph's 1955 founding of a company for new writing seems,
then, oddly timed. Alan Ayckbourn has spoken of a man who

> in the summer of 1955, in the face of intense competition from half a
> dozen other theatres in [Scarborough], managed to produce a series of
> new experimental plays by unknown writers, performed by unknown
> actors, in a theatrical format that was, at that period, completely
> revolutionary anywhere in the UK (Yaldren 2005: 41).

Joseph's summer 1955 activity in this field predates by several months the
1956 staging of new work at the newly renovated Royal Court Theatre.
Joseph initially drew writers from his own playwriting evening classes in
London; this allowed him not only a firm editing hand, but also reduced
costs by avoiding the need, initially at least, to negotiate with literary agents.
Joseph's staging of premiere productions also held out the possibility of
future royalties for his company, should Studio Theatre-initiated plays be
subsequently staged elsewhere.

Joseph's 1955 and 1956 summer seasons debuted a total of six new full-
length plays and two new one-act plays; previously performed work totalled

just one full-length play and one one-act play (Murgatroyd 2008). There was no dominant writing style within these new plays, or indeed those that followed. Joseph's point was to find new work and stage it; thus audiences were offered a varied diet, including James Saunders's Ionesco-like absurdism, David Campton's politically provocative comedies of menace and Alan Ayckbourn's quirky familial comedies. The repertoire included historical drama, modern blank verse, epic biography, a fresh translation of Sartre: Joseph would stage plays in almost any style.

The near-exception was what was to become the rule elsewhere: there remained an almost total absence of serious-toned, class-conscious and social-realist new writing in the style of early John Osborne, Arnold Wesker or Shelagh Delaney. Perhaps Joseph wanted to keep 'clear blue water' between his company and George Devine's Royal Court; perhaps his own controversial preference for 'sentimentality in the theatre, especially when it is combined with more or less epic treatment' (Joseph 1967: 155–6) steered him away from social realism. Perhaps he simply wished to sidestep a movement later characterized by theatre historian Kate Harris as 'theatre's attempt to catch up with what the dramatised documentary had been pioneering for almost a decade [before 1956] on television, and longer on radio' (Harris 2008: 178). It's possible too that Joseph was simply on the lookout for any strong new work, and little fitting the social-realist genre came his way.

In truth, a new playwright who placed work with a regionally located fringe company such as Studio Theatre was taking a risk. In 1958 Joseph admitted as much in a private letter explaining his decision to abandon regular touring visits to London:

> It is a sad thing but true that a try-out by a theatre such as ours (and the same thing is true for repertory theatres that do new plays) may actually do harm to a promising playwright since managers only read notices, and if the notices are few and unsympathetic (as is usually the case) the play (which may in fact be a good deal above average) never gets seen or read again. It is better for the playwright to send [their] play direct to a big manager and if it is turned down, burn it! Agents know this and very seldom allow us to do plays that have any chance at all (Joseph 1958m: 1).

Such a discouraging environment seems only to have spurred Joseph on in his hunt for new work. During his career-long search for new plays he used no fewer than seven routes towards unearthing new writing for the stage:

1. writing and staging new plays of his own
2. inviting direct submission from unknown and untried playwrights
3. developing new plays through playwriting courses

4. working in collaboration with those who already had access to high-quality new writing
5. challenging theatre company members to attempt playwriting
6. reaching out to emerging or established playwrights who had fallen foul of the English theatre establishment
7. offering theatrical staging to writers working in television

Joseph does seem to have briefly explored his first option, staging his own work. By 1955 he had quite a back catalogue of self-authored plays across a range of genres, much of which had already been tested on student casts. Perhaps highest-profile was his 1953 play *The Key*, performed in Bucharest for the communist World Festival of Youth and Students. Joseph's plot has fun with fourth-wall-breaking, and with a lost key that fantastically reappears within three different time periods; the time-travelling conceit allows Joseph to present modern naturalism, melodrama and Jacobean verse within a single piece – meaning that his student actors, and also audiences new to the theatre, would get to 'sample' different genres within the same story. This quasi-educational feature became less valid on the professional stage; additionally, the large cast size would have rendered production costs prohibitive.

Further, Joseph's sketch- and playwriting efforts had been staged at Central, and also at Cambridge University (cf. Lane 2006: 62–9; also Wood 1979: 7, quoted earlier); a *News Chronicle* review of the 1948 Cambridge Footlights production directed by Joseph records that he 'wrote the best sketches' (Wood 1979: 7). He also co-wrote with David Campton a play for television – *One Fight More* – broadcast by the BBC on 18 December 1956. Ten days later Michael Barry, Head of Drama at the BBC, offered a fairly damning criticism of the play and its production. Barry's comments suggest that Joseph and Campton had scripted a type of dramatized documentary:

> Some of the acting scenes flashed into life and gave the impression of belonging to a different play to the close-up method applied, for instance, to the magistrate (incidentally, an unconvincing moment). The period of close description showing the entrance test for an engine cleaner was completely unbalanced with the synoptic coverage of the Borstal and army period, and for this we were to blame (Barry 1956b).

Barry's final comments highlight that the co-writers were attempting something quite pioneering:

> I have no doubt that much can be done with this method of story telling, and personally I should be extremely interested in anything else you write as a result of thinking along these lines (Ibid.).

Joseph seems to have subsequently abandoned any further ambitions to write for television. He also deemed his own stage work unsuitable for professional production; although he did allow a single Sunday evening showing of his translation of Arthur Adamov's *Professor Tarranne*, performed in London's Mahatma Gandhi Hall in 1956 (Note 1 n.d.).

Joseph's second method for finding plays was to invite direct submissions from unknown and untried playwrights.

In 2012 former playwright J. W. James produced a small cache of previously unseen letters from Stephen Joseph, a donation to the Stephen Joseph Theatre. The letters offer useful insights into Joseph's handling of new writing talent. Joseph's first letter to James, written on 6 August 1957, is brief and direct. He offers: 'I am sure you have talent, but you seem to be following a false star' (Joseph 1957) – adding simply: 'Come and have a chat' (Ibid.). Joseph next commissioned James's 1958 play *A Sense of Loss*; by October that year James was receiving, along with promises of overdue royalty payments, a glimpse into Joseph's state of mind:

> The rigours of trying to keep a shoe-string company together are more of a strain than you may imagine and I'd rather be slow about these things than get them all wrong. Incidentally, please check that [the payments] are alright! (Joseph 1958t)

Joseph also shared his private disappointment at his company's reception in southeast England:

> We went out with a dull wheeze at Harlow – the coldest audiences we've ever met. You would have frozen in your seat (ibid.).

A little over a year later, following discussion around a possible James translation of work by the eighteenth-century playwright Pierre de Marivaux, Joseph wrote declining to stage two James scripts. He did however offer feedback:

> I enclose the one act plays. Each of them has attractive qualities (as you must know), but each of them also has what I can begin to rely on as a J. Jamesian defect – there is too much talk in relation to action. I'm not asking for murders, jumping from parapets and so on – though I'm not against these. I'm asking for the developing relationships between people. This *may* be shown physically, but its better shown emotionally through the progress of separate characters from one situation to another. After working on SENSE OF LOSS I felt that Jean was the most developed character, for this very reason. The least developed from this point of view was Jimmy. Result – trouble! But you know by

now I ask for a simple dramatic experience, not because I think the
audience is simple so much as because my own taste is simple. Which
is maybe why I enjoy Marivaux? (Joseph 1958u).

Ever-conscious of tight budgets, Joseph added:

By all means write for three women in the summer – not more than
four men (three if possible) to go with them, though! (Ibid.)

In the end, Joseph commissioned just two plays from James: the Marivaux
adaptation *Love and Chance* – staged in a double-bill with Pirandello's *The
Man With A Flower In His Mouth* – and the original piece *A Sense of Loss*,
staged immediately after. In fact the 1958 Scarborough season showcasing
James's work is remarkable in featuring plays by a host of non-British, mainly
non-contemporary dramatists. Alongside the Marivaux and Pirandello
pieces there were plays by Racine, Jean Jacques Bernard and Valentin Kataev.
Clearly, Joseph was determined to prove wrong the 'number of people' (Joseph
1955e) who had warned him 3 years earlier 'that Scarborough is incapable of
anything more than the lightest of entertainment and that we are wasting our
efforts here' (Ibid.).

Joseph's keenest ambition was, though, reserved for finding new work.
The Scarborough base had been founded on a conviction that 'the theatre
is badly in need of an organisation concerned with putting on new plays –
particularly plays that do not comply with the formulae of west-end comedy'
(Joseph 1955d). In fact Joseph's enthusiasm for provoking new writing seems
to have been almost indiscriminate. A letter from a theatre supporter and
non-writer received the following unsolicited 'call to arms':

Is agriculture going down the drain? Write a play about it. Let us have
scenes all over your offices and warehouses – perhaps you have written
one already? (Joseph 1958e: 2)

Alan Ayckbourn recalls an incident that exemplifies Joseph's risk-taking
commissioning strategy:

There was one wonderful [play] called *Halfway to Heaven* . . . which
was absolutely turgid. [Joseph] said, "Well, we're doing a new play, so
we'll just get on with it, people!" I wasn't in it, thank God. It started
with somebody trying to commit suicide, which is something I later
used in *Absurd Person [Singular]*. And then he invited the author to the
first night, because she hadn't been, and she was too old to travel! And
I said, "What has that done? Bored the pants off us all, and just made
her a bit happy." She was about eighty-nine or something . . . it was her

first play to be done – and probably her last, too. . . . I said, "Check their ages next time" (Ayckbourn 2007).

Alan Stockwell was another name new to Joseph. The playwright and director would enjoy limited success within children's theatre, eventually experimenting with in-the-round staging (The *Stage* 1962: 15). He first approached Joseph in 1961, writing as the self-styled manager of Bradford Experimental Theatre (Stockwell 1961a). In the same year, Stockwell submitted two scripts for Joseph's consideration. In April 1961 Joseph rejected both pieces (Joseph 1961f: 1); he wrote again the following month, having heard that Stockwell was seeking a base for his own theatre company. Joseph urged Stockwell to 'find a cellar, or some similar space wherever you can run a theatre club. I offer my services (free!) as adviser on converting *anything* into a theatre' (Joseph 1961b: 1). Joseph's offer of involvement went beyond the offer of free consultancy:

> . . . You will probably need some sort of list of patrons. You will know the sort of persons to get. Invite John Wood, Roy Shaw and myself, amongst others, we will lend you an air of respectability! (Ibid.)

Stockwell must have persisted in sending scripts, as a July 1961 letter from Joseph offered a single 'club' performance of a provocative new play titled *The Bed Life of a Mad Boy*. Joseph suggested himself as director, 'possibly with the help of Alan Ayckbourn' (Joseph 1961c: 1). Joseph's programme note for the production clarifies why he chose to stage the piece:

> THE BED-LIFE OF A MAD BOY is a vigorous expression of a young man's reactions to the sorts of problems that must claim the attention of everyone today. It is, of course, confused and confusing; it takes much of its sombre colour from the sombre world we live in; but its vitality is the vitality of a young artist, striving to find a pattern in the apparent chaos. The play is written in unconnected scenes which add up to present a vivid picture of the world that has been inherited by the younger generation (Joseph 1961e: 2).

The play – partly written in rhyming verse and lacking a traditional narrative structure – is likely to have been staged privately for two reasons. Joseph did not feel the play 'would attract enough people into the theatre to justify including [it] in our repertoire' (Joseph 1961e: 2) – although he added the hope that the audience 'will enjoy themselves, and encourage us to make more experiments of this nature' (Ibid.). Secondly, the Stockwell play contained highly controversial scenes – including the rape of a nun (Stockwell 1961: 33) and the onstage suicide of a character (Ibid.: 39), both of which would surely have provoked a ban from the office of the Lord Chamberlain. In the event *The Bed Life of a Mad Boy*, with its controversial scenes of violent behaviour by a group of youths, reached the stage some 4 years ahead of the Royal Court's club performance of Edward Bond's famously violent *Saved* (Ellis 2003). Joseph's own single club performance in Scarborough featured Ayckbourn as the rapist; Joseph appeared onstage too, as one of two 'madmen'. Perhaps predictably, Joseph then invited his audience to a post-performance 'informal discussion in the exhibition room' (Joseph 1961e: 2). Six years later Joseph would praise in print Stockwell's 'challenging and highly original script' (Joseph 1967: 155); between times he dared to workshop scenes from the play during drama demonstrations – including for members of the Women's Institute (Joseph n.d., f). Within these, Ayckbourn – despite confessing early on that the play had 'turned me off [poetry]' (Ayckbourn 1961: 1) – continued to reprise his role as 'A figure' (Joseph 1961e: 3).

Unsolicited plays did emerge via Joseph's third source for new plays – the ongoing intermittent short playwriting courses offered by Joseph under the auspices of the amateur British Drama League (BDL). Joseph's biggest 'catch' via this route was surely David Campton (Wood 1979: 51), who would later join up as a company regular. Campton's work with Joseph is discussed within the next chapter.

Another early discovery via the BDL courses was playwright Joan Winch. For her, as for Alan Stockwell, ongoing success as a professional writer would prove elusive; however, a close reading of letters between her and Joseph suggests that she was increasingly heading for success when an incident prompted Joseph to cut the cord between them. Curiously, Winch chose to write under the male pseudonym Jurneman Winch. 'Jurneman' does seem to have both tricked and impressed theatre critics, when her first play was staged during Studio Theatre's 1955 debut season: *The Stage* dubbed her 'A Playwright to Watch' (*The Stage* 18 August 1955), describing 'his *Turn Right at the Crossroads*' (Ibid.: 1955) as an 'unusual theatrical experience' (Ibid.: 1955); Scarborough's local newspaper praised 'Mr. Winch's dramatic style' (*Scarborough Evening News* 1955); and the *Yorkshire Post* considered Winch's debut play to be 'undoubtedly the most thought-provoking of the company's fourfold repertoire' (*Yorkshire Post* 12 August 1955). The piece in The *Stage* labelled Winch's 'morality play' (*The Stage* 18 August 1955) a

> dramatically exciting work. The author has somehow captured the style of modern cinematic ballet, albeit using words, and the watcher has a dream-like sensation, being of and yet outside action which is exaggerated yet perfectly credible (Ibid.).

Winch retained the male pseudonym for her next Studio Theatre commission, a theatrically impressionistic adaptation of Emily Bronte's *Wuthering Heights* for the 1956 Scarborough summer season. The *Stage* now praised Winch's 'virile' production, which was 'shot through with his striking dialogue in verse or poetic prose' (*The Stage* 1956). Noting the in-the-round staging, Ted Gomm at the *Socialist Leader* offered that he had 'no doubts now that drama is intensified by bringing it right into the midst of the audience' (Gomm 1956); he observed that 'one's close proximity to the players brought one into immediate sympathy with their problems' (Ibid.).

Some 3 weeks after *Wuthering Heights* opened, Winch wrote to thank Joseph for 'keeping me within your company's charmed circle' (Winch 1956a). Two months later she submitted a synopsis of her proposed play *Chopin*, along with a request for a tutorial. Did he agree that 'work should come before frivolity at a palais-prom?' (Winch 1956b).

In January 1957 an 'astounded' Winch (Winch 1957) announced that she had been invited to join a writers' agency. However her writing had simultaneously 'dried up, absolutely and completely' (Ibid.). She added:

> There's nothing there at all, though two plays were roughed. I am afraid
> the desert may last a long time for a similar period some years ago
> lasted nine months, and that wasn't as barren as now (Winch 1957).

Though this was clearly a cry for help and guidance, Winch's decision to sign with an agent seems to have alienated Joseph. Although he was no writers' agent, he had liaised with them often, and had dabbled – once even arranging publication of David Campton's *The Lunatic View*. Winch offered pre-emptively that she was 'sorry about all this, particularly my share in it' (Ibid.), before adding: 'A spot of dancing might do me a world of good. Would it you?' (Ibid.).

Did they dance, and more? This is a fragment of story told only in letters. In what may be the final correspondence between the two, a deeply impassioned Winch wrote in July 1958 that she was

> bursting with desire to write . . . and the themes that appeal wither when
> I think of human beings as their exponents. I feel I could thunder and
> lash and ecstacize and be lyrical about worlds beyond this one. Perhaps
> if I could have gods and devils and fairies as characters . . . and maybe
> some puppets called men. (Winch 1958)

Joseph never again commissioned work from Joan – although he did restage her adaptation of *Wuthering Heights* in a 1960 Scarborough production which was also taken briefly to London.

In April 1957 Joseph wrote to George Devine at the Royal Court. Joseph confessed that he was 'not getting enough playwrights to these classes or the right people' (Joseph 1957a) – before adding, with either surprising frankness or (more likely) playful irony, that his own company 'has managed to put on a number of what must be called "not very good new plays"!'(Ibid.). In fact Joseph's letter represents an example of his fourth route for finding new work: seeking collaboration with those who already had access to high-quality new writing. He continued:

> You may therefore consider the possibility of recommending young writers of promise to attend our tutorial classes. . . . Perhaps you could send us scripts which you consider to have promise but not quite enough to come up to the standard required in your own repertoire (Ibid.).

Joseph's April 1957 letter was one of at least two invitations to collaborate – with George Devine, and also with organizers at the *Observer* newspaper, to whom Joseph applied 'for the possibility of . . . staging some of the better non-prize-winning plays' (Joseph 1956b: 1) in their 1956 playwriting competition. Both were rejected. Perhaps Devine, Kenneth Tynan (at the *Observer*) and others privately agreed that Joseph was staging harmfully mediocre work; perhaps his early antagonism towards the theatre establishment (to be examined in Chapter Five) marked him out as an undesirable collaborator. Devine's rejection of several plays by female playwrights (reported earlier in this chapter) prompted Joseph to offer instead an early critical success – David Campton's darkly comic, somewhat absurdist quartet *The Lunatic View* (1957). Campton's play too was rejected.

The Campton rejection suggests just how hard it can be to identify an original playwriting 'voice'. *The Lunatic View* was dismissed by George Devine as 'a bit derivative, without making an original contribution to this kind of theatre' (Devine 1958). What kind of theatre was Devine referring to? Campton's play quartet had already sparked interest among critics; Irving Wardle had dubbed the piece a 'comedy of menace' (Billington 2007b: 106), marking the first use of a term that would quickly be adopted to describe an exciting and still-forming theatrical genre whose new-wave exponents would include N. F. Simpson and Harold Pinter.

It's possible Devine didn't read Campton's play. In fact he wasn't really required to, because then, as now, new plays submitted for possible production were typically allocated to a dedicated play reader. In the late 1950s, the Royal Court's self-styled 'best play-reader' (Johnstone 1981: 24) was Keith Johnstone, eventual author of the seminal handbook *Impro*. Johnstone's belief that 'ninety-nine per cent of the plays submitted were just cribs from other people' (Johnstone 1981: 25) led him to reject numerous plays that he deemed to be derivative.

It's possible that such a puritanical commitment to perceived originality excluded at least some strong new work. Presentation no doubt mattered too. What might have been the fate of James Saunders's *Alas Poor Fred* (1959), subtitled by the author 'a duologue in the style of Ionesco' (Saunders 1959: title page)? Perhaps Saunders's original phrase 'A Suburban Duologue' (Ibid.) would have opened doors at the Court. We'll never know: Joseph was to receive cast-offs from neither Devine nor Tynan; while Saunders would see his first professional work produced instead by Studio Theatre in Scarborough.

Stephen Joseph's work with James Saunders – a playwright described in The *Guardian* as 'one of the most distinctive voices to emerge from the wave of new British playwrights of the late 1950s and early 1960s' (jamesaunders. org, n.d., a) – stands as probably Joseph's most successful nurturing of a writer outside the Studio Theatre company. Here, the collaborative partner with access to high-quality new writing was actually Saunders's agent Peggy Ramsay – a figure central to new British and international playwriting throughout, and indeed beyond Joseph's professional career. Ramsay, who also represented Ionesco, recognized the need for Saunders to emerge as an original playwright; aware of the strength of this early influence, she carefully controlled Saunders's exposure to the critics. Four plays later given their professional debut with Joseph's Studio Theatre company – *The Ark*, (Joseph n.d., a), plus the triple-bill *Barnstaple* (Joseph n.d., b), *The Pedagogue* (Joseph n.d., c) and *Who Was Hilary Maconochie?* (Joseph n.d., d) – were initially granted amateur-only performances at London's Questors Theatre (doollee.com, n.d., a). It seems Joseph rather accelerated Saunders's entry into professional theatre when he commissioned a production of *Alas Poor Fred*, performed in June 1959 under the direction of Rodney Wood. *Alas Poor Fred* attracted critical praise during its brief touring visit to London in 1960. *The Times* critic – who enjoyed Saunders's 'wildly funny' (*The Times* 1960) dialogue – alluded also to the play's still-radical in-the-round staging:

> The Studio Theatre Company comes with missionary zeal to convert us to its principles; that, fortunately, is unnecessary. We are little concerned about the physical surroundings given to acting of Friday's quality in plays as wittily original as these (Ibid.).

Peggy Ramsay wrote soon after that Saunders 'has now emerged as an author with very much his own voice, so 'ALAS POOR FRED can do him no harm at all' (Ramsay 1960). Later that same year Saunders would receive an Arts Council bursary – meaning that 'he was able, two years later, to become a full-time writer' (jamesaunders.org, n.d., c). Saunders soon became known for using drama 'to play with philosophy, psychology, history and the vicissitudes of language' (Ibid.); as such he was an important influence on a young Tom Stoppard, whom he mentored at a writers' workshop in Germany in 1964. Critic Michael Billington has noted how Saunders's on-stage philosophizing – such as within his 1962 play *Next Time I'll Sing To You*, which examines whether a completely isolated person 'could in any real sense be said to exist' (Billington 2007: 155) – would later be 'explored in more depth by Frayn, Stoppard and Terry Johnstone' (Ibid.).

In 1978 Saunders was invited by Rodney Wood to share memories of Stephen Joseph. Saunders recalled meeting Joseph to discuss the need for a new scene for his 1960 play *The Ark* – a play which wittily examines the importance of thought and thinking, and is peppered with themes and flavours of Stoppard plays yet to be written. Having created the new section, Saunders – generally a forensic, tortuously slow writer – then received news from Joseph of 'cutting . . . by the chunk' (Saunders 1978). I hold what appears to be the typescript containing Joseph's cuts; my personal view is that Joseph's editing renders a good play excellent. In fact 2 years earlier, in a letter to emerging playwright J. W. James, Joseph offered a pithy glimpse of his approach as an editor:

> I have pencilled some tentative cuts in the first 18 pages. I'm not good at this. I'm much happier making terrifying cuts in rehearsal! But this is not such fun for the author . . . (Joseph 1958s).

James Saunders went on to supply Rodney Wood with a thumbnail sketch of Joseph: 'at the same time casual and businesslike' (Ibid.), [he was] 'an off-beat grand-seigneur, very secure in his position and able to delegate, never having to push rank' (Saunders 1978).

Saunders's death prompted the obituarist on the *Daily Telegraph* to reflect on whether his 'only intermittent popularity with the public and the critics . . . may have been [due to] a cerebral slant in his writing' (Billington 2007: 155). Whatever the reason, Saunders 'came to depend increasingly on his royalties from France and Germany, where his intellectual curiosity and constant flow of ideas, however abstract, found a faithful audience' (Ibid.).

In their 1984 book *The Repertory Movement: A History of Regional Theatre in Britain* (Jackson and Rowell 1984), authors Jackson and Rowell highlight Stephen Joseph's commitment to drawing writers from within a theatre company (Ibid.: 152). This, Joseph's fifth route for developing new work, required continuity. As funding grew, Studio Theatre was able to employ its cast and crew – Joseph's potential source of playwrights – for longer periods. Right from its launch in 1955, new work by David Campton, graduate of a short Joseph playwriting course, would form a central part of Studio Theatre programming. In 1957 Campton quit his secure job with the Gas Board (Wood 1979: 52) and was soon occupying a range of roles with Studio Theatre, from theatre manager to actor to playwright. Campton would quickly enjoy Joseph's invaluable guarantee of production; however his loyalty had additional roots. Campton thought Joseph

> a splendid teacher of playwriting – I did not so much learn from him, as realise the things I had known all the time. The first thing I learned from him was not to be afraid of any idea, however outrageous (Campton 1970).

Drawing plays from within a theatre company brought advantages: the playwright's craft was demystified; a speedy responsiveness to contemporary issues became possible; and editing and revision work could take place with the writer present, or at least quickly reached. The policy was also cheap, because a grateful first-time writer would almost always be unrepresented by a literary agent.

The presence of multiple playwrights within a single company also provoked competition. Alan Ayckbourn recalls that as an actor he 'was always . . . making up next to a bloke who's writing the next play – that was David Campton'. Ayckbourn remembers a season 'when it was play by him, play by me, play by him, play by me. We were vying with each other, almost . . . it was quite fun' (Ayckbourn 2007). Joseph's success in establishing a writers' company reached a peak in 1962 when the company produced *Hamlet* with 'six authors in the company. . . . Richard Gill (Ghost), Alan Ayckbourn (King), Peter Cheeseman (Voltemand), Stephen Joseph (Cornelius), Peter King (Laertes) and David Campton (Polonius)' (Wood 1979: 56).

Joseph's sixth method for finding new plays saw him reach out to emerging or established playwrights who had somehow fallen foul of the English theatre establishment. The ageing J. B. Priestley spurned such an approach; a young Harold Pinter embraced it. The story of Joseph's Pinter project was first reported in detail in my 2010 article for the journal *Studies in Theatre and Performance* (Elsam 2010: 257–66); below, I offer an updated record.

The first production of Harold Pinter's first full-length play *The Birthday Party* toured to Wolverhampton, Oxford and Cambridge, gaining some 'enthusiastic appreciations . . . [of] a play of original genius' (Day-Lewis 2008) from regional critics. The play opened in London on 19 May 1958 – and closed 5 days later, after a ferocious critical mauling. A comment from *Daily Telegraph* critic W. A. Darlington perhaps best summarizes the collective critical response: referring to the character of landlady Meg's husband, labelled 'a deeply depressed little man' (Darlington 1958), Darlington offers the character 'one word of cheer. He might have been a dramatic critic, condemned to sit through plays like this' (Ibid.). Pinter was left 'thinking of forgetting the stage altogether' (Pinter 1995).

Less than 2 years later – in March 1960 – a filmed version of *The Birthday Party* was broadcast to critical acclaim, and to a huge television audience. Four months later *The Times* was describing Pinter as 'virtually, our most popular young playwright' (*The Times* 1960: 16).

Theatre historians and even witnesses have long disagreed as to how Pinter's reputation was so profoundly revised in a period of less than 2 years. Credit has been offered to various sources, including critic Harold Hobson, the BBC, and *Encore* magazine. It's true that Hobson was a lone voice among major critics in the capital, partially echoing regional reviewers in asserting that 'Pinter, on the evidence of his work, possesses the most original, disturbing and arresting talent in theatrical London' (Hobson 1958a). However by the time Hobson's *The Sunday Times* review had reached publication the debut production of Pinter's play had already closed, its author's reputation in tatters. The BBC has rightly received credit for commissioning Pinter to write for radio; BBC Radio producer Donald McWhinnie, in particular, has been identified as Pinter's saviour for 'immediately offer[ing] Pinter commissions for three radio plays' (Chaillet 2008: 11) after the playwright's London humiliation. In fact Pinter was already under contract to the BBC when the London production opened (Billington 2007b: 87); and senior figures within BBC Radio declined even to broadcast *Something in Common*, Pinter's second offering (Ibid.: 95–6). The following year a 'radical wing' (Stokes 2001: 29) within *Encore* magazine's publishing arm demonstrated that it 'recognised something new and important in Pinter's work' (Ibid.) by publishing a small print run of *The Birthday Party*. For *Encore* co-founder Charles Marowitz this was the action of 'champions of the playwright [who] felt a heinous act of injustice had been committed' (Marowitz 2006). Such publication certainly represented a significant if small act of solidarity with Pinter; in making the gesture Marowitz was joining co-editor Clive Goodwin, a former student of Stephen Joseph at Central who had spent most of 1957 acting and directing with Studio Theatre. Also in 1959, in May, there was a first amateur staging of *The Birthday Party* at the Tower Theatre in Canonbury in London. Pinter was apparently present at the casting for this Tavistock Rep production; a former company member thinks that because Pinter 'lived within easy reach . . . it seems very likely that he would have wanted to observe rehearsals' (Harland 2008).

By 1962, when John Russell Taylor published his seminal book *Anger and After* (1962), Pinter was established as an internationally successful writer. Russell Taylor became one of the first to formally highlight the mystery of Pinter's speedy ascent, asserting that the playwright had achieved his stellar success without recourse to any significant patron – including 'any enterprising provincial company' (Russell Taylor 1962: 323). Yet the author was mistaken; the simple, mislaid truth is that it was Stephen Joseph who provoked a new start for Pinter, when he contracted the (by now former) playwright to personally direct a new production of *The Birthday Party*.

The key evidence can be read in letters and other documents, most of which are held in the Rylands archive at the University of Manchester. The first, dated 2 October 1958 – some 5 months after the London closure – records Pinter in restless mood. Writing to Joseph, his former teacher at Central, he confided:

All I've done recently is write a radio play for [the BBC Third Programme]. Acting at Richmond this week, but on the whole life ain't easy. Between ourselves, I don't think it was ever intended to be! (Pinter 1958b).

Joseph had recently contacted Pinter's literary agent Jimmy Wax to propose a second professional production of *The Birthday Party* – preferably with the author directing. Pinter continued:

Jimmy Wax told me some time ago that you said you might do "The Birthday Party" after Christmas, at Birmingham, I think, also that you suggested I might produce it. I hear from [*Encore* co-founder and Studio Theatre member] Owen Hale that you have been, and are, extremely busy, travelling from one place to another, and this enquiry may be premature, but I should be very interested to know whether you still consider putting on the play a workable proposition (Pinter 1958c).

Joseph had already begun seeking funding for what would be a last-minute 'extra' within Studio Theatre's Winter 1958/1959 touring season. Shortly before Pinter's 2 October enquiry Joseph had written a begging letter of his own – a request for emergency funding from the Arts Council. On 3 October 1958 N. V. Lintlaker posted a reply refusing Arts Council support – adding unhelpfully that

If you are desperately short of cash, the only alternative is to try and get the Secretary-General to authorise a payment in anticipation of the Council's approval to vary its original offer . . . [but] it lends an air of desperation and crisis which is bad for your general cause (Lintlaker 1958).

Notwithstanding this response, Joseph must have sent Pinter an encouraging reply: 10 days later Pinter wrote that 'To make no bones about it, I should be delighted if you do decide to do 'The Birthday Party', and very glad of the chance of producing it' (Pinter 1958d). At this point Pinter had no professional directing experience, and he asked for an early meeting with Joseph 'to get some red hot tips, as it were, on the technical problems of working in the Round' (Ibid.). But the prospect of leaving London for rehearsals in Scarborough presented Harold with a problem: as a married man and father to 'a fast-growing boy, at present eight months old' (Ibid.), he was keen 'to stay away from home with him as short a time as possible' (Ibid.). Joseph seems to have been offering a further two-week commitment – most likely, directing a production of Shaw's 'Heartbreak House'. Although tempted, Pinter asked if they could 'review the situation a little later on, do you think, in the light of the date for 'The B.P.' becoming definite?' (Ibid.)

On 6 December 1958 Joseph sent Pinter a contract for him to direct *The Birthday Party* alone. There would be one week of rehearsals in Scarborough, beginning on Tuesday 30 December; then a second week of rehearsals in Birmingham. The play would open in Birmingham on 12 January 1959, for a minimum of one week, with a possible further week in Leicester. Pinter's production fee was set at 20 pounds. Agent Jimmy Wax would receive a royalty of eight per cent – which, Joseph wrote, 'is the highest royalty we are paying on any play during this season' (Joseph 1958a: 1).

Pinter had a casting suggestion:

I should very much like my wife, Vivien Merchant, who is a very experienced actress, to play the old woman, Meg. This isn't a case of pulling a fast one! I recommend this with absolute confidence in her ability to play the part well. So what do you think about that? (Pinter 1958d)

It seems the budget would not stretch to accommodate Merchant. Studio Theatre regular Dona Martyn was cast as Meg, with the list completed as follows:

- Petey - David Campton
- Lulu - Faynia Jeffery
- Goldberg - David Sutton
- McCann - Rodney Wood
- Stanley - Alan Ayckbourn

A week before rehearsals began Joseph wrote to Jo Hodgkinson at the Arts Council, highlighting a secret plan to strengthen the link with his former student:

I am hoping that Harold Pinter will do a good job of producing his BIRTHDAY PARTY for us. If he does well and we all like each other when it is over, I should like to commission a play from him (Joseph 1958f: 1).

Pinter set to work, overturning some of the damaging creative choices imposed on the debut production. The spacious conservatory which had been the central feature of the original proscenium production was replaced with Pinter's intended claustrophobic seaside boarding house, here set 'in-the-round'. But the actors, beginning rehearsal, were wary. Ayckbourn, cast as Stanley, remembers that Pinter was 'in a very defensive, not to say depressed state' (Billington 2007b: 106); the actors were 'extremely suspicious of him, because we thought he was a complete charlatan . . . in his eyes anyway his play had been completely misdirected before and the fact that it had got a severe roasting merely justified his self-belief, which seemed quite strong' (Allen 2001: 78). Actor-playwright David Campton, who had recently impressed critics with his absurdist quartet *The Lunatic View*, reflected that Pinter's play 'might as well have been a Japanese Noh play for all the sense it made to me' (Ibid.: 77). Ayckbourn, badgering writer-director Pinter for information about the character of Stanley, was told to 'Mind your own fucking business. Concentrate on what's there' (Billington 2007b: 106). Faynia Jeffrey (now Williams), cast as Lucy, wrote in her diary after the first day's blocking: 'I think this is going to be a theoretical experience' (Williams 2008). She described Pinter's directorial approach as that of a 'meticulous but exciting producer' (Ibid.).

Though new to directing, Pinter was an experienced repertory actor; and his cast began to settle. Ayckbourn remembers in Pinter 'a passion behind his eyes . . . we were swept along by him' (Allen 2001: 78). The watching Stephen Joseph recorded a sketch of Pinter in rehearsal:

> The actors enjoyed working with him. He knew precisely how they felt about the play, and precisely how to help them. He seldom tried to explain "obscurities", but instead showed the actors how to do the action, thus giving even the most baffling parts of the play a conviction and organic logic of their own (Joseph 1967: 51).

Kept busy behind the scenes, Joseph secured bookings in touring venues in Birmingham and Leicester, and began lobbying critics to attend. Rehearsals moved from Scarborough to Birmingham. The midwinter journey south was remembered by Rodney Wood as 'quite terrifying. At times we wished we could have changed the lorries for Sno-cats' (Wood 1959). Rehearsals continued at the Theatre Centre in Birmingham, and were almost complete when the *Birmingham Post* printed a feature on Studio Theatre's forthcoming visit. The article noted how the company was 'blowing like a fresh breeze through the tinsel and gauze of pantomime [with] the work of two of the younger generation of playwrights' (Gascoigne 1959: n.p.); David Campton and Harold Pinter were linked together because 'both belong to a group which has been tentatively labelled the "non-naturalists"' (Ibid.) writing '"comedy of menace"' (Ibid.). The article noted that with author Pinter in charge, 'the production is likely to be rather different from what Wolverhampton and Hammersmith saw last spring' (Ibid.).

The date of the first performance arrived. The actors – poised to open only the second professional production of one of modern theatre's most derided plays – were understandably nervous. Ayckbourn remembers: 'we went on stage and we just electrified the audience. We just came off stage and stared at [Harold]!' (Ayckbourn 2002). Faynia Williams, fresh from her debut as Lulu, wrote in her diary that she 'wouldn't change places with anybody – I felt history was being made. Harold was thrilled to bits – hugged and kissed me afterwards. I hope for his sake the notices are good' (Elsam 2008).

In fact the notices were very good. The *Birmingham Weekly Post* reviewer was 'hit . . . between the eyes; it is a strange gust that leaves one a little breathless' (*Birmingham Weekly Post* 1959: n.p.). The *Birmingham Post* reviewer recorded that 'Mr Pinter handles his cast with masterly precision; his writing is universally admirable in its tautly theatrical effect, whether that be humorous or symbolic' (*Birmingham Post* 1959: n.p). The critic on The *Wolverhampton Express and Star* was able to compare productions, having seen the 1958 Lyric-bound production on its pre-London tour:

> This time the author himself is in charge . . . and if his main objective is to show how foolish were those of us who originally read into the play a wealth of complicated symbolism, he certainly succeeds . . . It is always difficult not to look for meanings, but the more one can be persuaded to feel rather than think about the play the more one will experience (*Wolverhampton Express and Star* 1959).

Just one national newspaper critic attended. The *Manchester Guardian* – whose London reviewer had damned the production in the capital – reflected now that critics of that earlier staging 'simply did not want to watch [Pinter's] sometimes comic, sometimes touching, and almost always frightening balancing act on the tightrope between sanity and insanity' ('D. G.' 1959: n.p.). Pinter's direction was praised too for drawing 'a whole series of first-class performances from a fine cast'. This was, the *Manchester Guardian* concluded, 'a play that ought to be seen' (Ibid.).

Creatively, Stephen Joseph's decision to employ Pinter seems to have been something of a catalyst. Indeed cast member Alan Ayckbourn, who had begun 'to get very fascinated by the way he wrote' (Ayckbourn 1991: 10), '. . . wrote a Pinter play soon after [the tour] just to see if I could' (Ibid.). But which play? During the tour, Ayckbourn scripted his debut 'Roland Allen' play *The Square Cat* (1959); this is a smart farcical comedy with a galloping plot, and not at all what we might now call a Pinteresque play. Another 'Roland Allen' play, *The Party Game*, is thought by Ayckbourn archivist Simon Murgatroyd to date from 1958 or 1959. Undiscovered until 2006, it seems closer in style to Pinter's early work. This unperformed, darkly funny single-location piece, 50 pages long, documents the apparent real-time progress of an alcohol-fuelled drinks party – offering a strong early glimpse of the type of dark-edged anatomizing of social relations Ayckbourn would begin to produce years after Joseph's death. It's possible that Ayckbourn, inspired by Pinter, showed him the play; it's also possible that Pinter, reading *The Party Game*, was inspired to take his own writing in a new direction. Actually we don't know, because Ayckbourn recalls little of the piece – other than the memory that a local amateur company rejected it for production.

Pinter was apparently also inspired to write during the tour: it seems likely that he worked on his second full-length play, *The Hothouse*, during this period. Harold's playful side emerged too: it's reported that he 'chuckled merrily when. . . . Ayckbourn and his magic tape recorder were involved in the first, and probably best, of two thousand million take-offs of Harold Pinter's dialogue' (Allen 2001: 79). Pinter's witty sketch *Trouble in the Works* was also probably created during the Studio Theatre tour: it's not hard to imagine this daft and partly northern-accented duologue emerging from spontaneous improvisations between the two London-born actors on tour, bonding among strong regional dialects.

Towards the end of the Winter 1958/1959 tour, Stephen Joseph – sensing, perhaps, that he had provoked a theatrical event of at least national importance – began pitching *The Birthday Party* to senior television executives. His efforts led directly to the televising on ITV of Pinter's play – and also, via a second ITV company, to the commissioning and broadcasting of a new Pinter drama. Harold Pinter, just months earlier a humiliated playwright, would soon be both revered and famous.

Stephen Joseph's retrospective view of the Pinter 'project' can only have been mixed. He succeeded in helping to rescue a former student's reputation, while forcing the theatre establishment into a critical volte-face; yet he failed to add a rising and charismatic young theatre maker to his Scarborough company. He failed too in his bid to direct the broadcast version of Pinter's play. Pinter's deserved success would take the playwright back to London, then abroad; new commitments would mean that Pinter's private offer to direct a new Studio Theatre production – a huge coup, should it occur – never materialized. In fact *The Birthday Party* did linger on in Scarborough without Harold: his scratch cast actually restaged first-act scenes for a bizarre evening charity fundraiser for World Refugee Year 1959. Pinter's young cast shared a theatrical bill with Mollie Sugden, Martin Grainger's Puppets, and Scarborough dancing group 'The Futurist Lovelies'. Ayckbourn later recalled the event:

> It was terrible – all the comics refused to get off, they were doing Frankie Howerd jokes, but we had him there as well. My company put on the first act of Pinter's *Birthday Party* . . . the audience loved it for the first original jokes they'd heard all evening (Ayckbourn 1974: n.p.).

The seventh and final route employed by Joseph to reach new theatre playwrights saw him offer his in-the-round stage to writers already working in another important medium: television. Independent Television (ITV) launched in 1955, just as Studio Theatre was completing its inaugural summer season. Suddenly there were opportunities for writers urgently needed to satisfy the 'lack of new scripts' (Harris 2008: 164) within the medium. Stephen Joseph was quick to engage with the expansion, even seeing it as a career opportunity. An August 1956 enquiry to the BBC (Barry 1956a) represented his first attempt to move into directing television drama; several further unsuccessful applications followed, including to H. M. Tennent Ltd (Beaumont 1956) and to ITV (Thomas 1959b). In 1957, ITV invited Joseph to submit work by his new theatre playwrights; the opportunity arose from a bold letter from senior Granada TV executive Ernest Borneman, seeking ideas for new plays in which 'no holds are barred. We want plays of real importance, both in context and in form. The only taboos are unintelligibility and preciousness . . .' (Borneman 1957a). Borneman even extended to Joseph the personal invitation that 'if you can receive our "workshop" productions, you might also care to let us know your criticism of them' (Ibid.). Joseph's swift proposal of Studio Theatre company member David Campton met with an equally swift and provocative reply:

> I hold David Campton in the greatest respect, but I have found that there is a vast difference between his superb realistic dialogue in "The Cactus Garden" and the lack of discipline in the short plays which you have directed. . . . If you can persuade him to write me an honest, realistic play about some vital social or personal issue of our day, I would be only too glad to put it on (Borneman 1957b).

Borneman's letter highlights that, within 2 years of Joseph launching his Scarborough theatre venture, he was developing a national profile as a champion of new theatre writing. It also underlines that Joseph's advocacy of non-realist approaches to politically provocative subject matter, was by no means to everyone's taste. In general, playwrights producing work for the Studio Theatre Company were using increasingly sophisticated theatrical techniques: Joseph encouraged them to explore in full the live event, using intimate in-the-round staging to examine the effects of poetic speech, direct audience address, time shifts and other features uncommon within the burgeoning social realist movement. Joseph was also regularly persuading playwrights – especially David Campton – to write on the looming nuclear threat; as early as 1956 Joseph produced radio dramatist (and later Oscar-winning screenwriter) Robert Bolt's first stage piece *The Last of the Wine*, an examination of reactions to impending nuclear war (Joseph 1967: 41).

It's perhaps unsurprising, then, that Studio Theatre's theatrically adventurous playwrights were rarely commissioned to write for the small screen. Although Joseph had 'thought that television might take to' (Joseph 1967: 41) some of the one-act plays offered by his company, in 1967 he stated simply, 'We were wrong.' (Ibid.)

There is however one stand-out example of a television writer placing their first theatre work with Joseph's company. In January 1963 agent Peggy Ramsay teased Alan Plater, a client with a growing track record in television drama, with the thought that 'one cannot say one is a playwright until one has written a [theatre] play that fills the whole evening' (Ramsay 1963a). At this point Ramsay had submitted Plater play synopses to a number of high-profile theatre managers; responses had been lukewarm. Producer Michael Codron replied twice – first noting how it was 'difficult to judge the merits of the finished article if one doesn't know the *style* of the writer' (Codron 1962a), before hardening into a view that ' "Playwrighting" [sic] seems to have become so easy – perhaps that is the fault of managers and T.V. producers too hungry for talent?' (Ibid.).

In my 2008 interview with Plater he recalled his first meeting with Stephen Joseph after a Joseph lecture in Hull. Plater introduced himself as a writer for television:

> "Oh God," [Joseph] said, "I hate television." I said, "What's wrong with it? What's wrong with it?" "I'll tell you what's wrong with television," he said, "If I'm watching television, and I think a man is a bloody awful actor, and I go up to the screen and I shout at the screen, 'You're a bloody awful actor!' nothing happens. If I do it in the theatre, something happens." Which was his way of, I think, defining the relationship between performers and audience (Plater 2008).

Joseph invited Plater to Scarborough. He was met instead by Peter Cheeseman, 'then his Number Two' (Ibid.). After an invitation from Cheeseman to 'Come and work with us at Stoke' (Ibid.), Plater's first pieces

for theatre – *The Referees* and *The Mating Season*, both originally short
television plays – were staged at the Victoria Theatre. Peggy Ramsay told her
client that she was 'delighted about this, probably even more delighted than
you are' (Ramsay 1962). The success of these two short pieces prompted a
commission for *Ted's Cathedral* (1963), an original full-length play, which
was produced in-the-round at Stoke. Soon after, Plater – now, therefore, a
writer of television drama turned playwright – was amused to see his first
full-length stage play bought for broadcast on television. Around this time
Margaret Ramsay offered a sketch of a 'little company [that] has been doing
remarkable work up north' (Ramsay 1963b):

> Nearly all the actors are writers in their own right and this was a group
> which was started by Stephen Joseph who has now handed over to
> Peter Cheeseman who is doing remarkable work, really unique in this
> country (Ibid.).

Plater remembers an atmosphere at Stoke where 'everybody kind of mucked
in . . . it was very healthy, because you didn't get any false ideas about the
glamour of theatre' (Plater 2008). Although he was never a regular Studio
Theatre member, Plater recalls 'a very tightly knit group [who] inevitably . . .
were almost huddling together for warmth and survival' (Ibid.). Although an
outsider, he remembers that 'once I'd proved myself, I was there' (Ibid.).

A second Plater play, *A Smashing Day*, was commissioned by Studio Theatre
for staging in 1965. The play – another development of a television script –
had been offered elsewhere since at least 1962, when the Theatre Guild in
New York rejected it as 'a gentle, charming play [which] is not really right for
our program' (Foster 1962). During the planning stages of the Stoke-on-Trent
production Peter Cheeseman approached The Beatles manager Brian Epstein
with a suggestion that John Lennon and Paul McCartney – who had by now
'already made their first couple of million quid' (Plater 2007: 4) – write the
music to accompany the piece. After attending a performance, Epstein began
planning for a new production in London's West End, which would feature
Hywel Bennett in the play's lead role. Plater remembers that, in the event,
music for the show was written by two lowly Stoke company members –
Robert Powell and Ben Kingsley, 'then Acting ASMs in the company' (Ibid.).

Plater noticed early on that 'radio plays could transfer to theatre-in-
the-round easily' (Plater 2008). His experiences at Stoke quickly converted
him to the new staging form. Describing a production of a play by Norman
Smithson titled *The Three Lodgers*, Plater remembers that

> the set was all on the floor of the stage. It was the ground plan of the
> house. You could see all the rooms, so [the actors] just walked in and out

of the rooms, but there were no walls and you'd have things happening in that room and in that room and in that room, simultaneously. It worked like a dream. You'd have great difficulty doing it . . . behind a prosc arch. (Ibid.)

Plater considers theatre-in-the-round to be

a very flexible form. . . . I like there to be as little as possible between the audience and the show . . . you can't tell lies. Whereas in a way big prosc arch theatres – the old traditional theatres – lend themselves to telling lies. The lies are almost a prerequisite (Ibid.).

It's noteworthy that there was a clear change in style and content within Plater's stage work during the 1960s; his earlier, more whimsical plays, such as *Ted's Cathedral* (1963) and *A Smashing Day* (1965), were to briefly give way to more openly agitational work. This change coincided with Plater's exposure to the ascendant musical documentary genre, particularly in the verbatim form pioneered by Peter Cheeseman; and it led to such hard-hitting and highly political work as the musical play *Close the Coalhouse Door* (1968), featuring lyrics (written with Alex Glasgow) which are openly agitational:

A is for Alienation that made me the man that I am /
And B's for the Boss who's a bastard, a bourgeois who don't give a damn (Plater 1969)

Close the Coalhouse Door received widespread regional production after its premiere in Newcastle-upon-Tyne, and the play with music was televised by the BBC (Plater 2007: 4). As such, Plater, debuted as a playwright by the Studio Theatre company, can himself be regarded as something of a political figure on the British theatrical landscape. Plater's influence on theatre for working class audiences also includes a little-acknowledged role as co-founder of Hull Arts Centre in an adapted church hall, which became Spring Street Theatre and was later the home of Hull Truck Theatre Company (Ibid.: 6). Plater would also become 'steadfast mentor and friend' (Roberts 2012: 5) to Lee Hall, award-winning playwright and screenwriter of *Billy Elliot* and *War Horse*; indeed Plater read and encouraged Hall when his first work was staged at Newcastle upon Tyne's Live Theatre.

Plater's own development as a theatrical provocateur can be linked back to both Stephen Joseph and Peter Cheeseman. For Plater this was to do with

the conspiracy between the audience and the performers of the play, and about the physical directness, and starting work in theatre. One of the things I remember the actors saying to me at Stoke was, "Your plays start so quickly"... there's a kind of physicality and directness, I think, in my work, that probably has it's roots in that, and certainly, I think, the Cheeseman tradition [which] was very much a Stephen Joseph tradition (Plater 2008).

In Plater's view Stephen Joseph 'was a very important person, and he should be airbrushed back into history' (Plater 2008). Plater has expressed strong views on how historians have misrepresented theatre activity beyond London: in his view 'the history of British theatre so much is about the history of London theatre – and it disregards the whole of the English regions, the whole of Scotland, most of Ireland . . .' (Ibid.). At the end of my 2008 interview with the writer, Plater observed wryly:

You've got to make your metropolitan gestures if you're going to be recognised on a national level. If you don't do that, then you're just a regional writer. Like William Shakespeare (Plater 2008).

4

The New Makers

Some years after Stephen Joseph's death, former Studio Theatre company member Rodney Wood wrote a letter to the artistic directors of Manchester's Royal Exchange Theatre. Wood, researching for a postgraduate degree, wanted to clarify Stephen Joseph's possible influence on the design and building of the high-profile new in-the-round venue. A January 1979 response sent on behalf of the directors confirmed that while they had in their formative years 'presented many plays at the [Manchester] University Theatre for which Stephen Joseph was responsible' (Marshall 1979), and Joseph was 'bound to have influenced the directors' feelings, perhaps unconsciously, towards theatre in the round' (Ibid.), they 'do not remember actually discussing [Joseph's] ideas when they were planning the new theatre' (Ibid.). Joseph's extracurricular work in Manchester included design input to the endstage University (later Contact) Theatre; conversion of a disused Lutheran church to form an adaptable black-box space which frequently employed in-the-round staging; and the publication of a book dedicated entirely to theatre-in-the-round. In short, in Manchester, he and his ideas were hard to ignore. Yet the Royal Exchange directors' denial of a Joseph design influence actually rings true: their stage was circular, not rectangular; there were two upper seating levels, including a West End-style upper circle with cheap seats; and productions often featured 'star' actors. (These features remain, more than three decades on.) It seems then that, just 12 years after Stephen Joseph's death, he had almost no influence on the design and construction of a new theatre-in-the-round built 'on his doorstep'.

Thomas Postlewait has observed that theatre historiographers need to be 'skilled in their spectral knowledge in order to recognise the incorporeal traces of the past' (Postlewait 2009: 16). So it is with Stephen Joseph and the Royal Exchange. The late Ian Watson, a former Joseph student and ex-Studio Theatre company member, said in 1998 that he felt sure Joseph's contact with directors Michael Elliott and Braham Murray had 'informed their decision' (Watson 1998) to build the Royal Exchange as a round theatre. George Taylor, another former Joseph student at Manchester University and a senior lecturer there when interviewed by Stacey Morley in 1998, went further: he recalled how colleagues were 'appalled by the publicity [for] this new, wonderful, first ever professional theatre-in-the-round [when Joseph's round theatres] were still functioning' (Taylor 1998: 5). Curiously, acknowledgement of Joseph's design presence is little more than spectral elsewhere in northwest England: his work on the large and astonishingly versatile Nuffield Theatre at the University of Lancaster – still one of Europe's most successful adaptable theatre spaces, more than half a century after its construction – seems to have had little public acknowledgement. Yet this is a space so flexible that it creates the unique problem that visiting artists 'imagine that they can have anything' (Sims 2013).

Issues of attribution are of course important, since strong evidence – including witness testimony – can offer context on whether Stephen Joseph 'matters'. Because there are gaps and uncertainties, this has meant finding and speaking to surviving artists and others who knew Joseph, and were willing to share opinions and memories. Such contact has revealed something of a hidden network of people who consider Stephen Joseph to have been a key influence.

Focus for this chapter will be, therefore, on theatre makers other than Alan Ayckbourn and Peter Cheeseman (already discussed in detail within Chapter 2). The term 'theatre makers' is used here simply to identify theatre practitioners who are not exclusively actors or playwrights.

The makers featured in this chapter either achieved particular success after meeting and working with Stephen Joseph, or interacted with him in ways that clarify his influence on others. Sir Ben Kingsley, the lone exception, worked for Studio Theatre in Stoke-on-Trent but never directly worked with Joseph. Yet my 2008 interview with Kingsley reveals both a sharp awareness of Joseph's methodology as a theatre maker and a sense of debt towards him – suggesting that a Joseph legacy had actually begun to develop prior to Joseph's death in 1967. The research for this chapter is presented mainly, although not exclusively, through profiles of individual protégés; the section draws, in part, on a range of recently recorded interviews, and on fresh correspondence.

Shortly after Joseph's death in 1967, a Stephen Joseph Memorial Appeal committee was set up in a fundraising initiative led by Ken Boden, a key figure within the British Drama League who had also been a longstanding and influential supporter of Joseph in Scarborough. Boden produced a one-page appeal letter (Boden n.d.) listing the names of 131 individual supporters and outlining the memorial project; Boden explained that the premises in Scarborough had already been identified for the intended purchase, and would allow for 'experiment in forms of staging' (Ibid.) including 'experiment in Peripheral (sic) staging, Prom Theatre (sic) and the more radical departures which Stephen Joseph was planning almost up to his death' (Ibid.). Boden's proposal describes a plan for a community-focused building that evokes both Joan Littlewood's Fun Palace – intended as a 'university of the streets' (Littlewood 1994: 704) – and also Arnold Wesker's Centre 42 initiative that 'pointed to a diversified future for participative, politically committed theatre that reached beyond large, static institutions' (Shellard 1999: 129). Building also on Peter Cheeseman's contemporary work in the Potteries, Boden proposed a building that would welcome local schools and amateur theatre groups, and would become a 'stimulating social centre [open] seven days a week, daytime as well as evening' (Boden n.d.). Proposed amenities and activities in addition to live theatre would include a restaurant, exhibition space and 'regular performances of folk song, jazz, chamber music, poetry and films'. A planned schools link would incorporate an outreach programme in which, in something of a departure from Cheeseman's base in the Potteries, 'members of the company could also do improvisation work with children . . . encouraging the children to explore imaginatively and to create their own plays' (Ibid.). There would be a continued focus on new writing: Boden recorded that 'we particularly want to find new Northern writers' (Ibid.). The whole enterprise was advanced 'in the same questing and questioning spirit in which [Stephen Joseph] challenged established ideas' (Ibid.).

The list of individuals comprising the Stephen Joseph Memorial Appeal committee might be expected to represent, at least in part, a list of noted figures within British theatre who had been influenced by Joseph during his career. This broadly seems to have been the case. Committee members were drawn from a wide variety of backgrounds. Several – including Millicent Martin, Sir Tyrone Guthrie, Sir Donald Wolfit, Sir Michael Redgrave and John Gielgud – most likely feature as a result of their international profile, along with, to varying degrees, their acquaintance with Joseph's mother Hermione Gingold. A second, much larger group represents people who had worked directly with Joseph; these individuals were most likely invited in recognition of their developing profile within British theatre and television. This list includes Alan Ayckbourn, Clifford Williams, Eileen Derbyshire, Henry Livings, Harold Pinter, Alan Plater, Terry Lane, Professor Hugh Hunt, Richard Pilbrow, John Neville and Margaret Rawlings. The remaining theatre makers may simply have considered Joseph influential; this list includes Adrian Mitchell, David Scase and James Roose-Evans, along with nationally respected theatre critics J. C Trewin, Irving Wardle and Milton Shulman.

It's interesting to note the significant number of theatre figures whose names are absent from the list. There's no nationally known politician; only Scarborough's Member of Parliament and the town's mayor are included. There are notable omissions from English theatre – Joan Littlewood, for example – plus theatre establishment figures Joseph had publicly criticized: Laurence Olivier, Harold Hobson, W. A. Darlington, Kenneth Tynan. Joseph's profile within British theatre was surely prominent enough to draw support from the likes of John Osborne, Noel Coward and Ralph Richardson. Director Peter Hall and playwrights J. B. Priestley and Arnold Wesker, who knew Joseph, are absent from the list. Peter Cheeseman's name is also missing.

Why so many omissions? Ken Boden's knowledge of Joseph's once-provocative relationship with some of these theatre makers may have dissuaded him from making an approach. Approaches may have been made and rebuffed. Perhaps Joseph, whose death was not sudden, had asked Boden to avoid making certain approaches. Perhaps, even, Joseph's recent identity – as a regionally based university lecturer and occasional fringe theatre practitioner – rendered him, to some, unimportant. Quite simply, we don't know. It is also, of course, too simplistic to claim that Memorial Appeal committee members were all inspired or influenced by Joseph, while all those noted theatre figures absent from the list were not; clearly Peter Cheeseman's absence unravels such a claim. Stronger evidence is needed: either archival re-examination, fresh interviewing, or (where possible) both.

For this chapter then, my approach is to look back over Joseph's lifetime both as a teacher and as a theatre professional, and to identify the different routes through which Joseph may have most strongly influenced other fellow theatre makers. The routes are:

1. through his teaching, both at
   a. the Central School of Speech and Drama and
   b. the University of Manchester;
2. through working with members of the Studio Theatre Company; and
3. through Joseph's 'missionary work' – offering consultancy support (usually unpaid) to others.

1a. Joseph's work at the Central School of Speech and Drama

Joseph's earliest substantive mentoring of future theatre makers took place during the pre-Studio Theatre period when Joseph worked as a teacher at the then Central School of Speech and Drama ('Central') beginning in 1949. Harold Pinter was a favoured student: Pinter biographer Michael Billington identifies Joseph as 'one of those influential father-figures who crop up throughout Pinter's early life' (Billington 2007b: 32); decades later Pinter remembered him as 'a very remarkable man' (Pinter 2008). The possible extent of Joseph's early influence on his student – in 1951, not yet a playwright – was highlighted in a 2008 interview with Pinter at the British Library:

> One day I wrote an essay and [Joseph] said to me – I was supposed to be a young actor – and he said to me "Why don't you stick to writing?" I said, "I probably will". (Pinter 2008)

Clive Goodwin was also taught by Joseph at Central. Goodwin co-founded the influential theatre magazine *Encore*, and was also briefly an actor and director with Studio Theatre. Terry Lane reports an image of the student Goodwin in a characteristically minimalist Joseph-directed production, 'play[ing] God at the top of a pair of steps' (Lane 2006: 95).

Surviving glimpses of Joseph's work at Central are intriguing, but sparse. Joseph studied and then taught there when the drama school was based at the Royal Albert Hall; parts of the archive were either lost or destroyed when the school relocated. During the summer of 2008 some rudimentary sorting of the remaining Central archive was undertaken, but 'nothing of significance relating to Joseph was found' (Loveland 2009). Joseph's surviving teaching colleagues at Central also seem unable to shed much light: Ann Jellicoe told me that she could remember nothing of Joseph; Cicely Berry wrote in 1978 that although she 'loved [Joseph] dearly and laughed with him a good deal' (Berry 1978), she could recall only a general memory of a man who was 'smashing and eccentric' (Ibid.). Fortunately Rodney Wood – also a Joseph student at Central – conducted his own appraisal of Joseph's work there for his unpublished 1979 Master's dissertation (Wood 1979). Three other Central graduates taught by Joseph have been traced and interviewed for this book: Harry Landis, who is recorded as working with the Studio Theatre company during the company's first season (Lewsen 1978); plus Walter Hall and Shirley Jaffe, both of whom would join the company for full summer seasons.

An analysis of Stephen Joseph's working relationship with students reveals that he 'fast-tracked' a few favourites, bringing them in to work alongside professionals. As reported below, this happened quite frequently when Joseph was later lecturing at the University of Manchester; he also debuted professional actors, and indeed his 1955 Scarborough launch of Studio Theatre involved 'a band of young actors – most of them ex-Central School' (Wood 2008: 44).

Alan Ayckbourn considers that Joseph 'loved students, who were completely open, and therefore would take more risk [than professional actors]' (Ayckbourn 2007). In a discussion of staging in *New Theatre Forms* (1968), Joseph records an Ann Jellicoe production in which a 'very inexperienced and tentative' (Joseph 1968: 40) student gave a strong performance despite tripping onstage and even forgetting lines. Joseph concluded that '. . . the very lack of . . . any technique, helped the young man to stumble toward an organic projection that was convincingly appropriate on a tiny thrust stage' (Ibid.).

The acting careers of each of my three interviewees span much of the postwar period. All are still working as professional actors, and all have directed fringe theatre work; Jaffe and Hall went on to join the Studio Theatre Company in Scarborough after graduating from Central. Harry Landis worked variously at the Royal Court Theatre, across the West End, in films and within 'about four hundred television shows' (Landis 2007: 1) before becoming President of the British Actors' Equity Association – a post he held until 2008. Curiously, although Landis is listed as appearing in a production during the inaugural Scarborough season for Studio Theatre company (Joseph1955a), in his recollection, '[Joseph] didn't invite us there, I was doing movies and stuff, and West End plays, so that never happened' (Landis 2008).

A factory worker at the age of 15, Harry Landis 'got a grant' (Landis 2007: 1) to attend Central after discovering live performance at Unity Theatre in King's Cross, London:

> The language spoken [at Unity Theatre] was the language I understood, coming from the East End – and the characters I recognised from people down my street, and I thought, "I can't believe it" – live theatre absolutely knocked me out (Ibid.).

Landis remembers Joseph – 'one of the tutors [who] directed plays' (Landis 2008) – as

> very accessible, very easy to talk to, not a bit school-masterly, and a great bloke who laid down an atmosphere in the rehearsal room that let you bloom, flower, because that was his style (Ibid.).

Walter Hall, who remembers Joseph as 'one of the glowing spirits there at the time' (Hall 2007), recalls feeling that

> I'd like to be with him, because he's exciting and youthful – I mean, he was older than us, but not – but there was a connection between him [and the students] because of his energy and personality (Ibid.).

Shirley Jaffe (known professionally as Shirley Jacobs) recalls Joseph as 'a sort of legend' (Jaffe 2007) among the students. Directed by him in a production of Oscar Wilde's *A Woman of No Importance*, she remembers provoking a lot of audience laughter at a dress rehearsal – only to be told by Joseph, 'now you must make it real' (Ibid.). Joseph was 'my guru . . . he was just a very exciting, very vibrant person to be with' (Ibid.)

Joseph's projects at Central were consistently adventurous, and placed the actor in a position to influence creative outcomes. Rodney Wood remembers Joseph as a director of student productions who 'encouraged his actors to experiment with their roles rather than giving detailed instruction as to moves and stage business' (Wood 2008: 44). For Jaffe, Joseph 'seemed to create an atmosphere in which people could be creative' (Jaffe 2007). Walter Hall recalls Joseph-led improvisation classes which were 'a kind of breakthrough into the future. . . . I don't think RADA did [them] at the time – and there was a great emphasis on relaxation, and of course voice' (Hall 2007).

Hall remembers his frustration at having to work with a different tutor, when Stephen Joseph directed his own cast in scenes from *A Midsummer Night's Dream*:

> All the students in my half thought, "Oh God, we wish we were in that"
> . . . it was just the sort of stuff that we wanted to do. It was contemporary
> . . . students were encouraged to do interesting things – and Harold
> Pinter, as I recall, played Bottom . . . it was rather exciting (Ibid.).

Jaffe recalls that 'Stephen had enormous knowledge of old plays [and] always wanted to do things that were a bit obscure' (Jaffe 2007). Joseph's published books suggest a deep knowledge of theatre history, including a familiarity with early-twentieth-century European theorists and practitioners whose work, he wrote in 1963, 'is now beginning to reach us, mostly through the USA' (Joseph 1963a: 127). In *The Story of the Playhouse in England*, Joseph's 1963 book for younger readers, he describes how 'The constructivist settings of Tairov, Popova or Rabinovitch often did without scenic flats and cloths, making use instead, of scaffolding, ladders, and huge platforms' (Ibid.: 139). Rodney Wood has noted that Joseph-directed student productions at Central encompassed the work of mainland European playwrights, including George Kaiser's politically provocative German expressionist play *Gas*; student and cast member Jeffery Dench remembers Joseph taking the cast to see Fritz Lang's film *Metropolis* 'to get the idea of how to do it' (Dench 1979). Joseph's production featured

> very "stylized" movements and grey-green make-up . . . [Joseph] spent
> hours of detailed work on the (to us) huge crowd scenes getting us to
> work with unison movements on specific words – large, angular arm
> movements and contorted bodies (Ibid.).

Dench also offers a detail of how

> [Joseph] spent hours arranging the music and sound effects and
> finished up sitting in the front-of-house with the adjudicators with
> the volume control in his hand actually dimming up and down to his
> satisfaction (Ibid.).

Rodney Wood recalls a Joseph production of August Strindberg's *Lucky Peter's Travels* which was 'performed on a constructivist setting of builders' ladders and wooden planks' (Wood 1979: 11): Wood witnessed 'a theatrically effective forest scene . . . achieved by actors sitting on top of ladders, waving branches and singing like birds' (Ibid.).

For Joseph's student tour to communist Bucharest, two productions were rehearsed – the Chester Mystery Play *The Deluge*, and Joseph's own play *The Key*. Jaffe remembers worrying over her additional responsibilities in charge of props:

> I said to Stephen, "Why have you done this?" and he said "I believe in giving people responsibility and they will rise to the occasion." And I must admit I rose to the occasion (Jaffe 2007).

Jaffe recalls a group trip 'to the zoo to examine the animals. . . . Stephen was encouraging people to do animal things around the zoo' (Jaffe 2007). Harry Landis – converted at Unity Theatre to the power of theatre portraying 'actual, real people who go to work and have struggles' (Landis 2007: 1), and several years older than most of his fellow students – reacted against Joseph's apparent preference for 'flamboyant themes – he wanted you to be animals, all sorts of things' (Landis 2008). In Landis' view Joseph 'never settled into reality-, Stanislavski-type reality plays'. Landis even offers a theory for Joseph's perceived stance against naturalism:

> He worshipped his mother. She was a review artist who I wouldn't say was superficial, but belonged to another area of performing, in review and comedy – [she] never played what you might call a real, real part. That's where [Joseph] was stuck. You couldn't get him to discuss deeper psychological things about characters, because he didn't do those kinds of plays. Restoration, flamboyance and all that stuff. And brilliant stuff! And I loved doing it. But you couldn't get him onto another level (Ibid.).

Walter Hall thinks that Joseph may have consciously explored naturalistic acting after leaving Central:

> Later on, when I worked in Scarborough, Stephen – I think at the time he'd seen Marlon Brando in *On The Waterfront*, and was impressed with the techniques of the Method (Hall 2007).

A curious feature of Joseph's mentoring style is that favoured students could be left unaware of his approval. Walter Hall recalls:

> I think I was rather bumptious at the time – I don't think Stephen even took me terribly seriously. I don't think I was a particular favourite of his while I was at Central (Ibid.).

One year after graduation, Hall was a member of Joseph's Studio Theatre group. He would go on to co-found a lunchtime fringe theatre company in London's Greek Street, where he staged early work by David Edgar, Trevor Griffiths and former Studio Theatre company members Mike Leigh and David Halliwell (Ibid.). Hall was even offered, and declined, the opportunity to lead Studio Theatre at Stoke-on-Trent; the invitation, provoked by Joseph's sacking of Peter Cheeseman, followed a similar one made to Alan Ayckbourn, and seems to have preceded Terry Lane's acceptance of the post (Ibid.). Yet Hall stated in 2007 that he 'always felt that Stephen had his reservations about me' (Ibid.).

1b) Joseph's work at the University of Manchester

More than 10 years later, a similar sense of uncertainty dogged Michael Weller, then a student on Joseph's Diploma course in Manchester. Weller is now an acclaimed playwright and screenwriter, a faculty member at New York's The New School and co-founder of the influential Mentor Project for playwrights at New York's off-Broadway Cherry Lane Theatre (New School 2009). Weller recalls an incident as a student that was 'quintessential Stephen' (Weller 2009a). Weller had written a play, *How HoHo Rose and Fell in Seven Short Scenes*, which was staged in the University of Manchester's black box theatre. He recalls:

> After the play Stephen called me downstairs to his office to, presumably, give me his response. When it was over I was devastated, and called [fellow student] Mike Stott for sympathy. Mike was stunned that Stephen hadn't liked the play. He'd been sitting next to him and seen him smile and laugh aloud several times. Finally Mike asked to hear exactly what Stephen said to me. And I reported: "He asked me if I had any questions. I told him no. Then he said, 'In that case, carry on.'" And that was it. He showed no interest whatever. Mike asked me to repeat this several times, and finally told me I had made history. For Stephen to say literally *nothing* was the highest accolade possible. His educational philosophy, according to Mike, was that the better a student, the more a teacher should step aside and leave well enough alone, as such people will always find their way. Whereas if someone had little talent, it was a teacher's obligation to talk to them at length, because the only good they could do was to try and make them feel a little better about the fact that they were without talent. This was Mike's explanation, but from the very little that Stephen said to me about my work throughout the year, I pray he was right (Ibid.).

A second email from Weller identifies the lessons he drew from this experience:

> The incident remains with me as a double lesson – the first: one should try to report exactly what happened and let it speak for itself, rather

than tell people how you felt about what happened . . . and the second is that when faced with a truly talented student, as a teacher it's best to say very very little, as they'll be bound and determined to find their own way (Weller 2009b).

Weller's 'old classmate' (Watson 2002) Ian Watson kept in contact with Joseph after graduation. A three-page letter written in November 1963 suggests that Joseph enjoyed discussing theatre history and practice with favoured former students. In the letter Joseph defended writer and critic Ferdinand Brunitière from 'pompous' (Joseph 1963b: 1) academic criticism, before confessing unease at developments at The Vic in Stoke-on-Trent. Joseph reported too his despair at the plight of theatregoers, suggesting 'a motto over every theatre entrance – enter here and stop living' (Ibid.: 3):

> Audiences are not allowed to cough, eat chocolates, talk to each other; when bored they must sit still (there is scarcely elbow room for figits). . . . Let the audience talk, eat, move about, make a noise – the actor's job is to win attention (not command it) (Ibid.).

Joseph was of course part of a team at Manchester. Former London Old Vic theatre director Professor Hugh Hunt – with a background that was 'very sort of Establishment' (Taylor 1998: 2) – brought with him an impressive list of 'international contacts [who] were a significant element' (Goodhead 2008) of the student experience; visitors included Peter Brook and veteran Russian actor Faina Ranevskaya. Young lecturer (later Professor) Peter Thomson, newly arrived from the University of Cambridge, brought along an 'historical understanding of drama' (Ibid.). Clare Venables, newly graduated from the university and not yet a theatre director, was an additional and provocative member of the teaching team on the Diploma (Ibid.).

A reading of a range of Manchester reminiscences – including those drawn together by Terry Lane, Rodney Wood and Stacey Morley – reveals Joseph as an important influence on teaching colleagues. Hugh Hunt is now credited with reintroducing audiences to the work of Irish melo-dramatic playwright Dion Boucicault through his 1968 Abbey Theatre, Dublin production of *The Shaughraun*; yet academic and former Joseph student George Taylor recalls that Hunt was 'horrified' (Taylor 1998: 3) at Stephen Joseph's 1965 plan for a production of the play. Hunt's reaction persisted until he saw that the piece was 'far better than its reputation [as a] dreadful Victorian play' (Ibid.); soon after, Hunt was planning his own production.

Former colleague Peter Thomson has reflected in depth on Joseph's influence on others. Joseph 'scared the living daylights out of me when I first met him' (Thomson 2008a); this reaction came in response to an intervention at a syllabus planning meeting, when Joseph said

> something like "Why do we keep talking about plays? Anyone can read a play. Let the students read plays. We need to talk about the difficult things. Anthropology. Electronics. Sociology. Group dynamics. Architectural space" (Thomson 2008a).

Although Thomson recalls that 'to my great relief Stephen's challenge to academic orthodoxy was evaded at the time' (Ibid.), he adds:

> The next time I saw him he was showing the Diploma students how to run a flat. We don't do much flat running these days – box sets having fallen out of fashion. But I got a huge sense of achievement out of doing it (Ibid.).

Thomson soon 'plucked up the courage to explain to Stephen the profound limitations of my own knowledge' (Thomson 2008b), which he remembers as 'youthful enthusiasm for teaching, an amateur interest in putting on plays and some ideas about Romantic drama's irrelevance to popular theatre at the start of the 19th century' (Ibid.). Thomson recalls that '[Joseph's] response was straightforward. "Knowledge doesn't matter. What matters is wanting to know – and knowing how to find out"' (Ibid.).

Thomson offers that 'there, if you like, is a basis of a worthwhile pedagogical system. Provided it's paired with curiosity rather than inertia, ignorance is the great incentive to learning' (Ibid.). Thomson offers a summary of what may be considered Stephen Joseph's approach as an educationalist:

> Stephen based his whole teaching of Manchester's unique one-year Diploma course on not teaching. His educational system was to allow, and if necessary to provoke, an ethos of enquiry to prevail. The next step after a Stephen Joseph class was to try it – whatever "it" was – to try it out (Thomson 2008a).

Joseph's posthumous influence at the University of Manchester is explicitly recognized by Thomson as 'the basis for the change of tactics that the younger staff at Manchester set their sights on in about 1970' (Ibid.). Thomson offers his own interpretation of the Joseph philosophy for teaching drama within a university setting:

> A theory whose significance cannot be demonstrated through practice is probably of no use to anybody, and certainly anathema to a working drama department (Ibid.).

Thomson – who considers that Joseph 'lived life as an adventure into the unknown' – offers a summary of Joseph's 'other incidental impacts' (Ibid.):

> his scepticism about directors, for example, with its concomitant preference for actors; his relish of melodrama as a theatrical mode . . . his delight in the belt and braces of theatre; his vision of a purposeful work space (partially realised by his designs for the Nuffield at Lancaster) (Ibid.).

A 1998 request from then drama student Stacey Morley for memories of Joseph, prompted Thomson to offer this personal sketch:

> He was fascinated by funfairs at night [for] the lighting effect they created in a city-scape . . . he liked motor-bikes . . . as a cowboy might love a horse . . . he loved good melodramas, because they told cracking stories; he liked actors with no arrogance [and] had no time for directors who didn't like getting their hands dirty. . . . I think he was shy, and coped with it sometimes by a show of aggression – but never to women (Thomson 1998).

Joseph's students mattered to him; and he would frequently use his Studio Theatre company to place them alongside professionals. Occasionally, he was willing to cast students in major roles – including within the 1965 Scarborough premiere of the play which would become Alan Ayckbourn's first West End success:

> *Relatively [Speaking]* had two women [who] were students from [Manchester University], Cathy Naish and Jo Tope – and the two men, David Jarrett and Peter King, were both professionals. That was how [Joseph] operated. But I mean it was quite an interesting mixture, it was sort of slightly different – I mean there was a sort of even more informal feel about it (Ayckbourn 2007).

Peter Cheeseman has recalled how his controversial (and shortlived) sacking by Stephen Joseph, when Cheeseman was running The Vic in Stoke, led to the theatre being temporarily run by 'a scratch company [comprising] an extraordinary group of people [drawn] from his students in Manchester' (Cheeseman 2008). Recent graduate Ian Watson found himself installed as Business Manager. Student playwrights too could find themselves suddenly professional – as when Joseph staged Mike Stott's play *The Play of Mata Hari* in Scarborough. Non-production roles, offered to provoke students' interest and creativity, were also granted: Clive Goodhead remembers working in 1965 as a publicity assistant, alongside fellow student (later film-maker)

Roland Joffé. Goodhead's role combined marketing work – mainly offering concessionary ticket deals at local hotels – with crew work specializing as a lighting assistant. Goodhead believes that

> one of the reasons Stephen regularly offered jobs to promising graduates and undergraduates from Manchester was that they would thereby solve the Equity conundrum and obtain the requisite means of entry to the theatrical profession (Goodhead 2007: 2).

As a student, Goodhead 'rarely knew what to expect' (Goodhead 2007: 1) from a class with Joseph. He recalls an activity involving spontaneous improvisation during a class in 1964:

> One of our first encounters as "freshers" involved us forming pairs to invent improvisations based on the nonsense phrase, "Down in the clutterbuck something glossopped". Another similar starting point – though exactly what, I forget – led to my friend Maggie Mash and me seeming to blow ourselves bigger and bigger until we burst. . . . I found such methods fascinating, challenging and immensely enjoyable (Goodhead 2007: 1).

Goodhead remembers a Joseph-supervised production by Roland Joffé which took round theatre staging in a surprising direction:

> [The production] was staged in the round but, instead of the audience encircling the actors, it was the other way round. The perimeter stage encircled the audience, who were (so to speak) in a pile in the middle (Ibid.: 3).

2. Joseph's work with members of the Studio Theatre Company

Stephen Joseph recruited dozens of theatre employees during his career. New recruits were frequently 'jobbing' theatre workers; their fixed contract work with Joseph thus represented just one part of their freelance activity as performers, directors or technicians. Joseph may have influenced such employees; but then, so may the numerous other employing directors. And anyway Joseph was frequently absent from the daily running of the company: Rodney Wood observed that 'as soon as [Joseph] had a suitable manager in Scarborough, he went off and drove coal lorries to "save a salary"' (Wood 2008: 44). Two years after launch Joseph noted that his company's 'financial crises' (Joseph 1957k) meant that there was 'not enough money in the bank for me to draw a salary' (Ibid.) – meaning that he had 'to work for a living' (Ibid.).

Joseph's employees on longer contracts, however, often found themselves quickly offered extra or new roles within the company. Some of these employees achieved considerable entrepreneurial success on leaving Studio Theatre.

The focus within the next section of this fourth chapter is, then, on employees whose contact with Joseph prior to joining his company was either minimal or non-existent. The text below offers a representative selection of such employees: theatre director and playwright Clifford Williams; theatre director, playwright, actor and manager David Campton; actor Faynia Jefferys (later, as Faynia Williams, a theatre director and BBC producer); and actor Sir Ben Kingsley.

Clifford Williams

When he died in 2005, theatre maker Clifford Williams had achieved sufficient status and fame to be accorded detailed obituaries in the British national press, including in The *Independent*, The *Guardian* and The *Daily Telegraph*. These sources noted in particular Williams's success as a director at the Royal Shakespeare Company (RSC) in the early 1960s. While they also highlighted Williams's pre-RSC work in dance, in regional theatre, working with Theatre Workshop and with his own Mime Theatre Company, no reference is made to Williams's ongoing intermittent work with the Studio Theatre Company between 1956 and 1962.

Williams's RSC success was achieved despite an alleged initial rebuff:

> The only senior RSC director never to have been to university, Williams had never thought of himself as a member of the company. Nor had Peter Hall, its founder. "You'll never be a producer here," he told Williams in 1961. There was "no room". He had no use for "outside people" (Shorter 2005).

Williams was eventually entrusted with the direction of a small range of theatre productions, and would become 'the RSC's best delineator of the company's house style' (*Daily Telegraph* 2005). Echoing the work of former employer Stephen Joseph, Williams was '[the RSC's] most resourceful and reliable investigator of forgotten classics' (Ibid.). Williams's RSC success led to a career directing productions in London's West End, for the National Theatre, and on Broadway. He directed the London version of Kenneth Tynan's review *Oh! Calcutta*, apparently ensuring that 'everyone – director included – [was] naked in the rehearsal room during the nude sequences'

(Strachan 2005). Williams's staging choices at the RSC are especially noted by one obituarist: his revival of Shakespeare's *The Comedy of Errors* was set

> on three planked and raked platforms with a few benches, and the cast were dressed in uniformly grey costumes. As the play progressed, decorative elements were added – a scarlet feather, a striking ruff, a ridiculous hat – until the scene gradually became a carnival of colour (Shorter 2005).

It seems Williams is another Studio Theatre recruit who was persuaded to write. He directed his own one-act piece *The Disguises of Arlecchino* for Studio Theatre in 1956. Subtitled 'a comedy in one act with music and mime' (Williams n.d.), the play attempts to authentically represent the work of the *commedia dell'arte* using four characters: Pantalone, 'an old and rich widower'; Arlecchino, 'his servant'; Clarice, 'an ugly widow'; and Columbina, 'her maid'. The setting is 'A street in an Italian city. Houses at either side'; the time is 'The 18th century – or any time'. (Ibid.)

The Disguises of Arlecchino, performed in-the-round in Scarborough, drew praise locally for its 'highly amusing frivolity, with a call on the imagination of the audience admirably suited to the round' (*Scarborough Evening News* 1956a). Williams's play was part of a double-bill which became a triple-bill after a *Scarborough Evening News* journalist complained that, minute-for-minute, the shorter evening was 'the most expensive show in town' (*Scarborough Evening News* 1956b): Williams also directed the

Figure 4 *The Disguises of Arlecchino*, written and directed by Clifford Williams. Courtesy of Scarborough Theatre Trust

other new play in the triple-bill, Eleanor D. Glaser's *Call The Selkie Home* (Joseph 1956b).

Williams's work as a Studio Theatre director locates him there at points that are historically significant. The completed typescript of *The Outsider* author Colin Wilson's first original play *Viennese Interlude* turned out to be so brief – reportedly as short as 17 minutes – that Stephen Joseph was forced to twin it with Strindberg's *Miss Julia*; *Theatre Record* praised Williams's 'fine direction' of the latter play (*Theatre World* April 1960). Williams also directed two of Alan Ayckbourn's earliest plays, *Love After All* (Allen 1959) – an Edwardian farce which toured successfully in early 1960 (Joseph 1959f) – and *Dad's Tale* (Allen 1960). *Dad's Tale* seems to have been a good project for dancer-turned-director Williams because the project threw together actors from Studio Theatre and dancers from Gerard Bagley's British Dance Drama Theatre group. David Harris – as an actor with Studio Theatre, David Jarrett – thinks Williams was also asked by Joseph to direct Ayckbourn's *Standing Room Only*, his first play to be considered for West End transfer: 'but he didn't do it, Stephen did it' (Harris 2007). Clifford Williams seems nevertheless to have been entrusted with an unusually wide range of genres while with Studio Theatre: he tackled serious psychological drama (*Miss Julia*); commedia dell'arte (*The Disguises of Arlecchino*); folklore drama (*Call The Selkie Home*); English farce (*Love After All*); and sentimental dance-drama (*Dad's Tale*).

Williams's genre-stretching achievements with Joseph's company must surely have influenced his subsequent work with the RSC and beyond. His exposure to in-the-round design minimalism – and Joseph's lesson that director and designer should be the same person (Joseph 1964a: 106) – surely guided Williams towards the bold stage minimalism that was to receive such high praise at the RSC. Likewise, Williams's post-Studio Theatre reputation as someone who 'took chances on scores of questionable new plays and on risky revivals' (*The Daily Telegraph* 2005) echoes Joseph's own passion for risk-taking play selection. But to what extent is my claim for a Joseph influence on Williams mere assertion? Williams is actually on record providing a flavour of Stephen Joseph's value to him as a mentor:

> We all rather courted Stephen's favour. People could easily be hurt by him, because he could forget your existence. He never seemed to have enough time for one. He had charisma, was intensely interesting. He represented a flag, a rallying point, for those who wanted to do plays by writers like Strindberg, and new writers. He was a big chap. You could always stand behind him, as it were. You felt he had muscle, clout (Williams *in* Lane 2006: 113).

David Campton

In the twenty-first century, playwright David Campton's legacy would appear to exist chiefly within the amateur theatre community. Campton's 2006 obituary in The *Stage* records that 'some [of his plays] are regularly performed in schools and festivals, both here and overseas' (Max 2006).

A 2006 obituary in *The Times* describes Campton as 'a prolific dramatist who wrote for the stage, screen and radio for 35 years' (*The Times* 2006). The unidentified obituarist adds the faint praise that 'While his plays achieved little national popularity, they were usually intelligent and easy for an audience to grasp' (Ibid.). While praising Campton's 'verbal ingenuity' (Ibid.), the obituarist states that his plays 'never began to have the same impact as the work of Harold Pinter, who was exploring similar themes and techniques' (Ibid.).

This somewhat indifferent view of David Campton's career as a writer is at odds with the version of Campton emerging through my own research. An appraisal of his work during the years of his collaboration with Stephen Joseph – between 1955 (when Studio Theatre was launched) and 1967 (when Joseph died) – posits Campton as an innovative and provocative figure who was central to the achievement of some of Joseph's aims. Campton's relationship with Joseph, and indeed with the Studio Theatre company, appears to have outlasted that of any other creative individual; at least one new Campton play featured in every Scarborough season during Joseph's lifetime – with the exception, ironically, of the amateur-run season of 1966 (Murgatroyd n.d.).

David Campton's playwriting career began in amateur theatre (Wood 1979: 51). In January 1955 he attended a playwriting course run by Stephen Joseph (Ibid.): at this time Campton was settled in employment as a clerk 'at the top of his grade' (Lane 2006: 131) in a 'nice, cosy, super-annuated job with the East Midlands Gas Board' (Ibid.). In the summer of that same year Campton's full-length play *Dragons Are Dangerous* (Campton 1955) was staged by Studio Theatre during the inaugural Scarborough season, with direction shared between Stephen Joseph and cast member John Sherlock (Joseph 1955b). In 1957, after Studio Theatre had staged Campton plays in each of the two previous summer seasons, Campton was persuaded to leave his job in Leicester and join Joseph. Doubtless at least part of the attraction derived from Joseph's 'guarantee of production' (Wood 1979: 52) for any future playwriting.

Campton's recruitment to Studio Theatre is likely to have brought twofold benefits for Stephen Joseph. Campton's former employment, and his ongoing presence as a company member working variously as a playwright, actor

Figure 5 *Usher* (1962), adapted and directed by David Campton. Courtesy of Scarborough Theatre Trust

and occasional company manager, provided the company with a degree of stability and administrative support. Lewin Goff, Joseph's former lecturer in Iowa, noted Campton's 'gentle, understanding nature' (Goff 1977: 2) during a working visit to Scarborough. Campton's skill as a playwright, and in particular, his willingness to respond to Joseph's suggestions and demands, further helped Joseph to fulfil a personal ambition to stage 'revolutionary theatre [that] makes its assault as best it can' (Joseph 1967: 139). Indeed, aside from Joseph's own provocations of the English cultural establishment (explored in the next chapter), his chief method of political agitation derived from his ongoing commissioning of provocative new work from David Campton. Seventeen new Campton plays (including one-act pieces) saw production during the lifespan of the Studio Theatre company; during the same period eight new plays by Alan Ayckbourn were staged, and eight by Peter Terson (mostly under Peter Cheeseman). Many playwrights received only a single commission (Murgatroyd n.d.).

For much of Campton's period with Studio Theatre, he wrote for specific audiences: 'light comedies and Gothic horror plays for the summer seasons at Scarborough, and black comedies for the winter tours of industrial towns' (Wood 1979: 53). It seems Stephen Joseph shares credit for the ideas behind some of Campton's earlier work – in particular, *The Lunatic View*, the quartet of one-act plays rejected by the Royal Court Theatre. A concise description of the 'comic macabre zanyhood' (*The Times* 1957) contained within the four pieces was supplied by a reviewer in *The Times* when the piece reached London in November 1957 (Ibid.). *A Smell of Burning* features 'a dim-witted young English couple at the breakfast table [who] remain blandly blind to the revolution and sinister uses of a hatchet that accompany the morning toast and correspondence' (Ibid.). *Memento Mori* relates how 'in an empty crumbling house a wife-murderer, boasting of his ability to live for himself alone, is hoist with his own petard by a dotard caretaker of the selfsame background' (Ibid.). In *Getting and Spending* 'a young married couple, ambitious for children and high political office, sink into a humdrum elderliness while endlessly working to keep their jerry-built house from falling about their ears' (Ibid.). *Then* glimpses 'in a Piccadilly desolate with atomic dust the last two creatures alive – a science teacher and the year's ironic dumb "Miss Europe" – fumblingly try to come to terms of intimacy heavily incommoded by the radiation-proof paper bags about their heads which have saved them' (Ibid.). Several critics highlighted Stephen Joseph's programme note that the quartet was 'written from the start for theatre in the round' (Joseph 1957i: 2).

The production programme for *The Lunatic View* identifies the Producer (the contemporary term for a director) as Rodney Wood (Joseph 1957i: 3). With an original cast including Clive Goodwin, co-founder of *Encore* magazine, the piece received performances in both Scarborough and London during 1957. Three years later it was restaged under Stephen Joseph's direction with a cast including David Campton, Alan Ayckbourn and Faynia Jeffery. Joseph supplied the linking voice-over for both productions – playfully billing himself as 'Heath Block' (Ibid.), a name also adopted for Joseph's pseudonymous letter-writing (discussed in the next chapter).

Terry Lane claims that *A Smell of Burning* sprang from a breakfast conversation between Joseph and Campton as they sat 'looking out of the window at the gasometer only yards away' (Lane 2006: 139). More persuasively, *Then* was apparently inspired by 'Stephen's fury at the critics' carping criticisms of not being able to see the actors' faces in the round' (Ibid.: 139–40): the provocative solution was to deny sight of the actors' faces to everyone, by using paper bags. Intriguingly, Rodney Wood states in a footnote that '*Memento Mori*, the opening play is based on one of Stephen Joseph's playwriting exercises' (Wood 1979: 52) involving a battle over disputed space: it's noteworthy that Harold Pinter's *The Room*, the hastily written debut play by another former student of Joseph, centres too on a claustrophobic battle for ownership of a mysterious room.

Stephen Joseph's 'very strange effect' (Ayckbourn *in* Watson 1981: 49) on David Campton's playwriting has been highlighted by Alan Ayckbourn, who recalls how

[Joseph] didn't necessarily give David the plots, but he certainly encouraged and channelled his writing towards what was then the comedy of menace school, and threw in his thoughts on nuclear disasters (Ibid.).

Ayckbourn – who politely but strenuously resisted Joseph's efforts to shape the content of his own work – reflects that he remains unsure

how David [Campton]'s talent would have developed, had he been allowed not to be quite so strongly dominated by Stephen saying: "This is what I want, David; can you write it?" (Ibid.: 50).

Ayckbourn has recalled how in 1960 Joseph unsuccessfully attempted to involve him in a collaboration on what was to become *Dad's Tale*:

I learnt quite an object lesson. He wanted me to collaborate with David; and David wrote a synopsis for *Dad's Tale*, based on *The Borrowers*. By the time I got it, I found I was unable actually to work to other people's ideas. I was maybe too undisciplined, I don't know; so I totally went my own way (Ibid.).

In 1970 David Campton delivered a lecture to the amateur Drama Festivals Conference. Within a speech which was reported in *Amateur Stage* magazine, Campton spelt out Joseph's role as a provocateur:

It was Stephen who encouraged me to think "the more way out the idea, the better . . . let's see how far we can go". The other thing I learnt was to be completely practical in writing plays. All the plays I wrote during this period all sprang from very practical beginnings (Campton 1970).

Far more recently, Campton spoke further on Joseph's influence on him – openly suggesting that his mentor frequently chose the subject for much of Campton's output:

Stephen would just come out with "I've got a splendid idea for a play." It was an almost continual process, so I'm never quite sure whether the idea started with me or with (him) (Lane 2006: 139).

In Chapter Three I noted how David Campton's early reputation for combining serious ideas with comedy – most notably within *The Lunatic View* – saw him labelled by critic Irving Wardle as a playwright who created 'comedy of menace' (Wardle 1958: 86). Wardle's September 1958 analysis for *Encore* magazine also made brief approving mention of an early play by John McGrath, who was identified as 'a third-year undergraduate who seems to have seen everything' (Wardle 1958: 87). McGrath, later co-founder of the influential 7:84 theatre group, had staged his play *A Man Has Two Fathers* at the Oxford Playhouse in June 1958. Wardle observed within McGrath's play a theme of 'inexplicable holocaust' (Ibid.) – remarking also on '[the play's] exhibition of fluctuating identities, its satire, its comic preoccupation with cliché, and its surrealist action [in which] a note of menace is constant' (Ibid.). Much of the early Campton work commissioned by Stephen Joseph was also concerned with holocaust; and it transpires that a young John McGrath had witnessed a performance of one of these Campton pieces during one of the famous anti-nuclear Aldermaston marches. Reviewing an early amateur production of Campton's *A View From The Brink* for the May/June 1960 edition of *Encore*, McGrath – who had been a member of an audience comprising 'two hundred youth Protesters [sic] just arrived from Aldermaston' (McGrath 2002: 16) in a school classroom in Reading lit only by 'two naked bulbs' (Ibid.) – deconstructed what he later described as an event that 'looked forward to much of my later work' (Ibid.). McGrath's short review focused both on the production, and on the atmosphere and circumstances surrounding it: this began with an unusually perfunctory pre-show ritual involving 'half-a-dozen dedicated actors from Oxford' (McGrath 2002: 16):

> Remove sleeping bags [from the stage], point Protesting Youth vaguely at the stage, switch on bulbs, shove on actors, and begin the most exciting evening of theatre for a long time (Ibid.).

In a partial echo of Irving Wardle's 1958 *Encore* piece identifying Campton as 'the only writer I know of who has adapted [James] Joyce's verbal techniques for the theatre' (Wardle 1958: 89), McGrath noted the influence of Ionesco and Joyce on Campton, praising the writing as 'meaningful and original in matter beyond doubt' (McGrath 2002: 16). After offering the non-professional production and acting 'a somewhat qualified appraisal' (Ibid.), McGrath then went on to deconstruct an 'exhilarating' (Ibid.) evening that seems to have shared some of the characteristics of the type of single-room, adapted-space, no-frills event which Stephen Joseph's professional company had been providing around England since 1955. A noted factor on this occasion was the audience. McGrath recorded how

> . . . the complete and vociferous solidarity between audience and actors was overwhelming; the speed and clarity with which points were made by the performers and grasped by the brightest and youngest audience I have ever seen made one feel some faith in the future of the theatre (Ibid.: 17).

McGrath concluded cheerfully that 'the babble of comment from this young, footsore audience made one feel more certain than ever that the youth of England demand something to think about in the theatre and appreciate it when they get it' (McGrath 2002: 17).

McGrath's *Encore* article dates the reviewed Reading performance to Good Friday, 15 April 1960; yet Studio Theatre's debut production of *A View From The Brink* in Scarborough did not take place until 5 months later (*Gazette and Herald* 1960). If these dates are accurate, Campton and Joseph must have provided an advance copy of *A View From The Brink* in time for the 1960 Aldermaston march – with the intention, presumably, of provoking a politicized young audience that happened to include John McGrath. As such, David Campton and Stephen Joseph can be said to have played a small but significant role in a formative moment for agitprop theatre within Britain. We might note too that the stripped-down performance recorded by John McGrath, in which actors and audience were thrown into close and informal proximity under two bare light bulbs, predates the first Western exposure to the stage-minimalist work of Jerzy Grotowski by some 8 years.

In August 1960 Joseph was again involved in encouraging students to stage Campton's agitational work; this time, he intervened to propose an Edinburgh Fringe Festival staging of *The Lunatic View* by students from Sheffield's University Union of Students' Dramatic Committee. An article in the local *Sheffield Star* described how 'the committee had read play after play, then ran out of them. They were resigned to producing an old one when "The Lunatic View" was sent to them by Stephen Joseph, of the Library Theatre, Scarborough. They liked it' (*Sheffield Star* 1960).

Also in August 1960, Stephen Joseph wrote privately to former company member Dona Martyn that 'David's fate is very much in the balance, and we simply do not know if he is to achieve "Success at last"' (Joseph 1960i). Success for Campton would require other professionals to begin staging his work – something that barely happened at any point in his career. In fact his limited success in receiving professional staging beyond Studio Theatre remains something of a mystery. Campton's work did reach beyond his mentor, including to television: his provocative one-act piece *Incident* (Campton 1967) tackling the absurdity of racial prejudice, was broadcast twice on the BBC during 1965 (Ibid.: 2). Early in his career he had been the recipient of an Arts Council bursary, awarded to encourage him to continue writing for the theatre; Campton's eventual body of work would comprise some 134 plays. It's true that many of these were one-act pieces – a genre typically more attractive to amateur theatre groups than to professionals; even so, the plays' comic yet provocative content might have attracted far more interest from professional managements. In 1970 Campton offered the reflection that

> . . . as soon as you put a serious idea behind a comedy script, people said, "how terribly way-out and avant-garde; this is not for us" – and sat on their hands all the time (Campton 1970).

In later life Campton rejected the 'comedy of menace' label, noting that the term had over time 'acquired a connotation of theatre of the absurd' (Campton n.d.). He suggested instead 'Laughter and Fear' (Ibid.) – observing wryly that

> the chaos affecting everyone today — political, technical, sociological, religious, etc., etc., — is so all-pervading that it cannot be ignored, yet so shattering that it can only be approached through comedy. Tragedy demands firm foundations; today we are dancing among the ruins (Campton n.d.).

It is possible that Campton's movement away from professional theatre was intentional – both as a source of regular income, and as a way of continuing to agitate within amateur and student theatre communities. Publisher Samuel French Limited, which retains in print 21 of Campton's plays, quotes BBC journalist John Florance saying that 'there is hardly an amateur dramatic company in the country which won't have done one of his plays at some time' (Florance n.d.). On the Samuel French website Campton states:

> I have always written with production in mind . . . an idea can always be developed towards a particular medium, be it experimental theatre in the round or an all-female group performing in a converted schoolroom (Campton n.d.).

It's also possible, however, that Campton had little choice in committing himself to non-professional theatre. Campton's close association with the anti-establishment Stephen Joseph may have damaged the playwright's reputation, and perhaps even his chances of securing further regular employment within professional theatre after the death of his mentor in 1967. Terry Lane reports that a performance of Campton's provocative *Little Brother, Little Sister* was visited by the British government's Home Office department, which 'sent a Colonel from Intelligence to report on its seditious nature' (Ibid.) in response to a 'strongly worded The *Guardian* review' (Lane 2006: 164). Lane offers no specific dates – the piece was produced more than once by Joseph's company – but a January 1961 preview in The *Guardian* praising plans to stage the play located Campton as 'the nearest thing the

Campaign for Nuclear Disarmament has to an official playwright' (The
Guardian 1961a). Tellingly, a subsequent unattributed The *Guardian* review
speculated that the production would leave Joseph and Campton 'well on the
way to success which will earn them a place in the pages of Britain's artistic
annals' (The *Guardian* 1961b). Much, then, was at stake in 1961 for Campton,
Joseph and the Studio Theatre company; and the London press now joined
the Manchester-based The *Guardian* in offering comment. A piece in *The
Times* headed 'Theatre in the round to get £99,000 home?' (*The Times* 1961)
combined a supportive reporting of Studio Theatre's well-developed plans
for a new round theatre in Newcastle-under-Lyme, with praise for the 'wildly
funny' (Ibid.) production of Campton's controversial quartet. However a
review in the *Daily Telegraph* took a starkly different view of the production,
dismissing Campton as

> A somewhat derivative writer . . . [who] has an acute ear for the sounds
> and symptoms of very sick humour [and] does not appear to have the
> discipline – even the sense of when to stop (*Daily Telegraph*, 31 January
> 1961).

Just weeks later, the British government's Ministry of Housing and Local
Government effectively blocked local council funding for the proposed
Newcastle-under-Lyme round theatre – provoking the collapse of the new-
build project.

The Victoria Theatre, adapted from a former cinema, opened in 1962. By
this time David Campton had, according to Peter Cheeseman, already 'left
the company to earn his living as a full-time writer' (Cheeseman 1970: ix).
Rodney Wood suggests that from 1966 Campton 'turned his back on the
professional stage' (Wood 1979: 53) in response to Joseph's 'dispute with his
manager at the Victoria Theatre' (Ibid.). Although Campton continued to
produce new work after leaving Studio Theatre, during Joseph's remaining
years Campton's work was mainly premiered within the continuing, mostly
Joseph-directed summer seasons above the central library in Scarborough
(doollee.com n.d., c) – an early gesture of loyalty, perhaps, towards a man
whose ideas and suggestions had so often inspired Campton's work.

Faynia Jeffery/Williams

Faynia Williams – Faynia Jeffery when working as an actor, including with
Studio Theatre between 1958 and 1960 – has worked variously as a BBC
radio producer, film maker, freelance director of opera and as a freelance
and resident director of theatre (Debrett's n.d.). She was also the first artistic

director of Glasgow's Tron Theatre (Glasgow University n.d.). Williams has developed an unusually wide and eclectic international profile in a variety of non-performing roles that continue to provide opportunities for her to influence the work of theatre makers worldwide. A former director of the Directors' Guild of Great Britain, she is Honorary President of the Unesco International Theatre Institute (ITI) Dramatic Theatre committee, directing and exchanging directorial information and contacts in countries including Iran, Mongolia, Bangladesh and the Philippines (Williams 2009). Williams has stated that in her work she chooses to 'speak out and lobby for the power of theatre, both here and in areas of conflict, to contribute to a sustainable and better world' (Ibid.).

Williams is one of a number of former Studio Theatre company members who have in some way championed Stephen Joseph as a significant theatre figure – here, mainly through *Surrounded* (Williams 2005), a 2005 BBC radio documentary presented by former Studio Theatre actor Robert Powell. In 2008 Williams also wrote to the *Guardian* newspaper to remind readers – and, specifically, theatre critic and historian Michael Billington, whose May 2008 article (Billington 2008) had prompted Williams's response – that Stephen Joseph had helped 'save [Harold] Pinter's career after the withdrawal of the Lyric Hammersmith production of *The Birthday Party*' (Williams 2008: 29).

Williams has a clear memory of a party at Joseph's flat in London representing 'the most extraordinary kind of gathering of people who were going to be there for the next [Studio Theatre] season' (Williams 2008). The gathering also featured

> People who'd been there from the previous season, playwrights, people like Colin Wilson, all the sort of people [who] were interested in this very unknown company called Theatre in the Round (Ibid.).

Throughout the interview, Williams (like other former company members including David Harris) uses the term 'Theatre in the Round' in place of Studio Theatre, the company's official title. An artefact held by Williams – a beer mat, produced to publicize a company tour to Hemel Hempstead, Southampton, Scarborough, London, Totnes and Newcastle-under-Lyme – announces (along with the names of the host towns and cities) that 'Stephen Joseph presents Theatre in the Round' (Elsam 2008). The title – used to identify the company on a range of company literature, including programmes – serves to highlight the continuing absence of any other theatre-in-the-round in Britain some 4 years after the launch of Joseph's company in 1955.

Williams recalls Joseph at the party as a 'huge bear of a man . . . not seeming comfortable in his own flesh, really . . . a big kindly bear' (Williams

2008). Williams describes Joseph as 'Amazingly charismatic' (Ibid.) – citing, intriguingly, the following memory as an illustration:

> One of the things I remember about him in rehearsal was he often . . . used to come into rehearsal with a motorcycle magazine . . . in his full gear, and sit at the back, and he would not look up from the magazine until you gave him something to look up for (Ibid.).

Williams regards Joseph's rehearsal room behaviour as an aspect of his role as a teacher and mentor. As an actor, Williams developed 'an awareness' (Ibid.) that the focus was 'about the work. . . . You couldn't rely on him doing the work for you' (Ibid.). Echoing this, former actor David Harris offers his own view of Joseph's attitude towards actors:

> . . . providing they know what they're doing, just let them get on with it – no point my telling them where to go. They know the scene, they should know – they've got the characters – they move where the emotions, the situation takes them (Harris 2007).

Faynia Williams describes her time with Joseph's company as the 'formative experience in my life, actually' (Williams 2008). She considers Studio Theatre to have been 'the first Community Theatre . . . we ate together, we worked together, we did everything together, and he expected you to explore all your own talents, even if you didn't know you had a talent' (Ibid.). She recalls 'one of the sort of credos . . . that you did everything. You weren't starry at all' (Ibid.). Williams recalls:

> . . . you had to be prepared to sit on the box office, to sew costumes, to design Stephen's famous "Penny Theatre" – I did all the interior design for his famous Penny Theatre . . . (Ibid.).

Williams goes on to explain this Penny Theatre – a promotional tool employed when touring to theatreless towns and cities:

> [Joseph] believed, if councils put a penny on the rates, you could build a theatre . . . and he would make a little model one, and then I was responsible for doing the interior painting and sort of design of the interior, and he'd take these models to council people, you know – "Put a penny on rates so we can have this theatre in your town!" (Williams 2008).

Williams credits Joseph with strongly influencing her own subsequent work as a professional theatre director, including highlighting the value of 'doing really good research for a production – your own research' (Ibid.). Joseph – 'a real avant-garde, before we even used the word' (Ibid.) – helped to inspire Williams's interest in nurturing a theatre culture in which non-British theatre was welcome:

> British theatre was not very conscious of European work and Stephen brought in Marivaux, Sartre, he brought in plays outside the British sphere (Ibid.).

Williams – one of Britain's most internationalist theatre makers – considers that Joseph 'opened me up to a world outside theatre' (Ibid.). He 'saw that I was a pioneer' (Ibid.):

> He really showed me that that was an advantage, and I shouldn't be afraid of that, and I should always try and pioneer, and not go back to doing what other people had done (Ibid.).

Joseph's nurturing of Williams suggests that she might have been offered a leadership role with Studio Theatre, most likely at the point when Joseph was considering a move into academia; however between late 1960 and 1961 Williams was otherwise engaged, contracted as an artist with MGM Studios in the United States (Debrett's n.d.). In the event her first work as a director took place at Oxford Free Theatre, a company she founded at a time when 'everyone was whinging about grants' (Williams 2008) as an experiment in examining 'how much you could do for free, for how long' (Ibid.). She was also interested in exploring 'how free you could be in what the word "theatre" meant' (Ibid.). Williams considers that 'from that point of view Stephen's breaking boundaries was very influential' (Ibid.) on her work in Oxford. Williams's innovations in staging non-British theatre – an area she was able to take 'much further than Stephen did' (Ibid.) – saw her stage the first British productions of work by Aleksander Solzhenitsyn and Mikhail Bulgakov. In 1980 Williams founded Brighton Theatre, continuing the ensemble work she had experienced as an actor with Joseph's company. She was 'one of the first [to] mix students with professional actors' (Ibid.). Williams notes too, in relation to her work as a director and academic at the University of Bradford, that 'a lot of people would see the formative influence of Stephen on my work there' (Ibid.).

Stephen Joseph 'really, really created in me an interest in the architectural use of space – theatre in non-theatre spaces' (Ibid.). She notes too how the Pinter-directed production of *The Birthday Party*, in which she played Lulu, inspired her 'interest in rhythm in theatre, and that took me into music in theatre' (Ibid.).

Williams's own reflection on how her desire to innovate may have inhibited her own reputation, may offer insight too into Stephen Joseph's current anonymity:

That's why I'm not as famous as other people might be, you know? I'm much more interested in breaking barriers than actually repeating what I've done before, or going the safe way (Ibid.).

Ben Kingsley

Sir Ben Kingsley is one of Britain's most successful contemporary actors. Nominated four times for Academy awards for film acting, Kingsley won the Best Actor 'Oscar' for his portrayal of Mahatma Gandhi in Sir Richard Attenborough's 1982 film *Gandhi*. A former member of Joseph's Studio Theatre company, Kingsley worked under Peter Cheeseman during the early 1960s.

Kingsley did not attend drama school; he entered professional theatre directly after gaining experience as an amateur actor with the Salford Players. He considers himself 'very very fortunate' (Kingsley 2008) in his early theatre career because 'I'd gone from proscenium arch as an amateur actor, and my first job was in the round. No hiding place' (Ibid.). Employed first to act within 'very challenging' (Kingsley 2008) theatre-in-education productions for theatre entrepreneur Brian Way – noted by Kingsley as being 'linked with Stephen' (Ibid.) – the actor was 'persuaded' (Ibid.) by Way to audition for Peter Cheeseman at Stoke-on-Trent:

> So although I never met Stephen Joseph face to face I knew that under his ethos, his guidance, his principle of "No Hiding Place", of accessible theatre for communities, of the arena, – all these wonderful things contributed to my first two jobs (Ibid.).

Kingsley credits his early experience working in round theatre as being central in his own development as an actor working 'in that classic Stephen Joseph's arena' (Ibid.). Kingsley further identifies how working in the round shaped his understanding of truthfulness in performance:

> The important thing for all of us then, in Cheeseman's company, under Stephen's guidance, was that we didn't cheat the audience – there was no hiding place, and there were no tricks (Ibid.).

Kingsley summarizes some of what he learnt about acting in the round:

> You must have the energy in your body language and your vocal range to include the people sitting behind you. And how you do that is that you bounce the energy off your fellow actor, who, he or she will then project your energy to the people sitting behind you. And you also can change your positions in a very graceful and elegant way (Kingsley 2008).

Kingsley offers a view on a Studio Theatre approach in which 'nothing was diluted' (Ibid.):

> I can remember the whole of our audience in the round being completely enthralled by what we were doing . . . we did some pretty strong stuff at Stoke-on-Trent (Ibid.).

He further articulates how Peter Cheeseman 'was determined to be relevant to the people of Stoke-on-Trent' (Ibid.) – an aim which was achieved

> not by distorting anything that we were presenting them with, but by bringing the audience up to a level at which they comprehended, and were thrilled by, beautiful dramatic poetry and language (Ibid.).

Kingsley quotes Cheeseman's belief that audiences 'pay money to be stimulated, not to be anaesthetised' (Ibid.). He recalls working on

> a beautiful documentary called "The Staffordshire Rebels," which was based upon the history of that area . . . Beautiful songs, and delightfully bizarre sequences, tragic sequences, sequences of great historical potency, and relevance – nationally, and to their area (Ibid.).

Kingsley articulates too his own experience of an ensemble approach to working, in which company members were encouraged to explore other skills and techniques. Invited to compose music for a production of *As You Like It*, Kingsley – at this point working as an Acting ASM and 'not yet good enough to be in plays' (Plater 2008) – then

> wrote the music for a play by Alan Plater called *A Smashing Day*, which then went to London, and I went to London, and then to Chichester after that. Then at the Royal Shakespeare Company [I] was also invited to write the music for *The Tempest*, and for Bertolt Brecht's *Baal*, and sing the songs in both those plays (Kingsley 2008).

Kingsley's now little-known talent for songwriting received an outlet via another recent Studio Theatre company member who was working, during Kingsley's time in Stoke, as a BBC Radio producer:

> I worked with Alan [Ayckbourn] on a *Calendar* programme, a monthly *Calendar* programme – must have been what we now call [BBC] Radio Four, – and it was a monthly celebration of northern songwriters, poets – Roger McGough, I remember, was on the programme – comedy sketches, relevant current affairs items, once a month – so I used to write a song for them every month, for Alan, and read poetry for Alan too (Ibid.).

Asked about the political dimension of his early work, Kingsley offers a reply that would seem to echo Joseph, Ayckbourn and Cheeseman's collective belief in the potential for theatre to influence society:

> All good theatre is serious political theatre . . . [Art and Politics] are absolutely intrinsically linked, when you're talking about good art and good theatre – completely locked together (Ibid.).

Kingsley, born near Scarborough, ends his interview with a reflection on seeing for the first time the Stephen Joseph Theatre – named after someone who 'means a lot to me' (Kingsley 2008):

> We stopped on the corner, and there was – I'd never seen his theatre before – and there was the Joseph theatre, there it was. It was lovely to see it (Ibid.).

3. Joseph's missionary work

Much of Stephen Joseph's missionary work served as a route for recruitment – either of students for the full-time courses he taught at Central and at the University of Manchester, or of professional theatre workers. As such, the development of individual Joseph protégés can therefore be quite difficult to categorize. At least one Joseph employee, actor Ann Summers, progressed directly from a missionary event – a 1957 Summer School at North Riding Training College in Scarborough – to become a member of the acting company from 1957 to 1959 (Wood 2009). David Campton arguably belongs in all three of my categories, because Campton's attendance at an evening playwriting class run by Joseph at Central led to a commission as an outside playwright, after which Campton was persuaded to leave his regular employment in order to join the Studio Theatre company.

This final category of three offers, then, an opportunity to record and assess the testimony of two Joseph acquaintances who, although clearly influenced by him, had never been long-term students of Joseph, and were not at any point in their careers commissioned or employed by him.

Ian Hogg

The theatre work of former RSC actor Ian Hogg has included the role of Prospero in Peter Brook's 1968 Paris production of Shakespeare's *The Tempest*, the title role in Trevor Nunn's 1972 production of *Coriolanus* and parts in Brook's *Marat/Sade* and *US*. After training at Central, Hogg was involved with 'one of the student walkouts' (Hogg 2008) after which 'we formed the Drama Centre' (Ibid.) to establish drama as 'a serious platform [with] a social intent – a place for debate and experience' (Ibid.).

Hogg's interest in training as a professional actor was provoked by his participation, while still at school, in a 'very respected' (Ibid.) three-week residential course in Scarborough that was led by teachers including Stephen Joseph. Hogg remembers Joseph as 'very energetic, very down-to-earth – [there was] no pretension about him at all in terms of intellect, or the grandeur of what was being done' (Ibid.). Hogg remembers 'The Fireman's Outfit' (Ibid.) – striking clothing Joseph wore for rehearsals and teaching, comprising 'jean material, kind of bib and braces . . . belt, quite heavy shoes, maybe boots on' (Ibid.).

Hogg reflects that Joseph was 'extremely reachable' (Ibid.) during the short course. He recalls a rehearsal of Chekhov's *The Seagull* in which the nineteen-year-old Hogg was meant to 'kiss this similar girl – seventeen, eighteen years old' (Hogg 2008). He remembers being

> so bloody "Public Schoolboy" . . . very embarrassed by this, you see. And I can remember, when the moment came, I used to chicken out of it, you see. And Stephen found this a) amusing and b) irritating, and I can remember him saying "Come on! Come on Ian! For Christ's sake it's so easy!" And he took the girl and went [mimes a kiss], and put her gently back and said, "There – didn't hurt!" (Ibid.)

Hogg also recalls Joseph as 'the first person to say "Come along and see theatre-in-the-round" ' (Ibid.).

Trevor Griffiths

Born in Manchester in 1935, Trevor Griffiths worked variously as a schoolteacher, liberal studies lecturer and further education officer for the BBC, before becoming a full-time writer in 1970. Stage work includes *Comedians, The Party* and *Occupations*; screenplays include the Oscar-nominated *Reds*, co-written with Warren Beatty; *Country*, directed by Richard Eyre; and *Fatherland* directed by Ken Loach. Griffiths has also produced a range of important original work for television.

Griffiths first met Stephen Joseph while working as an assistant lecturer in Liberal Studies at the Stockport College of Further Education. At this point he 'had very little understanding of theatre, very little experience of theatre and very little interest in it to be honest' (Griffiths 2008).

The new Principal of the college wanted to build a theatre within a gymnasium on campus, and Griffiths agreed to take on the project – even though 'I didn't know what a bloody theatre looked like or how to design one' (Ibid.). Griffiths remembers that 'people kept mentioning this guy Stephen Joseph' (Ibid.), so, sometime during 1963, he 'met up with Stephen – he came up to Stockport, and we hung out for two hours and wandered the space.... I was learning on the job, and he was teaching on the job' (Ibid.). Griffiths remembers two unpaid consultation visits from Joseph which were

> informal, uncontracted . . . this was an active site, and things were changing. He came over and he said, "those are dangerous, don't have those there; you don't want those in the wings, you don't want any wings", you know, all of that stuff. And I, as I say, I'm struggling to understand what the fuck he means by wings (Ibid.)

Griffiths remembers Joseph regretting that 'you hadn't got me earlier so we could have talked this thing out . . . [about] designing a circle somewhere in this gym' (Ibid.). Griffiths was unable to arrange for plans to be abandoned, so Joseph 'started looking at ways of just opening the thing out, until we had a kind of an end-stage, rather than a prosc arch' (Ibid.). Griffiths remembers how Joseph 'began to design all kinds of little curves that would begin some kind of circle that wasn't ever going to be completed, but nevertheless, it was there. And I got it, you know, and I could see what he was after' (Ibid.). Griffiths places Joseph alongside playwright Henry Livings – whose new work was staged by Studio Theatre on a single occasion in 1965 – as

> probably the two most important people in my life, as far as theatre's concerned. [Joseph] showed me that theatre was a life and death activity. It wasn't trivial. It really meant something much more important than changing your frock, you know, and becoming some other person (Griffiths 2008).

Griffiths recalls Joseph's approach to theatre as

> completely unpompous, it was completely practical, and he loved talking in practical details . . . which swamped me because I had no way of catching up with him – he was hundreds, thousands of miles beyond where I was. It took me a whole decade to get anywhere near Stephen Joseph's grasp of space and time inside these structures we call theatres (Griffiths 2008).

Although Griffiths recalls having seen no more than 10 professional theatre productions by the early 1960s, he remembers noticing the shift, in some theatres, away from purely proscenium auditoria. During a visit to the new Festival Theatre at Chichester in 1964, Griffiths recalls that:

> while it wasn't theatre-in-the-round, nevertheless [the theatre] had an extraordinary roundness to it. It had that circle on stage. And then it spread itself out into the auditorium, so that people seemed to be crowded round the front of it (Ibid.).

Griffiths's social background was a strong influence on his attitude towards live performance. Although he felt fully at ease with circus and music hall, he remembers that 'finding space for theatre was quite problematic for me . . . it was to do with the class of theatre. The way that class impinged on every judgement you made about the theatre – the people who went to theatre, the people who saw it as birthright, as it were' (Ibid.). As a result Griffiths's role in the design of the Stockport College theatre space was limited; Stephen Joseph 'did all the designing he could, and I simply passed it on, I was just a vehicle for that' (Ibid.). Griffiths recalls being able to 'see the differences that [Joseph] was making, I could see why he was making them, and I began to think now about theatres as open spaces' (Ibid.). Griffiths notes how 'by the end of the '60's and the beginning of the '70's, the notion of the open space had been immortalised by Peter Brook for example, by Charles Marowitz, who opened a theatre' (Ibid.). He recalls how, despite his own early resistance to round theatre staging, his work was soon performed in such a space:

> I had a play in 1972 called *Sam, Sam,* at the Open Space. And it was more or less in the fucking round. I hadn't written it for the round, and I didn't even adapt it for the round, but somehow it got in there – and it worked (Griffiths 2008).

Indeed one of Griffiths's own directed productions while working at Stockport College was staged in the round, in the adapted theatre 'which Stephen Joseph gifted that college' (Ibid.):

> I produced and directed two plays, Arnold Wesker's *The Kitchen*, and Arthur Miller's *The Crucible*. Both of them large cast, needing quite different space to operate in. This *The Kitchen*, I played as if in the round! Though I didn't have a circle, I had a rectangle. But the audience sat round it (Ibid.).

Griffiths recalls how working in the college's Joseph-designed adaptable space taught him 'more about theatre in those eighteen months, than I'd learned in the whole of my life' (Ibid.). Although Stephen Joseph didn't manage to see Griffiths's student productions, his influence continued once Griffiths began writing professionally for the stage. His first play, *Occupations*, was staged at the Stables Theatre, run in Manchester by Granada Television – 'the great Mecca of anybody who wanted to be a writer' (Ibid.). Griffiths recalls 'an unrolling, a roll-out situation that affected me profoundly. Stephen Joseph was so at the heart of it' (Ibid.). Describing the debut production of *Occupations*, Griffiths remembers how

> [The actor playing] Gramsci . . . stood on a chair in the middle of this room, the lights went down, and suddenly he was surrounded by the audience . . . I learned that through just talking with Stephen Joseph. I'd learned that space is anywhere, and it's everywhere (Griffiths 2008).

Trevor Griffiths considers that Stephen Joseph's essential lesson to him was that a theatre space 'can be yours, you can make it yours, in no time at all. These look like simple things to people who are . . . doing a drama course. But to me it was extraordinary that these things could happen' (Ibid.).

5

Joseph and the Establishment

Section one: Overview

Was there an Establishment campaign to silence, or at least sideline Stephen Joseph? Predictably, it's hard to establish the truth. Not much was written down; even where it was, information is controlled: decades on, there are still Arts Council files to which access is restricted.

During my 2008 interview with Trevor Griffiths, he shared with me a personal example of how and why a living artist might begin to fade from theatre history. Following a 1982 British Council-sponsored visit to Australia, Griffiths declined to provide written information on people he had met during his three-week trip, telling authorities that their request was 'wholly improper' (Griffiths 2008). Other than an activist visit to the West Bank during the Second Intifada – a trip facilitated by a Council 'renegade' (Ibid.) – Griffiths would have no further contact with the Council. He believes that 'somebody thought that I had declared myself anti-British, anti-state, and therefore could not be trusted for anything else' (Ibid.). Some years later, when the Council began promoting British writers online, Griffiths – dubbed in 2006 'Britain's most mature political dramatist' (Billington 2006) – learnt that 'I was chucked out – I simply wasn't there' (Griffiths 2008). Targeted enquiries by others eventually restored Griffiths to the Council's list of profiled playwrights.

Writing in 1964, literary agent Peggy Ramsay recorded how criticizing people with influence can backfire:

> The trouble is that fame and reputation [grow] by *what one puts in*to ones work. . . . If one fusses about these things, the odd thing is that the reverse takes place (Ramsay 1964).

Ramsay is here commenting on a complaint, not from Stephen Joseph, but from Peter Cheeseman. Cheeseman resented the lack of credit given to Studio Theatre for staging television writer Alan Plater's first theatre work. Here, from an agent operating at the centre of British playwriting in the 1960s, is a key insight into one of the informal protocols of the English cultural Establishment: *Don't Make A Fuss*. This same unwritten rule served, I believe, to hasten Stephen Joseph's speedy posthumous disappearance from theatre history.

The term 'Establishment' is defined as 'a group in society who have power and influence in matters of policy or opinion, and who are seen as being opposed to change' (Oxford Dictionary and Thesaurus 2007: 348). Here, I refer to England's postwar cultural Establishment – a small, influential group located within English theatre, broadcasting, government and printed media. During Stephen Joseph's working years key figures included critics Kenneth Tynan, Harold Hobson, and W. A. Darlington; BBC Head of Drama Michael Barry; and Arts Council Drama Director Jo Hodgkinson. Some of the public and private disagreements between Joseph and Establishment 'members' will be examined during this chapter.

As a student at Cambridge, Joseph produced and directed two successful Footlights reviews including *La Vie Cambridgienne*, parts of which were later broadcast by the BBC. Joseph's active Footlights role saw him mix with others who would later achieve considerable influence within English culture and media, including: Michael Westmore – later a television executive at Associated Rediffusion; Charles Parker – later a key figure within the BBC, pioneering documentary recording; David Eady – later Director of the British Film Finance Board; Richard Baker – later a BBC broadcaster; and Stephen Garrett – later an architect and Getty Museum director. Joseph seemed well placed to join the Establishment – perhaps initially as a London-based theatre director or producer: after all, young graduate Peter Hall was soon to be found running 'my own theatre in the West End with the responsibility of doing a play every five weeks' (O'Mahoney 2005). In fact Joseph's first theatre work after university was in 'a series of short engagements including work as an assistant scene painter and as a stage manager' (Wood 1979: 8).

Joseph's taste for directorial experimentation emerged early on. Staging 'weekly rep' at a proscenium theatre in Lowestoft, some 140 miles from central London, he directed his actors to turn their backs during a naturalistic production; such a break with British stage convention 'led to the biggest batch of letters in the history of the Lowestoft Theatre, all complaining' (Ibid.: 9).

Joseph's 1949 move to a teaching role at Central temporarily freed him from paying audiences, and facilitated bigger risks. Former student and recent Equity union president Harry Landis remembers exploring theatre-in-the-round with his new tutor. Landis remembers too a distinctly non-realist Joseph production during the 1953 World Festival of Youth and Students in Romania, in which '[we] told a story of some sort, so we all had to be monkeys and birds . . . people in Bucharest wondered what the bloody hell was going on' (Landis 2008).

In fact the Joseph-led trip to Romania represented something of a provocation. Staged immediately following a war in Korea that had killed civilians in their millions, the festival (slogan: *No! Our generation will not serve death and destruction!*) featured a ceremony honouring North Korean war veterans (Lane 2006: 95). The trip is remembered by participant Shirley Jaffe as 'really quite an extraordinary thing to do' (Jaffe 2007); Harry Landis recalls pressure to abandon the visit:

> They would rather you didn't go. They'd talk about, "you're in trouble" – they tried to put you off. That was their kind of censorship. But if you say "balls, I've got a passport, I will go where I like, they'll let me in, I'll go there!" (Landis 2008)

A surviving working typescript of Joseph's play *The Key*, set in Britain and performed in Bucharest, features what purports to be a spontaneous argument between two front-of-house theatre workers. One rails against her country's leaders who 'never stop having wars and talk, talk, talk about peace – while they're killing our boyfriends' (Joseph 1953: 6). All in all it seems likely that Joseph – essentially a decorated British war hero turning towards pacifism – would have attracted attention from the security services, perhaps on both sides of the Iron Curtain.

The launch of Studio Theatre promised first exposure to new plays staged in-the-round. A pre-season profile in the June 1955 edition of *Plays and Players* argued that round theatre staging would satisfy both theatre managers and actors. The unnamed journalist wrote that Joseph had

> recently been to America and studied the methods of the arena theatre at first hand. He believes, I think quite rightly, that the new form gives actors the finest training and offers them wonderful opportunities. Costs are cut to a minimum, which reduces the backing needed for such an enterprise (*Plays and Players* 1955).

Noting next that 'In England the professional arena theatre has mostly been used by people who have no idea of the potentialities of the new medium' (Ibid.), the author challenged Joseph to 'remedy that and make it a real theatrical experience' (Ibid.). The anonymous article could not have been more enthusiastic if it had been written by Joseph; I rather suspect that it was.

Just before the start of Studio Theatre's inaugural 1955 season, Joseph launched a campaign of letter-writing designed to secure the involvement of at least one celebrated English theatre figure. Tyrone Guthrie, invited to direct, replied diplomatically that he was 'flattered [but] not free for over a year' (Guthrie 1954); while J. B. Priestley unhelpfully urged Joseph to 'express the inadequacy of your [adapted] buildings all the time' (Priestley 1955a).

A reply from John Perry at H. M. Tennent Ltd. highlights just how alien theatre-in-the-round was in England in 1955:

> I think a theatre in the round might well be a success in England if only one could rely on the weather. That seems the problem to me (Perry 1955).

Critical reaction seems to have provoked a defensiveness, later an aggression, in some of Joseph's own responses – in particular, in his dealings with the press. A summer 1955 letter to The *Stage* challenged newspaper editors – several of whom had printed gossipy reports of Studio Theatre's fragile financial state – to 'hold their prophetic tongues about the theatre at large and print their obituaries as small news' (Joseph 1955a). A 1958 Joseph letter written privately to critic Harold Hobson found Joseph rueing his failure to secure patronage from 'the Philistines' (Joseph 1958i: 1) in England's capital, despite 3 years of touring there. It seems Joseph had already come to view the Establishment in distinctly confrontational terms: it was 'awful', he confided, 'to be forced to conduct an artistic venture like a battle' (Ibid.). Publicly, he was optimistic. In March 1959 – fresh from Harold Pinter's acclaimed restaging of *The Birthday Party* – Joseph summarized the progress of his company in *Theatre World* magazine:

> After five summer seasons at Scarborough, the company has proved that it can attract all sorts of people into the theatre, and hold their attention with all sorts of plays. Touring round theatreless towns, the company has proved that theatre on a shoe-string need not be of a low standard. But the people who have witnessed this near-miracle have been few, there being terrific resistance to going to the theatre anyhow. The idea will catch on. Each visit the second time round brings a bigger audience. Soon it will be full houses. If the money lasts till then! (Joseph 1959n: 46).

Soon afterwards, Joseph was presented with the most exciting publicity opportunity of his career. In March 1959 he wrote to Mervyn Edwards at Scarborough Library to request 'carte blanche' (Joseph 1959h: 1) access for a BBC film crew. Joseph reported that

> They are particularly interested in my claim that all sorts of people see the plays in Scarborough who would not usually go to a theatre at home – and that they enjoy them! (Ibid.).

In July 1959 David Jones, a producer-director at the BBC, wrote to inform Joseph that

Harold Pinter will be coming up to Scarborough to do a little piece, and it looks as though I shall be able to get pithy comments from Messrs. [John] Fernald and [Bernard] Miles, and possibly from Madam [Margaret] Rawlings (if I can keep her down to under a minute!) (Jones 1959a).

Suddenly, Joseph – privately, poised to give up on 'lousey Londoners' (Joseph 1958q: 1) – was about to receive very public support from important theatre makers in the capital. Significantly, director and RADA Principal John Fernald – named by Joseph only a year previously as opposed to theatre-in-the-round (Joseph 1958a) – was now a keen supporter of the form. David Jones requested a copy of *Alas Poor Fred*, James Saunders's newly commissioned play, before adding:

[*The Outsider* author] Colin Wilson tells me he is not only interested in Theatre-in-the-Round, he has almost finished a play for it. Is this news to you?! (Jones 1959a)

The prospect of a visit from the BBC represented a huge opportunity for Joseph and Studio Theatre. The plan was to produce a special *Monitor* programme on Studio Theatre: *Monitor* is remembered to this day for its opinion-shaping, stylistically adventurous content. Three years earlier, the BBC had committed itself to a sustained campaign of support for George Devine's English Stage Company at the Royal Court – even, on one occasion, using a memo from a senior executive to secure an 'extremely favourable preview' (Harris 2008: 153) of a television excerpt of *Look Back in Anger* in the *Radio Times*. It must have seemed to Joseph that it was his turn at last: the BBC had swept aside Establishment concerns about him to spotlight his radical, class-conscious little theatre group.

In August 1959 Jones, returning from a three-week holiday in Italy, found that he needed to write again. His note to Joseph, brief and apologetic, announced the wholesale abandonment of the project. The last-minute yet permanent cancellation was due, Jones claimed, to unexpected crew and equipment shortages (Jones 1959b).

Joseph replied to 'accept your explanation' (Joseph 1959j: 1). He complained, too, at the 'positive if inexplicable antagonism that so many people have to what we are doing in the theatre' (Ibid.) The following day Harold Pinter wrote to express dismay at the BBC's 'amorphous dithering' (Pinter 1959) – hoping Joseph had already 'blown it all away with a great fart' (Ibid.). He added:

I can't afford to come up and have a look [at the summer season] without the BBC paying the fare, and now they're not going to do it. Bugger them (Ibid.).

Neither Pinter nor the BBC's *Monitor* team would return to the room above Scarborough library.

A survey of Joseph's record of publication following the BBC withdrawal, suggests that he had learnt something of a lesson. For 2 years he ceased all public criticism of the Establishment. In March 1960, now busy developing a permanent base in the Potteries, Joseph declined to write a full article for *New Theatre* magazine on the grounds that he was 'far too busy working against the oppressive commercialism of the theatre to find time to write a decent article' (Joseph 1960b: 1). Enclosed nonetheless was a 'badly written little piece in case you might actually want something crude and rude and not know where to find it' (Ibid.). Joseph's article, dryly titled '*Forward – to 1890*', lambasts the ongoing building of 'out-of-date' (Joseph 1960c: 6) proscenium theatres. However it's clear that Joseph's targets are in local government in the provinces: no London or southeast England-based Establishment figure comes in for criticism. Indeed the capital receives implicit praise for hosting and supporting the Questors in Ealing, an impressive 'flexible theatre' (Ibid.: 7) built by amateurs. Four months later, a letter was despatched to the drama critic at the London-based *Punch* magazine, criticizing the publication's failure to mention the work of Studio Theatre (McAlpine 1960). However the letter was signed, not by Joseph, but by employee and theatre manager Joan McAlpine.

Section two: Case studies

Case study 1: A speech to conference

In June 1961 Stephen Joseph was given a place at the podium for the third biennial congress of the Association Internationale de Techniciens de Théâtre (AITT) – an event carrying sufficient status to merit an opening keynote speech from Royal Shakespeare Company founder Peter Hall. The official transcript of the conference, edited by Joseph, records the highlights of a range of speeches by important international theatre makers.

Joseph's selection as a speaker provided him with what he described in his editor's introductory notes as 'a rare opportunity and an invaluable experience' (Joseph 1961a). Suddenly he had a forum for two key related ambitions: publicizing his theatre-in-the-round mission, and signing up allies from among some of the most influential non-performers in world theatre. In fact he clearly had, too, a third aim – also related: to expose and damn prejudice against open staging within England's cultural Establishment.

Joseph's presentation was crafted to achieve maximum impact on an eclectic audience that included, alongside members of Britain's local and national government, delegates from Germany, France, South Africa, the United States and India. He opens with the assertion that he 'should not be here' (Joseph 1961a: 67): Joseph was appropriating a conference on adaptable theatres, in order to promote fixed theatre-in-the-round staging, with its 'emphasis placed on the human material in the theatre resulting from the absence of what is usually called scenery' (Ibid.). Joseph would be sharing details of a proposed new theatre-in-the-round at Newcastle-under-Lyme – a project that is 'very small' (Joseph 1961a: 67) and not even adaptable. He notes next that

> this form of theatre has aroused a widespread, and often vicious, opposition in this country. . . . Famous actors, authors, producers, critics and designers have opposed the idea – and the fact (Ibid.: 67).

Joseph offers himself as someone labelled by others as 'eccentric, ignorant and, even, dangerous' (Ibid.) – someone willing to 'shoot ink-pellets at authority' (Ibid.). He adds, with perhaps a targeted look around the conference hall, that he would 'try to resist this temptation' (Ibid.: 67–8).

Joseph next shares his 'special excitement [for] the all-embracing effect of an audience that completely surrounds the actors' (Ibid.: 68) – reflecting too on his company's use of resident playwrights who were also actors. Focus then turns to plans for the new theatre in Newcastle-under-Lyme. Joseph reveals that local councillors had jeopardized the project by demanding a proscenium theatre alongside the planned-for theatre-in-the-round. Joseph offers:

> The confusion arises out of ignorance. It is common in this country to assume that any big space with a large number of seats is a proper theatre, provided they all face a hole in the wall got up to look like a proscenium arch. Sight-lines matter little, backstage equipment and working space even less (Ibid.).

Joseph now develops the theme that theatre design in Britain is unsophisticated, citing specific recent examples of poor theatre design in new or renovated theatre buildings. The new Coventry Belgrade theatre has 'inadequate backstage space, and a grid too low for functioning' (Ibid.: 69); Peter Hall's year-old RSC base at Stratford suffers 'wingspace . . . insufficient for the machinery installed' (Ibid.: 69); while London's recently closed and short-lived Royalty Theatre conversion is 'the laughing stock of the theatre profession' (Ibid.: 69). England – a 'conservative nation [that] will spoil any

new idea for the sake of a compromise and a good deal of talk' (Ibid.:70) – is
no role model for Joseph's international theatre audience:

> You must remember that we do not have a tradition of theatre-going
> and theatre-building such as there is in Germany and so many countries
> in Europe. We do not have a flair for the aesthetic as in France, or the
> brilliant as in Italy, or the beautiful and practical as in India and the Far
> East. We do not even take our theatre seriously and study it as they do
> in America (Ibid.: 69).

Finally he spotlights Britain's government – the source of a recent and
'unexpected setback' (Ibid.: 70) to his Potteries project. The refusal to allow
Newcastle-under-Lyme councillors to raise capital by loan represented
nothing less than

> absolute idiocy . . . it is, I suppose, part of the Government's fiscal
> policy. As far as drama is concerned, the policy appears to be one of
> broken promises, meanness and deliberate destruction of what is vital
> in our theatre. This, finally, renders me speechless (Ibid.: 70).

We can imagine the dramatic silence that must have followed Joseph's walk
from the podium.

What prompted him to do it? There's a range of possible factors: Studio
Theatre's forced withdrawal from London, after years of staging poorly
attended and sporadically reviewed theatre there; the cancellation, rather
than postponement, of the 1959 BBC *Monitor* television programme; George
Devine and Kenneth Tynan's apparent dismissal of Joseph as a potential
collaborator in developing new plays and playwrights; Joseph's repeated and
total failure to secure directing work with the BBC. Finally, his two-year-long
self-censorship had failed to secure him Establishment support for a creative
home in the Potteries. No longer, it seems, would he remain a dim figure at
the margins: fading fast, Joseph was shouting for help.

The first public response was immediate, passionate and unequivocal.
Speaker and internationally respected theatre and film designer Clifford
'Disley' Jones – a man whose work 'often irritat[ed] directors by earning
better notices than they did' (Robinson 2005) – offered open praise for
Joseph's 'splendid, indeed, enviable, single-mindedness' (Joseph 1961a: 79).
Jones added:

> At this point I must tell Mr Joseph once and for all, that as from 11am on
> the 29th June 1961 – this year of grace – I could never oppose his [in-the-
> round] form of theatre as such and would never want to, because, I would

like to think, I have sufficient intelligence to appreciate the value of truly original, considered and objective thought. And although I may never agree with him on certain technical and aesthetic principles, I realise that he is sincere, does know what he wants and therefore should jolly well get it. If he can get his theatre in Newcastle – and we should do all we can to help him . . . he has my unfailing support (Ibid.).

Jones – himself a 'handful' (Robinson 2005) – went on to issue an explicit public warning against pricking what some 'consider to be a balloon [when] they run the danger of making themselves the pawns in a game played by the establishments which they think they are fighting' (Joseph 1961a: 79).

Why did Jones not offer this last bit of advice in private? His distinctly upbeat conclusion provides a possible explanation:

> . . . I welcomed Mr Joseph's speech yesterday, because I suddenly saw at last a glimmer of hope that people in the theatre and at war with one another could work together to achieve what we all consider vital – the survival of the theatre (Ibid.).

Disley Jones's response was not the only one to lack equivocality. State funding for Joseph's proposed Newcastle-under-Lyme theatre was entirely refused; and soon afterwards, Joseph moved sideways into the university sector. Joseph's attritional war with the Establishment would, though, rumble on until his death in 1967. During that year, writing in *Theatre in the Round* (1967), Joseph openly restated his theatrical call to arms:

> A revolutionary theatre makes its assault as best it can. I am attracted to the possibilities of assaulting an audience, but I don't intend to take vigorous physical action until I find myself in a partisan group with something important to say. If we are to get into trouble with the police, I want it to be over an issue of real importance (Ibid.: 139).

Here can be found, I think, the central tenet of Joseph's vision for theatre: a belief in the power of communal theatre to provoke revolution – theatre as activism.

Case study 2: Heath block and other inventions

Stephen Joseph seems to have been willing to take sizeable risks in his public criticism of critics Kenneth Tynan and Harold Hobson. He also conducted what appears to be a short but elaborate 'sting' against *Daily Telegraph* critic W. A. Darlington. These correspondences are examined below. His provocative public pronouncements could also be more general: Alan Ayckbourn remembers 'letters Joseph wrote to the papers when he said everyone ought to be communists, which was the most awful word you could call anyone' (Ayckbourn 1996).

Although Stephen Joseph always signed letters offered for publication, sometimes the name was not his own. Always, his infrequent pseudonymous letter-writing – generally for publication – was intended to provoke or continue discussion. Joseph typically adopted the name 'Heath Block' – occasionally, 'R. Heath Block' – a tribute, perhaps, to former Central teaching colleague Heather Black. Initially this was a stage name: it appears in the cast list for the 1960 published version (Campton 1960) of David Campton's 1957 play *The Lunatic View* (1957).

In February 1962 – 7 months after Joseph's incendiary speech to the AITT conference – 'R. Heath Block' wrote a letter to the Editor of the *Stage*. Block begins by offering a muddled argument that appears to parody another letter in the Stage written by E. G. Bottle. Bottle had earlier criticized Joseph's published opinion of plans to renovate London's Prince Charles Theatre, which Joseph had thought ill-considered. Writing now as the London-based 'R. Heath Block', Joseph proclaimed:

> Sir, – Vote for Bottle! Of course we should have all forms of theatre side by side, and I cannot for the life of me see why Stephen Joseph should object to this situation. The fact that there is no theatre-in-the-round in this country simply proves that it is no good. This is a free country, and the monopoly of the open stage must be resisted (Joseph 1962: 14).

Next, Block personalized his attack on Joseph, wilfully misinterpreting Joseph's criticism of the planned redesign of a theatre that happened to have a royal name:

> I deeply resent Mr. Joseph's tone in attacking the Prince Charles Theatre. As if two foot of wing space mattered! Why, it is possible to act without any wing space at all. No, the truth is that Mr. Joseph is making a dastardly attack upon the Royal Family. Remember that it is his company that recently shocked the Midlands by playing no National Anthem in the theatre, and by presenting disgusting plays by John Osborne and Strindberg. The theatre must resist these communistic moves – and thank goodness we can rally behind the Bottle party! (Joseph 1962: 14)

It is difficult to know, more than 50 years on, how readers of the letters page of the *Stage* on 1 February 1962 would have responded. Joseph's lampooning may even have been read by some as a sober and authentic summary of what was wrong with his missionary work. Perhaps recognizing the risk, Joseph co-opted two company members to write more measured letters of support for his views for the same *Stage* edition; thus the balance of letters supporting Joseph outweighed, or at least outnumbered, the criticism by Block. Playwright David Campton, who felt that 'Mr. Bottle has gone slightly astray in his comments on Stephen Joseph's letter' (Campton 1962: 14), looked forward 'to the time when we have many forms of theatre – picture-frame, end-stage, round, and arena, all playing their part in a healthy theatrical climate' (Ibid.). Ian Watson derided the 'petty conservatism which is doing its best to murder theatrical excitement' (Watson 1962: 14), before claiming that Joseph 'certainly did not decry the proscenium arch theatre . . . [but rather] the attitude of Alfred Esdaile, who wants the Prince Charles Theatre to be as outmoded as possible' (Ibid.).

Heath Block wrote at least two more letters to the *Stage*. The first attacks a 1964 report from the Council of Repertory Theatres (CORT) which concluded (as summarized by Joseph/Block) that 'provincial theatre [is] a thoroughly lifeless and degraded activity' (Joseph 1964d: 14). At the time of the report's publication, the Vic in Stoke was breaking new ground under Peter Cheeseman, while Joseph was seeking improvements to his nine-year-old Scarborough base. 'Block' provides a fresh interpretation of the CORT report:

> If you're in the mud, drag others down too; it won't be so lonely. Unfortunately this sort of widespread mud culture is very dear to such bodies as the Arts Council, and it is thus taken seriously by local authorities. We could even arrive at the point where theatres are vital issues in council rooms and other debating chambers, but have little meaning to playgoers (Ibid.).

Joseph now rather abandoned efforts to hide his own identity, naming Studio Theatre as a company which 'to the best of my knowledge . . . has been staging a large number of new plays every year for ten years' (Ibid.). Block asserts reasons for the company's success – almost of all which were due to economies provided by the in-the-round staging – before slipping into the parodic observation that despite the company's success 'its productions are very, very bad' (Ibid.). Joseph's letter ends with a dismissal of the CORT's views as 'a coward's cry' (Ibid.).

A third *Stage* letter from Block tackled children's theatre, before dismissing many of the features of contemporary English theatre in general. While praising the work of Brian Way and Gerard Bagley, Joseph dismisses plans to take 'the dames and the knights' (Joseph 1964b: 14) into schools as 'sheer cant.

Children are indeed entitled to the best, but let it be suited to their tastes and capacities' (Ibid.). Block's argument was partly motivated by a conviction that children's behaviour often ruined classical theatre performances; not that the children were always to blame:

> When I was at school I was part of an audience that utterly destroyed a performance of "King John". It deserved to be massacred. Only adults with cultural blinkers or with a sadistic streak could have asked for our attention to this awful performance (Ibid.).

Finally, Block examines the low level of theatre-going nationally. Conclusions drawn – and actions needed – match those previously and often stated by Joseph:

> . . . standards are low, because our theatres are stuffy, old, out-of-date buildings, because our plays are tame stuff, because our acting is convention-ridden, because, except to the enthusiast, our theatre has little real contact with life, and isn't even as exciting as the dull rubbish that can be more easily watched on the TV (Ibid.).

Why did Joseph feel the need to create such an outspoken public 'other'? Perhaps he was trying to reach two audiences: those who might enjoy provocative and apparently genuine correspondence from an unknown author; and 'insiders' who might spot and enjoy the wit of the man behind the intermittent parody.

In fact there were other pseudonyms. Joseph's 1964 article *Letter to a Ratepayer* for *New Theatre Magazine* (Joseph 1964c: 15–18) saw him adopt the curious name 'Leslie Upton Brocket' (Ibid.: 15): the accompanying article, written in a playfully mocking tone, purports to be a private letter to his uncle 'Mr. E. Brocket' (Ibid.), published because the editors supposedly found comment 'difficult and pass it on to our readers for assistance' (Ibid.). Anonymity was clearly not Joseph's aim, because Leslie Upton Brocket is revealed to have apparently 'been working for some years with the Studio Theatre company' (Ibid). The article amounts to a summary of lessons Joseph had learnt, after almost a decade of struggle to establish a permanent theatre-in-the-round in England; it includes advice to ensure that 'there is an inbuilt device to burn the [new] theatre down after ten years' (Ibid.: 17). There's also an intriguing reference to a Joseph proposal for a revolutionary theatre-in-the-round in Southampton 'to be housed in a geodesic dome' (Ibid.) – 'filed away, without, I believe, anyone in authority ever looking at it' (Ibid.). Here Joseph may have been mistaken: such a design was to become a key feature of the in-the-round Royal Exchange Theatre in Manchester, more than a decade later.

In 1959 Joseph adopted a third pseudonym for his witty 'sting' on *Daily Telegraph* critic W. A. Darlington. Two years earlier Joseph and Darlington had exchanged letters, after Joseph had complained that his personal invitations to the critic had been ignored. Darlington replied:

> I don't get what you send to us. It's hardly possible I should, since my job is peripatetic and I don't keep regular office hours. . . the main trouble is space . . . if at any time you have something cooking which you think will do you special credit, by all means draw my attention to it and I'll do what I can (Darlington 1957).

Joseph, having failed to attract Darlington, wrote again. He received instead a note from the Deputy Editor of the *Daily Telegraph*:

> Here we have many theatres, and theatre in the round takes its place as an experiment rather than a necessity. . . . As for your more general complaint, I must say I find it unfair. No paper notices try-outs of new plays in the provinces more than we do. Our Drama Critic's interest in new playwrights is well-known (*Daily Telegraph* 1957).

Joseph began a fresh correspondence in 1959. At a point when Studio Theatre's acclaimed Pinter-directed production of *The Birthday Party* was touring alongside another new play by David Campton, Darlington had published a piece labelling the Royal Court 'the only nursery for young dramatists now operating in this country' (Joseph 1959b: 1). An incensed Joseph wrote privately to the critic, asserting that 'this is not true . . . my own company is quite definitely providing the sort of nursery you seem to refer to' (Ibid.). He continued:

> We are a small company, and you may wish to deny our existence . . . [however] in The Stage Yearbook of 1957 only four companies appear to have presented more than a dozen new plays during the year. They are the Royal Court, the Arts, Worthing Rep, and ourselves. No west-end [sic] management rates more than two . . . we are doing exactly what you have said no-one besides the Royal Court is doing. Further, we have been doing it for a slightly longer period! (Joseph 1959b: 1)

Darlington replied immediately to say that he should have written ' "the only nursery of national importance", or some such phrase' (Darlington 1959a) – before adding, 'People like you . . . are always a headache' (Ibid.). Joseph's four-page response, sent 4 days later, complained that 'if the important critics do not consider it their duty to find out what is going on in the theatre, no wonder the public is so ill-informed' (Joseph 1959c).

Darlington appears to have considered their correspondence closed. Clearly, Joseph disagreed. On 6 March 1959 he wrote privately once more – this time as 'Stephen Savage', an enthusiastic compiler of challenging historical theatre quizzes, who wanted to offer Darlington a special quiz for inclusion in the *Telegraph*. Although the critic declined it for publication, he couldn't resist attempting to complete it. He dispatched the quiz by return post with a note to say that

> it is a remarkably interesting questionnaire, on its merits as a collection of pontifications . . . it is too hard for me! . . . if you can spare time to send me the answers, I'd like to see if any of my guesses are on target (Darlington 1959b).

Ten days later, 'Savage' replied with the correct answers – adding, in conclusion, that the questions so intriguing to Darlington were in fact all drawn from a playwriting course taught by Stephen Joseph. *Now* their correspondence was closed.

Case study 3: Joseph, Tynan and Hobson

Letters between Joseph and Kenneth Tynan and Harold Hobson, the two most influential critics at work during the lifetime of Studio Theatre, involved no pseudonymous writing.

An undated letter from Tynan to Joseph (Tynan n.d.) – most likely written prior to the summer 1955 launch of Studio Theatre – highlights the remoteness of Joseph's Scarborough base from England's cultural Establishment in and around London. The tone of Tynan's letter is friendly, even conspiratorial; he writes of Joan Littlewood's Theatre Workshop:

> [They] really came a cropper at Barnstaple. I begin to give them up. The neurotic isolationism of their behaviour there was beyond belief – accepting no advice from anyone, even the charming young man whom Brecht sent over to assist them. Too bad (Ibid.).

Essentially however this was a letter warning Joseph not to expect a Tynan visit to Yorkshire. Although the critic was planning a trip to the Edinburgh Festival – a route that could easily take Tynan to Scarborough – Joseph was told that 'the editor wants me to make the trip by plane' (Ibid.).

Joseph seems to have responded critically to Tynan's absence in Yorkshire. In May 1955 he received a letter from Tynan's editor at the *Observer*, defending the critic from an accusation of regionalism. In fact, the editor's supportive reply rather underlines Joseph's point:

[Tynan] gets about in this country too – to Oxford, Cambridge, Bristol and Salisbury (not to mention Ealing, Bromley and Notting Hill Gate), and is, as you will have noticed, a constant champion in our columns of Theatre Workshop in the East End (Observer 1955).

Aside, then, from trips to the Establishment strongholds of Oxford and Cambridge, Tynan had made no review visits at all to English theatres north of London. In response, Joseph decided that he must bring his company to the capital.

Soon afterwards Tynan did see a Studio Theatre production in London. Joseph must surely have regretted his own lobbying. Tynan's *Observer* review (Tynan 1955) – expanded and repeated in 1956 for the South African press – derided Joseph's work for '[featuring] twice as many false moustaches as members of the company' (Tynan 1956). The critic's dismissive portrait of Joseph's 'guerilla outfit' (Ibid.) featuring 'inadequate actors and a bold but bad choice of plays' (Tynan 1955), ended with advice to readers to 'think twice before committing himself (sic) to Mr Joseph's creed' (Tynan 1956). Most of all, Tynan condemned Studio Theatre's staging:

One admits that "theatre in the round" costs very little, in that it cuts down the scenery to a bare minimum and needs only an auditorium with an open space in the centre and chairs around it. But its aesthetic advantages are extremely dubious. The argument that it produces a "three-dimensional effect" is particularly specious. In a conventional theatre the effect is just as "three-dimensional"; the individual spectator sees a group of actors in depth, just as he does at "theatre in the round." Strip a normal stage, put a semi-circle of chairs around the back of it and you have "theatre in the round": the question is, to what conceivable purpose? (Ibid.)

Joseph's eventual response came in the June/July 1957 edition of *Encore*, in a wide-ranging article examining a situation in which it was 'still modish for journalists and drama critics to insist that there are no new plays to see' (Joseph 1957e). Joseph used the article partly to mount an attack on the 'double standard' (Ibid.) he felt had been shown by Tynan, a critic who claimed to support new writing for the theatre even though

A new play put on by a commercial management is forgiven all sorts of absurdities and faults that are given very black marks in a little theatre production; and in general, of course, the commercial production gets much more space – no matter what the relative worth of the plays (Ibid.).

The critic did though receive some small credit for reviewing recent new work in London; whereas the Europhile tastes of Harold Hobson, reviewer for *The Times*, drew open sarcasm from Joseph:

> Mr. Hobson at this critical time had a good excuse for writing nothing about any of these seven [new] playwrights because a well-known French actress was playing again in London (Ibid.).

Joseph reflected this situation back on himself, noting how

> . . . philanthropists in the theatre [are] ready to throw away the small savings they have for the sake of experimental theatre. What happens to these noble managers afterwards? Fortunately, in the semi-welfare state, there is almost no queue at the labour exchange and they may be found, after their pathetic little failures, working as plumbers' mates, lorry drivers, or in the mines (Ibid.).

Some months later, provoked by the circumstances surrounding a play competition in the *Observer*, Joseph made an appeal 'for some honest reviewing' (Joseph 1958n: 1). In particular, he summoned fresh criticism of Tynan:

> Mr Tynan is a talented and well-known person, and his reviews of plays, particularly of what are usually called "serious" plays, determines to a great extent whether an audience goes to the plays or not . . . [yet] I must risk questioning Mr Tynan's integrity (Ibid.).

Joseph's objection – in what would be a rejected proposal for an *Observer* newspaper article – was that Tynan's 'supervision' (Ibid.) of the *Observer* playwriting competition should have disqualified him from championing a first production of N. F. Simpson's commended piece *A Resounding Tinkle*. Joseph dismissed Simpson's play as 'a pale imitation' (Joseph 1958n) of Ionesco and Beckett, in which 'the characters were feeble and the story dull and I was thoroughly bored' (Ibid.); while a new piece by John Mortimer, offered as the second piece on a double bill from the Royal Court Theatre, was branded 'phenomenally dull' (Ibid.). Although Joseph's uncharacteristically flippant treatment of new playwriting was written under his own name, he does seem to have been indulging in a spot of mimicry: George Devine had earlier rejected David Campton's quirky and original anti-nuclear *The Lunatic View* as 'a bit derivative' (Devine 1958); while 3 years previously Tynan had yawningly declined to read the same play, blaming 'laziness, I expect' (Tynan n.d.). Joseph's proposed article also targeted Tynan's championing of Theatre Workshop – a company which had recently been threatened with prosecution for an unscripted lavatorial joke aimed at Winston Churchill. Joseph's demand here was for 'some honest reporting' (Joseph 1958n), because Tynan had called for *Observer* readers to defend Joan Littlewood without, he felt, providing details of the case.

In fact, elsewhere, Joseph was very much in sympathy with Theatre Workshop. In another letter for publication, written this time in response to criticism from author and critic V. S. Pritchett, he observed that

> The important thing about this company is that the actors' approach is creative, and that it can give us fine acting, based on improvisation. The necessity of submitting scripts to the Lord Chamberlain rules out the possibility of such creative work (Joseph 1958v).

He added ruefully:

> I must admit I seldom find many people in the auditorium [at Stratford East]. It seems to me that the oppression is a minor disgrace compared with the lack of appreciation shown by the public to this excellent company. The prosecution may bring publicity to the theatre, and therefore an audience – probably the wrong audience for the wrong reasons (Ibid.).

Hinting darkly at Establishment favouritism, Joseph noted too that although George Devine's Royal Court Theatre was 'one company that is trying to discover new playwrights of real importance' (Ibid.), the group had

> put on so many plays that trespass on ground that we might suppose after reading Pritchett's article would be forbidden – this company is in a position to know how elastic our present system of censorship is (Ibid.).

The denunciatory tone found in these two pieces intended for publication, seems unwise: surely any attack, however retaliatory, on Establishment power-holders who manage media access, would only harm the public profile of a theatre producer. Indeed Joseph's confrontationalism worried his allies: for Alan Ayckbourn, Joseph's tendency to 'lash into the Establishment quite openly' (Ayckbourn 1997) and 'piss critics off quite a lot' (Ibid.) rendered him 'his own worst enemy' (Ibid.). This was especially true with regard to Kenneth Tynan, who 'loathed [Joseph] – he presented a threat' (Ayckbourn 1996). For former Studio Theatre manager Ian Watson, Tynan 'hated theatre-in-the-round, he wrote article after article about having to look at the buttocks of actors and seeing their sweaty backs' (Watson 1998: 8).

Joseph's interaction with members of the Establishment does however need to be placed within a personal context. Joseph's own view of his life away from the theatre will be assessed later in this chapter; at this stage it's worth noting that, at around the same time that Joseph was composing these letters, his father died suddenly, leaving his son 'very shocked' (Joseph 1958j).

Joseph's correspondence with *The Sunday Times* critic Harold Hobson is perhaps more fruitful in highlighting Joseph's complicated relationship with the Establishment. At different points Joseph seems to have regarded Hobson as anything from a barrier to the success of Studio Theatre, to a confidante – someone to whom he could even unburden details of his struggles with others in authority. While critics Kenneth Tynan and W. D. Darlington tended to keep Joseph at a distance, Hobson responded. In 1955 he found himself drawn into a provocative correspondence with Joseph on the responsibilities of a professional theatre critic: although some of Joseph's own letters are missing, Hobson's responses offer strong clues to content.

On 24 June 1955 Joseph wrote to Hobson (Joseph 1955b: 1) in an attempt to persuade him to review a production during the inaugural Scarborough season. This does not seem to have happened; indeed Hobson's first Studio Theatre review appears 2 years later, for the company's 1957 in-the-round production of Ruth Dixon's *Honey in the Stone*. Joseph subsequently wrote privately to Hobson, apparently asking him why his criticism had been ungenerous. Hobson replied:

> I am not sure what part generosity plays in dramatic criticism. A dramatic critic goes to the theatre not to be generous or ungenerous, but to say what he feels. If he does anything else than this he will inevitably lose his integrity. The sad truth is I did not like "Honey in the Stone" and do not think that it gained anything from its method of production (Hobson 1957b).

Hobson added encouragingly:

> It may very well be that I shall like some of your future plays better and perhaps feel that their production methods have values which other types of production have not. If I do feel this I shall certainly say so and it always gives me more pleasure to praise than to condmn [sic] (Ibid.).

Harold Hobson was not of course not alone among London critics in rejecting both Studio Theatre's new work, and its in-the-round staging. In late 1957 Joseph reflected privately that one reason why 'the London season was a reasonable failure' (Joseph 1957d: 1) may have been the degree of innovation offered to audiences in the capital:

We did unwisely to put on a young company, two new plays, in a new
form of theatre, before the critics . . . only a few of whom came. They
had no mercy on us! (Ibid.)

The majority of Joseph's 1957 correspondence with Harold Hobson occurred
against a curious backdrop: Joseph was in secret negotiations to stage a first
play by working class author Colin Wilson, international bestselling author
of the philosophical meditation *The Outsider*. Wilson had turned to Joseph
after receiving a critical lambasting for his second novel, *Religion And The
Rebel*: the story of Wilson's link-up with Studio Theatre is described later in
this chapter. It may be that Wilson's sudden enthusiasm for working with
Studio Theatre – and his proposal to '[build] up Theatre in the Round as the
rival to the [Royal] Court, and the mecca to young writers' (Wilson 1957) –
emboldened Joseph to demand greater attention from critics. However,
Joseph's now-lost response to Hobson's earnest self-defence (Hobson 1957b)
served, it seems, only to exasperate the critic:

Surely you must see that you pose to me a problem which can be solved
in only one way. If a theatre manager on the one hand wishes a critic
to attend his performance and on the other asserts that all his notices
do is put him out of business, this in most cases admits of only one
solution (Hobson 1957c).

Here then was a frank and transparent warning to Joseph to draw back in
his criticism of Hobson, and, by implication, other senior theatre critics.
Joseph had recently published his recognition of the 'simple' (Joseph 1957e)
truth that 'audiences follow the critics' (Ibid.): he needed them to come to his
productions and write favourable reviews; they needed theatre managements
to offer due deference, to respect their power and knowledge.

By late 1957 plans were underway for Studio Theatre to abandon
touring to London, because 'the travelling theatre has exhausted our capital
resources' (Joseph 1957f: 1). First, though, was Joseph's London swansong – a
new in-the-round production of Racine's *Phèdre* featuring celebrated actor
Margaret Rawlings in the title role. *Phèdre* – adapted and even part-funded
by Rawlings – would be Joseph's most expensive production to date; director
Campbell Allen's fee alone was set at 50 pounds (Joseph 1958r). Clearly, some
diplomacy towards the critics was needed. Instead a frustrated Joseph seems
to have provoked an increasingly wary Hobson, who wrote:

What splendid examples of resolute good temper we are displaying
towards each other! Whatever else it may be I am sure this
correspondence is an admirable character building exercise and that
we shall both emerge from it finer and better men (Hobson 1957a).

In his witty and bridge-building letter, Hobson offered to review a specific performance on 10 November 1957, requesting that Joseph send him tickets. Hobson then added what sounds like an explicit threat:

> I hope my notices will not finish off theatre in the round. But who can possibly foretell what the result on this occasion will be? (Ibid.)

The threat was however tempered with self-deprecating humour. Hobson continued:

> I once wrote a book which I hoped would be read by Ralph Richardson. Richardson never looked at it but it did get me elected a member of the M.C.C. [cricket club]. After all there must be quite a number of people in London who will go to see plays simply because I don't like them (Hobson 1957a).

Hobson's wit, and his willingness to correspond, warmed Joseph to the critic; when Joseph decided in 1958 to withdraw from staging work in London, Hobson was seen as a sympathetic confidante. Eleven days after unsuccessfully lobbying Michael Barry at the BBC that he was 'anxious to do some television directing' (Joseph 1958p: 1), and shortly before *Phèdre* left London for a brief provincial tour, Joseph complained privately to Hobson that

> Apart from the critics, few public figures have come out in our defence. [J. B.] Priestley might have done, but has yet to see one of our performances. The new movement of theatre people – Norman Marshall, John Fernald, Andre von Gyseghem [sic] – have talked about theatre in the round, condemning it for various reasons. None of them has been to see one of our productions... (Joseph 1958k: 1)

Joseph even added the *cri de coeur* that

> another promising theatre venture has been destroyed by the Philistines! We shall go away to the country and breathe in the fresh air, and return when we are strong again (Joseph 1958k: 1).

Joseph's confidence in Hobson would be short-lived. In April 1961 Joseph submitted a sharp little poem to *The Sunday Times*, Hobson's employer. The poem distils two Joseph objections regarding theatre critics: their overzealous championing of individual authors, and their preference for reviewing European theatre (including, for Hobson, anything featuring actress Edwige Feuillère) at the expense of theatre in the English regions:

> Harold Hobson's gone religious.
> Puffs for Pinter grow prodigious.

Nowadays Edwige Feuillère
Isn't quite so often there.

Must he do such names to death?
Praise them, yes – then save his breath.

That'll be the day that he
(Quote from who?) "Impresses me". (Joseph 1961g: 1)

The Sunday Times declined the opportunity to publish. No matter: Joseph had written it, and no doubt felt better for sending it.

Three months later Joseph was once again using the 'Letters' pages of the *Stage* to provoke the Establishment. This time Joseph was responding to shocking news of Joan Littlewood's mysterious mid-1961 decampment abroad. Littlewood would later write that while she 'had tried in England – I hadn't succeeded' (Littlewood 1994: 749); she felt that she 'wasn't often made welcome' (Ibid.: 752). In July 1961, amid mounting speculation that her self-exile would be permanent, Joseph wrote to defend Littlewood's move abroad. His charge – made just weeks after his damning speech the AITT conference – was specific and, viewed now from a historical perspective, partly self-referential:

The fact is that the whole business of theatre in this country is so utterly discouraging to anyone, particularly a producer or director, who has wholly original ideas and a real creative talent (Joseph 1961h).

Joan Littlewood's recent struggles in a range of Establishment-controlled areas – including failure to secure significantly improved Arts Council funding, and the refusal of planning permission for a new, easy-to-disassemble theatre space – clearly reminded Joseph of the difficulties encountered, not only by himself, but by earlier British theatre makers:

A director of [Littlewood's] calibre has the choice then of staying in this country and growing increasingly bitter and frustrated, of compromising and joining the "business", or of leaving the country. This last course is the one chosen by [Edward Gordon] Craig, by [Tyrone] Guthrie and by Littlewood. Those who have compromised are not worth mentioning (Joseph 1961h).

Hinting at an undercurrent of xenophobia within English theatre, Joseph next identified specific non-British victims of indifference or antipathy:

It is interesting to note how many great directors have visited this country under conditions that might have encouraged them to make this their home. Such Europeans [sic] as Michael Chehov [sic] and

Michel St Denis spring immediately to mind. They have not stayed here because there is no room for their brilliant talents (Ibid.).

Joseph's letter ends with what can be read as a simple condemnation of the Establishment – and a stern warning to those who fail to stand up to it:

> Joan Littlewood has done the right thing. We are the poorer for it, and it is our fault. There is no mystery. We have chosen to organise our theatre as a rather mean little gambling business, and we shall pay the price (Ibid.).

Joseph's quick and passionate defence of Littlewood may have played some small part in persuading her to return to England; certainly, others were soon adding their support – including *Theatre World* writer R. B. Marriott, who blamed the 'shattering blow' (Marriott 1961: 47) of Littlewood's flight from England on 'The Government, the Arts Council, local authorities, all who are supposed to have an interest in the culture of the nation [but had instead] treated her extremely shabbily' (Ibid.). Marriott highlighted too a lack of fairness among critics visiting Theatre Workshop's base in East London – recalling

> the galling fact that productions at the Theatre Royal which were not "winners", but still contained more of interest than twenty ordinary commercial efforts, began to be condemned out of hand by the critics (Ibid.: 48).

Joseph, it seems, had allies.

Case study 4: Colin Wilson

One of the most intriguing accounts of an artist's relationship with the Establishment relates to the writer Colin Wilson, bestselling author of *The Outsider* (1956). The story of Leicester-born Wilson's clashes with a post-war cultural Establishment encompassing both theatre and literature, offers useful insights into the strength and depth of feeling – arguably, prejudice – within that group. While Wilson's link to Stephen Joseph has so far remained unexplored, his short play *Viennese Interlude* has been noted as part of an 'astonishing' (Allen 2001: 77) repertoire of touring productions during Studio Theatre's 1959–60 winter season.

The morning after the 1956 publication of Wilson's first book *The Outsider*, the 24-year-old author 'literally woke up one morning and found myself famous' (Wilson 2006). *The Outsider* drew critical acclaim from the most respected national literary critics. Philip Toynbee in the *Observer* thought it

'Luminously intelligent' (Toynbee 1956: 14); Cyril Connolly in *The Sunday Times* labelled it 'one of the most remarkable first books I have read in a long time' (*Guardian* 2006a: n.p.). The initial print run of 5,000 books sold out in a single day; the author would earn around £20,000 in royalties – a huge sum in the 1950s. Wilson – in 1956 'the most photographed author of the year' (*Guardian* 1956a: 5) – soon found himself mingling with other major writers, including Kingsley Amis and John Osborne. Branded a 'genius' (*Guardian* 2006b) by iconic writer and photographer Daniel Farson, Wilson quickly became something of a mouthpiece for his peers – labelled, as they were, the 'Colin Wilson generation' (*Guardian* 1956b: 5). Wilson had been named in the *Daily Express* as one of a group of four Angry Young Men alongside John Osborne, Michael Hastings and Kingsley Amis (Ritchie 2006: 18); to this list Wilson has added 'John Braine, Alan Sillitoe, Stan Barstow [and] Arnold Wesker . . . all from working-class backgrounds' (Wilson 2007: xv). Now moving in literary, academic and theatrical circles, Wilson had developed a yearning to write a stage play, and had been approached by George Devine at the Royal Court Theatre:

> [Devine] told me to regard the Royal Court as a kind of playwright's workshop. If I had ideas I wanted to try out, to write them down in the form of dialogue, and then listen as a group of actors read them aloud (Ibid.: 59).

Part of the developing mythology of Colin Wilson derived from the author's background as being self-educated and working class; this placed him among 'the first *group* of working class writers that had ever existed' (Ibid.: xv) and set him apart from 'the majority of writers [who] had come from middle-class or upper-class backgrounds, and been to university' (Ibid.: xv). However Wilson's debut book – written during research visits to the British Library, a feat made affordable by his sleeping rough on Hampstead Heath – adopted a style much closer to the work of the latter group.

Soon after publication of *The Outsider,* Wilson's public reputation began to deteriorate. He suffered heavy criticism from the press after a series of revelations, including his decision to leave his wife and child (*Guardian* 2006b). In 1957 Wilson's second book *Religion and the Rebel* came out to excoriating notices: Philip Toynbee now re-remembered Wilson's 'Luminously intelligent' (Toynbee 1956: 14) *The Outsider* as 'A vulgarising rubbish bin' (*Guardian* 2006b), and dismissed its sequel as 'clumsily written and still more clumsily composed' (Ibid.); others thought the new book 'Half-baked Nietzsche', 'highly embarrassing', 'Folie de Grandeur' (Lewis 1978: 168). The feeding frenzy crossed the Atlantic: *Time* magazine captioned a photograph of Wilson 'egg-head, scrambled' (Ibid.), while the *New York Times Book Review* offered a list to describe the author: Wilson was 'brash, conceited, pretentious, presumptuous, prolix, boring, unsound, unoriginal and totally without intellectual subtlety, wit and literary style' (Ibid.). Fifty years on from the publication of *The Outsider*, John Sutherland in the *Daily Telegraph* recalled that

> The philosophy establishment – from the fastness of their Oxbridge High Tables – were quick to put the upstart in his place. A. J. Ayer proclaimed Wilson "a dancing dog", a jumped-up oick who'd infatuated himself with difficult books he didn't understand (Sutherland: 2006: n.p.).

Peter Lewis, former theatre critic for the *Daily Mail* and author of *The Fifties* (Lewis 1978), has written that 'There could scarcely be a better illustration of how the Establishment operates [to] reassert their natural prejudice against anyone who had come up from the ranks' (Wilson 2007: xv–xvi). Wilson had, it seems, fallen foul of the English cultural establishment.

Just as Wilson was himself becoming an outsider, his draft play *The Death of God* – scheduled for development at the Royal Court Theatre – was summarily rejected, wittily dismissed by George Devine as 'not dramatically alive' (Wilson 1957b). A 'furious' (Wilson 2007: 67) Wilson wrote a critical open letter to Devine, provoking a public argument in the national press between the author and the Royal Court's management (Wilson 1957b: 67–8). Wilson, now in hiding in Cornwall, wrote to Stephen Joseph – promising a copy of his rejected play, which he claimed Joseph had offered to stage 'if the Court rejected it' (Ibid.).

Wilson's first letter to Joseph in September 1957 revisited some of the public humiliation the author had suffered after his unperformed play had been publicly condemned by English Stage Company co-founder Ronald Duncan. Wilson then added:

> IF, after you've read it, you think that Duncan's assessment of it [in the *Mail on Sunday*] – ("Children's hour stuff" "bad science fiction", etc) is nonsense (as I do), and that something might be made of it, I think it would be to our mutual advantage to discuss the possibility of your doing it (Wilson 1957b).

Wilson then drew on three factors to persuade Joseph to stage his play: his own fame and connections; his link to David Campton, a friend from Leicester; and the sense of empathy he guessed Joseph was feeling as a result of his own marginalization by the English cultural Establishment:

> Dave [Campton] tells me that you are getting rather exhausted with the difficulties that Theatre in the Round is running up against, and this *could* be an opportunity to give it a lot of publicity. A first night of

a play by me would inevitably have full press attendance, and would probably get quite a deal of publicity. If it was a success, it would point an accusing finger at the [Royal] Court – and I wouldnt [sic] be slow to take advantage of it to make my point that the Court has failed young writers – is not our 'Abbey' Theatre – and that it has been left to a small and by no means rich theatre to take up their cause (Ibid.).

Having made explicit his desire for revenge against the Court's management, Wilson next envisioned a scenario that would place Joseph at the very core of experimental English theatre. Wilson even implied that he had already discussed his plan with selected literary friends. The scale of Wilson's plot warrants quotation in full:

We could then begin a full scale press campaign. I would write another play for you. Bill Hopkins (whose first novel will be out in November, and who appears with me, Stuart Holroyd, Osborne, Tynan, etc in this "Credo" volume on Oct 14th) has also finished a play which he intended to rewrite and send to the Court. Stuart has done 2 acts of a play and already submitted them to the Court; he could easily be persuaded to let you do them. And I have 2 other close friends who have not yet appeared in print, but who are working along our lines, who would also write plays which you could hack around or rewrite (Wilson 1957b).

Wilson next set out for Joseph a long-term vision of Studio Theatre achieving a status Joseph had never dared to voice in public:

This would give Theatre in the Round the advantage of standing out as a rival of the Court, and also having a definite school of writers (and the most controversial young writers in England at the moment – or so the press would alledge) [sic] treating it as their vehicle of theatrical expression. If we could use all the publicity that we've had so far, it couldn't fail to make a success (Ibid.).

Wilson may have been aware, through David Campton, of Joseph's recent offer to collaborate with George Devine in providing tutorial support for playwrights (Joseph 1957a: 1). Joseph's comments in The *Guardian* less than a month later – criticizing 'people [who] profess to be concerned about the shortage of new playwrights . . . [when] the only shortage is of notice taken' (Joseph 1957b) – suggest that Joseph's proposal was either rejected, or ignored. Wilson now cleverly called on Joseph as a playwriting tutor:

I am not saying all this to try to bribe you to present The Death of God. Obviously, if it is a rotten play, and the critics say "No wonder Devine rejected it", it would only damage me. Obviously, the whole thing depends on whether The Death of God really *has* more possibilities than Devine and Duncan allowed. IF it has, then I think we have a perfect opening for building up Theatre in the Round as the rival to the Court, and the mecca to young writers! (Wilson 1957b)

Having provoked Joseph with the tantalizing twin prospects of attracting the best new young playwrights, and sharing status with the Royal Court – Wilson now focused on his rejected script:

A word or two about the play. It is *not* science fiction. It is an existentialist study that depends entirely on clash of character, and its setting in the future is relatively unimportant. All of the more obvious "futuristic" elements could be cut out without affecting it (Ibid.).

Wilson ended with a teasing request for Joseph to

Let me hear what you think as soon as possible, wont [sic] you? Dave [Campton] thinks [literary agent] Jimmy Wax may try to get the Arts, or some other organisation to do it. If so, I will definitely persuade him to give you first rejection (Ibid.).

Here we see Wilson in somewhat Machiavellian mode. His second book had been condemned by critics, his first play had just been dismissed by George Devine, yet he was still positioning himself as a revered and well-connected writer whose agent (also representing David Campton and Harold Pinter) could secure him access to Peter Hall at the Arts Theatre. An alliance with Hall would clearly threaten Joseph's chances of tutoring 'the most controversial young writers in England' (Wilson 1957b), whom Wilson claimed to lead; Wilson was willing, if Joseph moved quickly, to commit loyally to Studio Theatre.

On 9 October 1957 Joseph provided Wilson with feedback on his play, delivered in a stern parental style and offering 33 lines (in contrast to George Devine's six-line rejection slip) of clear, specific commentary – plus an offer to go through the script on a one-to-one basis. He provided too an overview:

The parts of your play I liked most were the opening dialogues, and the closing dialogue. Here I felt there was some pressure of ideas driving the characters, the lines and the story along . . . The worst parts of the play (apart from a few details) are the "story" parts – when you seem impelled to put *action* on the stage (or what passes for action in our theatre) (Joseph 1957c: 1).

Joseph urged Wilson to think in a more original way about his writing, exhorting him to break from a form which even new young playwrights like

John Osborne were adopting with their own full-length plays. Here Joseph offers a glimpse of his broader missionary plan, while clarifying his own radical requirement that plays require no interval:

> It is as though you were cautious of breaking with tradition. You see, the play is in three acts . . . why? Three acts arise only so that there shall be two intervals in which the audience can go and drink at the bar, thus enabling managers to survive, and deadening the audiences [sic] appreciation of the drama. . . . This, and other traditions badly need breaking – by writers and all other theatre artists – if we are to have a living theatre (Ibid.: 2).

Joseph's feedback to Wilson followed the confidence-building assurance that 'I'd like to put on the play. I'm not sure which would be better – a Sunday show, or a two-week run at 41 Fitzroy Square' (Joseph 1957c: 2). Joseph was effectively offering to invest heavily in Wilson with a resource-sapping London run at the Mahatma Gandhi Hall.

Joseph was careful, in his reply and in subsequent letters, to write nothing in support of Wilson's deep criticism of the Royal Court's management. Perhaps he wanted to sidestep negative publicity that might damage his own company; after all, George Devine and Ronald Duncan were far closer than he to the core of the Establishment. In fact Joseph had already provoked a snub through an inflammatory letter sent to The *Guardian* a few months earlier: he claimed then that the newspaper's enthusiasm for the Royal Court's new Sunday evening performances – something Joseph's company had been providing for 2 years, to little press interest – showed that critics were not 'the least bit interested in new talent until somehow – and without the evidence of their own eyes and judgement – they learn that it is good' (Joseph 1957b). Worryingly for Joseph his speculative plans for a theatre-in-the-round, offered for publication soon after to the same editor, had been rejected on the curious grounds that 'we do not have the space to do them justice' (The *Guardian* 1957).

Perhaps Joseph simply respected Devine and Duncan, and did not wish to criticize them personally. He may also have agreed with the Devine judgement of Wilson's play – a monastery-set drama featuring a paranoid dictator with amnesia – if not with the rather curt manner of Devine's delivery. Certainly, Joseph's vision was trained on other future projects: his letter to Wilson concluded with 'the hope that you will be able to find, before long, a really exciting way of expressing yourself in terms of theatre' (Joseph 1957c: 2).

Wilson's elated response to Joseph's feedback – 'HOORAY. . . . It is a sheer joy to know that some of it was successful' (Wilson 1957c) – was tempered by the thorny revelation that in fact Wilson's agent Jimmy Wax knew nothing of the proposal:

> About presentation. Naturally, I'd prefer the longer run, but can see the difficulties that may arise. The first, of course, is Jimmy. Do you think you could get David [Campton] to ring him and put it to him? (Ibid.)

Wilson added unhelpfully:

> If Jimmy [Wax] blows his top, naturally, I don't want to alienate my agent while he is handling his first job for me; so the whole of that aspect is really between you and Jimmy (Wilson 1957c).

It may be that Wax did disapprove; certainly, *The Death of God* was never staged by Joseph's company. Instead, Joseph commissioned Wilson to write a new piece. During progress towards Studio Theatre's staging of what would be Wilson's play *Viennese Interlude* – lasting for between 17 and 25 minutes, depending on the reviewer – Wilson and Joseph continued their correspondence. But Wilson's unfamiliarity with playwriting hampered his ability to produce a full-length dramatic project. This was a trait apparently shared with potential Studio Theatre playwrights Stuart Holroyd and Bill Hopkins – both, like Wilson, 'angry young men (and therefore not very practical about scripts, it seems)' (Joseph 1958c: 1). All in all, it seems to have tested Joseph's resolve. On 4 May, 1958, he wrote to Wilson:

> I hope before you get too involved with another play you'll take time off to look at the theatre itself. Including our own theatre. Further, as you know, I believe there are certain technicalities of playwriting that a writer does not necessarily know by instinct, and that he may not learn by observation of other plays (Joseph 1958b: 2).

Wilson responded immediately with a fresh play proposal, and an enquiry as to whether 'any of the women [in Studio Theatre are] good enough character actors to play a queer abbott [sic]' (Wilson 1958).

In due course Wilson delivered a theatrical imagining of a meeting between August Strindberg and a doctor. Joseph's production of *Viennese Interlude* opened in Scarborough in December 1959, reaching the Mahatma Ghandi Hall in London on 7 March 1960. The shortness of the play forced Joseph to twin *Viennese Interlude* with another play, Strindberg's own *Miss Julia*. Although national critics did attend, they were either amused (at Wilson) or disapproving (of Wilson's play): the *Daily Telegraph* thought the piece 'hardly revealing a specifically dramatic talent' (*Daily Telegraph*, 8 March, 1960); *Theatre World*'s reviewer dubbed the play 'rather disappointing . . . there was a certain surface glitter but nothing of import underneath' (*Theatre World* April 1960). The *Daily Mail* noted dryly that 'It had been a long struggle for Mr. Wilson to breathe fresh intellectual life into the English theatre as he had promised a few years ago' (*Daily Mail* 1960), concluding that 'it wasn't really a play . . . it wasn't really a stage . . . But it was a beginning' (Ibid.). The *Stage* critic considered the play 'remarkably successful' (*The Stage* 1960), but felt the need to add that 'it must be borne in mind that [Wilson's] ideas are not his own' (Ibid.).

For Joseph, this was to be one of a series of promising projects that would end in disappointment; he would have to seek new playwriting talent elsewhere. In fact his attention had already intensified towards members of his own company – including David Campton, whose 1957 quartet *The Lunatic View* had secured for Campton an Arts Council playwriting bursary; and Alan Ayckbourn, whose first public play – *The Square Cat* (1959) – merited firm encouragement. Plus, he had already provoked a dramatic reappraisal of the first work of Harold Pinter.

Section three: Joseph and the Establishment – personal factors

Much of Stephen Joseph's missionary work within English theatre saw him pursue an agenda that was anti-authoritarian, and broadly anti-hierarchical. The hegemony of the English cultural Establishment was for him a bad thing; its champions were wrong-headed devotees of a socially divisive two-room theatre; their National Anthem, with its invasive, spoilsport air of 'tremendous solemnity' (Ayckbourn 2007), merited excision. Audiences – especially working-class audiences in England's theatreless towns and cities – deserved a new type of theatrical experience which would be inclusive, meaningful and egalitarian. Studio Theatre would lead the way in offering a playfully eclectic repertoire staged in intimate, in-the-round spaces.

Perhaps above all Joseph wanted people to share power. Terry Lane asserts that Joseph was responding to his own history as a victim of 'tyranny' (Lane 2006: 59): abuse from his father and stepmother at home, but also from elsewhere – including within the Royal Navy during wartime, with its humiliating initiation ceremonies (Ibid.). Peter Cheeseman remembers Joseph telling him that 'in adult life you try and create around yourself the atmosphere of your childhood, and mine was insecurity' (Cheeseman 2008). Whatever the stimulus, Joseph appears to have developed a strong need, at times strenuously resisted, to be in control of things – including his own company, and critical responses to his company. This seemed to combine with an incendiary instinct for anarchism – his teacher's desire to 'blow up the classroom' (Ayckbourn 2012).

Studio Theatre was Joseph's laboratory – his personal vehicle for effecting change within theatre, and, he hoped, within society. The company hosted and facilitated almost all of his more radical theatre initiatives: the establishment and development of a new (to Britain) form of egalitarian theatre that placed the audience in the same room as the actors; the defence and support of rejected working class writers, including Harold Pinter and Colin Wilson; the championing of overtly political work – including the anti-nuclear comedies-of-menace of David Campton, which saw performance at CND demonstrations and at Arnold Wesker's Centre 42; cheap seating and travel subsidy for people on low incomes; the banning of the British national anthem at performances; free programmes; the relentless missionary touring of in-the-round theatre productions to London and to a wide range of theatreless towns; and finally the establishment of community-rooted northern repertory theatres, under the emerging leadership of Peter Cheeseman and Alan Ayckbourn. All were developed under the umbrella of a company that operated, for the vast majority of its lifetime, through a Board handpicked by Joseph.

One curious aspect of Stephen Joseph's life relates to his employment away from Studio Theatre. Before going to Cambridge University, Joseph spent two terms teaching at Heatherdown, seemingly a school for young offenders. In a quotation attributed to David Campton, Joseph's witnessing of a senior school colleague's abuse of power left him reflecting that he would 'rather cart coal than teach' (Lane, 2006: 61); and indeed, at points throughout his subsequent long leadership of Studio Theatre, Joseph would often take on manual work – selling coal or paraffin, driving a lorry, digging roads – which denied him a supervisory role.

Joseph's sudden disappearances to take on temporary manual work may have helped to pay the bills at Studio Theatre; but did such work also provide him with some sort of necessary emotional escape route? Terry Lane remembers Joseph as 'manic depressive – either high as a kite or suicidal' (Ibid.: 101). While Lane has been judged 'too closely implicated' (Watt 2007) in key aspects of Joseph's story to be considered an objective commentator, and while none of my own interviewees paint Joseph this way, it nevertheless seems curious that Joseph should periodically vanish from his own busy company in Scarborough only to reappear on a London doorstep, carrying a sack of coal. It seems unlikely that Joseph would regularly need such work to keep his company solvent. Studio Theatre was run with great economy: the hire of the Scarborough Library space was, in effect, heavily subsidized by the local council; salaries were kept low, at times through mixing students with professional actors, and generally through requiring company members to 'multi-task'; the use of in-the-round staging vastly reduced the need for set construction, transport and the full-time services of a designer; and substantial support was available, at least in Scarborough, from local amateurs and other volunteers. Also, Joseph's family enjoyed a level of wealth that allowed him to obtain help, including occasional loans from his Uncle Lionel; and on at least one occasion his mother Hermione intervened with an unrequested gift of money.

It may be that Joseph's longstanding sense of personal discomfort – both as an employee under the control of others, and as a man with privileged status within English society – provoked and maintained his focus on wider social inequality, and kept him thinking about ways to actively rebalance society. In particular, Joseph's post-Royal Navy job teaching children from underprivileged backgrounds, will have heightened his awareness of social and class inequality in post-war Britain. Terry Lane quotes a poignant letter written in 1946 while Joseph still held his difficult teaching post:

> I detest the barriers (built so well in my own mind) that separate class from class in our society – but if I have any ambition to break those barriers, it is to go down. . . . I know I suffer fiercely in high places and among high people (Joseph *in* Lane 2006: 61–2).

Joseph's ideological opposition to social inequality was, then, entwined with strong personal feelings of anxiety. His ongoing search for 'the most perfect way of living' (Ibid.: 61) suggested that a downward social move might offer contentment: he had after all 'only learned so far that I find good things, more in humility, than in richness' (Ibid.). Cambridge University – his next major stopping point – would hardly be the place to mingle with the English working classes; likewise a post-war professional London theatre scene – firmly in the grip of a conservative Establishment, and poised to welcome to the top table the 'university men' (Shepherd 2009: 13) – could promise little in the way of authentic class revolution.

Twelve years on, Joseph was to be found running his own small revolutionary outpost at a temporary base in northern England. A May 1958 letter underlines just how important this theatrical missionary work had become to his personal well-being. Joseph's correspondence – very likely with Mary James (née David), a once-close friend in Wales who had declined his offer of marriage 'in the early war years' (David 2004) – followed the recent death of his estranged father Michael, an event which Joseph claimed elsewhere had left him 'very shocked' (Joseph 1958j: 1). In the letter, Joseph uses fresh contact from his old friend as a spur for some deep self-analysis. He begins:

> A letter from you is a pleasant surprise, and a reminder of all sorts of happy times, and also a cue for judgement. I have become one of these busy people who never stop working. The important questions remain unanswered and I am afraid to take time off to think because I know I am so ill equipped to do so. Besides, I seem to have become reconciled to being a haunted, hunted person, and I don't believe I could find an answer if I tried (Joseph 1958d).

As early as his second sentence, then, Joseph's self-analysis takes a dark turn. Attempting a more positive tone, he continues:

> Of course I have mostly been busy in the theatre. The theatre in the round has all sorts of excitements to offer, and it has opened up my ideas of drama a good deal. If I came to look at the new Church Hall you mention I should probably disturb you by suggesting the stage and the curtains are out of date – you need (I guess) a space in which various arrangements can be made to relate audience and actors! (Ibid.)

Despite a sharp reference to his recent bereavement, Joseph next manages a second, fairly upbeat paragraph – chatty, even:

> My father and I were not on close terms and his death meant very little to me. I have since got to know my stepmother more and find that she is a likeable person. I have accepted some responsibility for my step-brother (Shirley's young brother – by my father's second wife) who is coming to live here when he leaves school this summer (Ibid.).

Settling now into a darker groove, he continues in language and thought more typically suited to a private diary than a catch-up letter with an old friend:

> I suspect I have changed a good deal during the last ten years – not to advantage. The two elements that used to show perhaps as self-consciousness and conceit warring with each other, these have now become on the one hand thorough self-contempt masked on the other hand by energetic activity. There are times when the appalling inadequacy of this balance makes me paralysed – but empty and depressed, not still and wise. Wisdom is out of reach, and I am straining in another direction, meaninglessly. When I have not been working in the theatre I throw myself into the most energetic and meaningless tasks I can find! Yet, for the life of me, I do not know what it is I am

afraid of facing. And I cannot see where such irrational, unnatural and senseless behaviour is leading (Ibid.).

Finally, as if drawing back from the depths:

> If it is fair to judge on slender evidence, you must admit this is not cheerful. But, as ever, part of the irony is that one is cheerful in spite of oneself, and I have more than my share of enjoyment. I have grown fond of all sorts of music, and am beginning to enjoy chamber music in particular. I've just bought a lovely set of the late Beethoven quartets on LP records (Ibid.).

It would be easy to misinterpret and distort the significance of this deeply confessional letter. Joseph was after all grieving – working through a long process of acknowledging condolences from former friends and acquaintances; the 24 May letter represents just one such acknowledgement. We can compare it with a shorter Joseph letter written a month earlier to 'Elma' (Joseph 1958q: 1), a friend of his mother; this presents a more traditional response to offers of condolence in which Joseph thanks the letter-writer's 'kindness' (Ibid.) before adding that 'there is nothing I can ask you to do [because] my step-mother has the burden of difficulties' (Ibid.). This earlier letter goes on to offer a brief summary of Joseph's theatre activity – plus a statement that 'we do not expect to do anything more in London for some time' (Ibid.). Finally, there is a rather poignant request for news of his mother, Hermione, because 'I have no idea what she is doing on Sunset Boulevard' (Ibid.): at this point, neither parent is in Joseph's life.

A sense of defensiveness would stay with Joseph for his remaining 9 years. Peter Thomson, a teaching colleague at the University of Manchester from 1964, recalls:

> the two weaknesses in Stephen that caused him the most suffering in the years I knew him – the first, a certain weariness of fighting; and the second, a not-always balanced sense that he was being persecuted (Thomson 1977: 2).

Thomson recalls Joseph's belief that stage designer and teaching colleague Alan Barlow, who visited Joseph's home in Scarborough to discuss designs, had come 'in order to spy on him' (Ibid.). Thomson offers that Joseph's 'sad sense of having been betrayed by people' (Ibid.) was

> part of a melancholy that, in conversation, always carried Stephen back to his childhood. The impression I have of that childhood is over-simplified. A mother who had left him and his brother; a stepmother who bullied and hated them; a largely unknown father (Ibid.).

Joseph's confrontational behaviour – often surprising, although almost always motivated by the urge either to correct a perceived mistake, or highlight a perceived wrongdoing – will have been coloured, at times even prompted, by his psychological distress. It seems as though his 'haunted, hunted' (Joseph 1958d) nature increasingly blinded him to the possible consequences of his various provocations. If they had known of his plight, might Joseph's targets have responded sympathetically? It's an important question: sympathy for Joseph, rather than antipathy towards him, might have led numerous others (both critics and theatre makers) to embrace, during Joseph's lifetime, his radical ideas around innovative use of space within British theatres. For many in Britain, between 1955 and 1967 Stephen Joseph *was* theatre-in-the-round. To *Daily Telegraph* critic W. A. Darlington he was also 'a headache' (Darlington 1959a); to Kenneth Tynan he was 'a threat' (Ayckbourn 1996). Did a theatre Establishment wary of Joseph's 'pricking [of their] balloon' (Jones 1961) throw the baby out with the bathwater? In twenty-first-century England, open staging – although reasonably widespread – remains almost always 'thrust'; indeed there's only one permanent theatre-in-the-round in London and the southeast, the little 172-seat Orange Tree in Richmond. But thrust stage theatres are problematical; to this day, Stephen Joseph's point that 'there must be no feeling that the seats at either side are not so good as those centrally placed' (Joseph 1968: 56) is almost always ignored. Recently Sir Peter Hall criticized the dynamics within thrust-stage theatres – including at the RSC's new space in Stratford-upon-Avon:

> You come on down that vast diving board of a stage and address the person you're speaking to with your back to half the audience. So the moves tend to be based on whose turn it is to [speak] text (Hall 2010).

Twenty-first-century British theatre – indeed, Western theatre – remains dominated then by linear, rather than organic acting.

Of course there have been, and there still are, theatre makers who think deeply about space. Jacques Copeau is still given credit in some quarters; Sir Tyrone Guthrie also. Sir Peter Brook and the late Jerzy Grotowski continue to enjoy the patronage of selected British critics and commentators, who preserve both as innovative and experimental theatre makers and deep-thinking internationalists. Indeed Grotowski enjoyed, and Brook retains, statesmanlike status on an international level; as such there's little need to pick fights with the English cultural Establishment.

Joseph did, though, need to pick such fights. Some battle or other would be rumbling along almost constantly during his career, until he tumbled out of full-time professional theatre and into higher education. Interestingly, this move was strongly encouraged by Jo Hodgkinson, Joseph's former supporter at the Arts Council. Hodgkinson – to Joan Littlewood, a 'middle-aged gent in a dark suit [with] charm as removable as pancake makeup' (Littlewood 1994: 188) – wrote an ostensibly sympathetic note to Joseph advising that he was 'just the person who ought to be [in academia]. . . . I do know how much torturous frustration you have endured in the last few months' (Hodgkinson 1962). Someone close to Joseph did, it seems, understand – and they knew how to help him: he must leave the industry which had sustained and inspired and obsessed him since the war, and instead become a teacher. To borrow from the vernacular – who was playing who? A March 1977 letter from Arts Council Drama Director N. V. Lintlaker to Rodney Wood would seem to obscure, rather than clarify matters. Lintlaker – replying on behalf of Hodgkinson, who was by now his predecessor – claimed that although 'Theatre in the Round was novel to us in England. . . . I don't think we were ever resistant to the idea' (Lintlaker 1977). Noting Wood's intended research on Stephen Joseph, he observed that, although Hodgkinson 'might be' (Ibid.) willing to talk to Wood, 'I doubt that he would want to write it all down' (Ibid.).

In the summer of 1962 Joseph took Hodgkinson's advice and moved into academia. Instantly, he began writing and publishing books. These were books filled with important ideas – but also with stern criticisms of those with power: in a 1967 discussion of the 'collapse' (Joseph 1967: 55) of the Newcastle-under-Lyme new-build venture, he recorded how an 'unexpected obstacle [was] put in [our] way by the Minister of Housing and Local Government' (Ibid.). Meanwhile, Joseph's protégés began to shape their own careers. Peter Cheeseman – in 1959, an enthusiast with 'no professional theatre experience' (Cheeseman 1959) – had begun to model his overtly socialist community-based English theatre-in-the round: here was a space within which, through Cheeseman's invention of verbatim theatre and the musical documentary, authentic working class voices could be heard on the English stage like never before. Alan Ayckbourn – at the age of just 23, already vastly experienced both on and off the stage – would continue writing, move into radio production, and eventually take over and grow things in Scarborough. Both would encounter some of the hostility previously aimed at their mentor. In 1983 Ayckbourn told *Marxism Today* that he was 'still . . . inside me, in quite a feud with the establishment, especially the theatre establishment' (Ayckbourn 1983: 39). Ayckbourn – like Cheeseman, by now rooted firmly in the north – added simply: 'That's partly why I live so far away from it all and I'm not seen amongst it' (Ibid.).

But that was all still to come – as were the most visible legacies of Joseph's missionary work: two permanent, world-class theatres-in-the-round, sprung directly from the tiny company he had founded.

Work-wise, Joseph's Studio Theatre years were by no means settled; indeed, he periodically sought directing work outside the theatre. Although he once told writer Alan Plater that he 'hate[d] television' (Plater 2008), the medium seems to have held a particular attraction for him. In October 1956 he offered himself as a television drama director to H. M. Tennent Ltd (Beaumont 1956). During the same month, he began pressing Michael Barry, Head of Drama at BBC Television, for freelance drama directing work (Barry 1956). Joseph didn't let go easily: in February 1958, still 'anxious to do some television directing' (Joseph 1958g: 1), he rather optimistically asked Barry whether 'since you haven't called me as a freelance . . . there [is] any chance of joining the [permanent] staff?' (Ibid.) His 1959 championing of Harold Pinter led him to apply to direct the first broadcast version of *The Birthday Party*. In fact earlier, during 1957, Joseph did manage to secure freelance television work, directing children's programmes at the independent Associated Rediffusion company. Joseph reported at the time that he was 'not enjoying' (Joseph 1957: 1) working for a company he dubbed 'Associated Reconfusion' (Lewsen 1978). But if his plan was to graduate from children's television to adult-orientated drama, it was in vain: each of his offers to direct was declined.

Of course Joseph could not know this. So long as he was able to consider an alternative career as a more permanent employee – either within television drama, or indeed within education, because he appears also to have made a number of enquiries into university teaching – Joseph had also to imagine Studio Theatre going on without him. It was even possible that he might go abroad: in June 1958, he was offered – and presumably declined – the post of Director of Winnipeg Little Theatre (Campbell 1958). By late 1960 there are clear signs of Joseph's plan to settle in northern England: a 15 October letter to his bank reports that he has seen a run-down house he might like to buy, Scarborough's former St Thomas's Vicarage (Joseph 1960d).

Two days before the close of 1960 Joseph wrote to director Tyrone Guthrie to report that, although 'when we met a year ago I was planning to return to America and to teach at a university' (Joseph 1960h: 1), he had 'now changed my plans' (Ibid.). In the same letter Joseph asks Guthrie to supply a reference, should a new teaching job become available at the University of Manchester.

The 29 December 1960 date of Joseph's reference request to Guthrie raises interesting questions because the letter was written while plans for a proposed new-build theatre in the Potteries were still being finalized. Was Joseph seeking an escape route? Did he already suspect that public funding would be withdrawn from the project? Or was it that he actually feared it would all go ahead – jeopardizing the childhood insecurity he once told Peter Cheeseman he would 'try and create' (Cheeseman 2008) in adulthood? Alan Ayckbourn recalls that during the previous year, Joseph had declined to run a fully funded theatre-in-the-round project in London:

> I was staying in [Joseph's] flat in London and the phone rang, and he asked me to answer it – and it was a bloke from Croydon who said, "Hello. I'm part of the theatre committee down here, and Mr. Joseph was interested in starting a theatre in the round. Well, we think we have got enough money now to build a theatre, and we wonder if we could talk to him." And I went, "Oh! Oh yes – right." So I said – Stephen came in through the door and I said, "Look – oh! This is fantastic! These are the people from Croydon and you know you were down there the other week", and he said, "Oh Jesus no. It's not worth it." And he completely ignored it (Ayckbourn 2007).

In the event Croydon's Pembroke Theatre project – subsequently run by Clement Scott Gilbert – was to be short-lived, operating only during 1961 and 1962.

The letter to Guthrie also precedes by a full 6 months Joseph's incendiary AITT attack on the British government's 'absolute idiocy ... broken promises, meanness and deliberate destruction of what is vital in our theatre' (Joseph 1961a: 70). The speech can be read as a near-spontaneous final flourish – a dramatic public signalling of Joseph's now-and-for-ever abandonment of his long-held ambition to create a new and different professional theatre in England. Yet even as Joseph gave his speech, Peter Cheeseman was already in post, brought in 'to increase [Joseph's] permanent staff to run the new theatre' (Cheeseman 1998: 1). It's even possible Joseph's ambush on the Establishment was brewing months before the event; a 10 December 1960 letter from theatre designer Richard Southern, inviting Joseph to help form a British branch of the AITT (to become the ABTT), met with the instant reply that he was 'very keen to join any group of this sort' (Joseph 1960f): at long last he would get to be an insider.

Peter Cheeseman has described the extent of Joseph's disillusionment and withdrawal once the British government had refused to allow funding for the proposed new theatre. Cheeseman suggested they find and convert a building:

> ... first he said "no" – but eventually I got him to allow me to go and look at possible buildings. So I did, and he pooh-poohed it initially, but

then he started to give in. And we found this theatre, and we did [the conversion], and so he endorsed it, and said he would put me in charge of it – he was going to . . . work at the university and I could run the Vic (Cheeseman 2008).

Joseph initially accepted a one-year Fellowship at the University of Manchester – a move which academic colleague Peter Thomson thinks was perhaps one of *reculer pour mieux sauter* (Thomson 1977: 1). Whatever the motivation, Joseph's participation in the day-to-day running of The Vic was suddenly reduced; indeed, he received no production credit in any of the six theatre programmes following the launch of the inaugural Winter 1962 season. Yet Joseph had claimed to want a permanent, year-round ensemble theatre since at least 1954; for years he had nurtured the slow growing together of Studio Theatre's summer season and the winter touring schedule until finally, in 1960, the company could operate 'for nearly a full year' (Joseph 1967: 51). Thereafter, 'many actors stayed with the company for more than one season and benefited from the continuous experience' (Ibid.). A Gulbenkian Foundation grant, also in 1960, meant that Studio Theatre was further 'able to rehearse for three weeks or more, to add another actor to the company, and to improve advertising and public relations' (Ibid.); in October 1960 Joseph commissioned 'a further 10,000' (Joseph 1960e) beer mats to promote forthcoming productions via public houses in the north – a sure sign that he was reaching for a new audience. Studio Theatre was at last operating on a relatively secure basis – producing work at a pace that could ensure high performance standards, promoting shows effectively, expanding cast sizes, retaining company members; the company was in good shape.

Why then the 'vanishing act' at such an important time for Joseph and his company? Why, after years spent working towards a specific goal, would he hand control of the emerging professional theatre base in Stoke-on-Trent to two relatively inexperienced employees? Newly appointed theatre manager Peter Cheeseman had quite briefly run a traditional regional repertory theatre in Derby that featured a proscenium stage. Associate Director Alan Ayckbourn, although experienced in theatre-in-the-round, was still untried in an ongoing company leadership role.

Joseph's decision to 'hand over the keys' may have been, at least in part, a response to a growing sense of personal discomfort at the prospect of leading a permanent company. Studio Theatre had previously operated only intermittently, allowing Joseph time to teach, plan and recuperate. A risky new venture such as the Victoria Theatre – launched before a silent national press (New Vic Theatre n. d.) as Britain's first permanent round theatre, in a theatreless town with (as Joseph noted 5 years after the theatre's opening) 'small potential' (Joseph 1967: 109) to attract a large and loyal audience – needed a leader with sustained energy, a talent for community engagement and strong people-management skills. Joseph's instant rejection of a leadership role in Croydon suggests he lacked confidence in his own suitability for the role. Peter Thomson, who saw Joseph transform aspects of the drama provision at the University of Manchester, was surprised that Joseph 'didn't fight with passion to push his vision into actuality. It's even possible that this is because he was inured to failure' (Thomson 1977: 2).

In fact despite Joseph's move into higher education – first as a Fellow, then as a lecturer at the University of Manchester – he managed to maintain a squeezed Scarborough summer season. The Scarborough Theatre Trust – the new name, once Joseph had lost his final battle in the Potteries – would be the launchpad for would-be professionals including Mike Weller, Mike Stott and Roland Joffé. It would also launch the play which would become *Relatively Speaking* – Alan Ayckbourn's first genuinely successful transfer to the West End. This new group mixed Joseph's students with theatre professionals, including within Alan Ayckbourn's *Meet My Father* – later, in the West End, *Relatively Speaking*. But with each successive working summer Joseph found that he was losing energy, and he began to realize that he was dying. Rodney Wood, who stepped in to oversee the 1967 Scarborough summer season, recalls that

> like some others who are terminally ill [Joseph] had a double vision of life. They know they are dying but part of them is frantically making plans for the future. In 1967 Stephen had Ken Boden and I inspecting and measuring various buildings [in Scarborough] which might provide a site for a permanent theatre in the round (Wood 2009).

Lewin Goff – years earlier, one of Joseph's lecturers at the University of Iowa, and later employed by Joseph as a visiting director in Scarborough – thought Joseph 'a truly gentle theatre artist, the only one I have known' (Goff 1977: 2). My own interviewees remember him with warmth and affection. Yet he had, too, a tendency to lash out – not only at perceived enemies, but also at allies and supporters. Even strangers asking for help could become targets. In a May 1957 letter to a representative for an intended new adaptable theatre in Harlow, Joseph dismissed the proposed design as 'utterly inadequate' (Joseph 1957b: 2) – asking his correspondent whether 'you [are] deliberately forcing people to stay at home and watch the television? This is what you will certainly do, but surely you do not wish to spend £100,000 doing so' (Ibid.: 1–2). Phyllis Kramer, an American would-be playwright who had pressed Joseph for an opinion and the return of a mislaid play (Kramer 1960), was dismissed with a note that her play was 'a good piece of writing but it does not appeal to me personally. I found the incidents are a little arbitory [sic] and the characters become melodramitic [sic] in order to complete your story' (Joseph 1960a: 1). The normally grammatically precise Joseph seems here to be mocking his correspondent's own style and spelling. Alan Ayckbourn remembers Joseph's tendency to 'fire from the hip' (Ayckbourn 2007) – even at friends and colleagues. Former fellow Cambridge student Stephen Garrett – co-designer of the cancelled Newcastle-under-Lyme theatre, and later Director of the J. Paul Getty Museum in California – thought Joseph 'one of the most fascinating and irritating people that I have ever known' (Garrett 1977). Peter Thomson remembers Joseph's 'very deflating' (Thomson 1977: 1) reaction when Thomson first met his new colleague in Manchester: 'somewhere between matter-of-fact and contemptuous' (Ibid.). Even Peter Cheeseman – full of praise for Joseph when I interviewed him in 2008 – recalled 'some paradoxical things' (Cheeseman 2008) in Joseph's style of leadership, including during the frequent overnight touring trips:

> When we struck the shows at Scarborough . . . [it] took twenty-four hours to then drive to Dartington, [going] the long way round. . . He used to make a song-and-dance about, reveling in staying up too late. It was a bit unfair . . . He was a little bit unreasonable about that (Ibid.).

Joseph was willing to risk alienating even his most loyal company members through his occasional sharp criticism. Joseph 'said some quite hurtful things' (Ayckbourn 2007) to Alan Ayckbourn regarding his staging of Joan McAlpine's version of *David Copperfield* – only his second production as director:

> I was rather pleased with [the production] because I'd managed to make it fairly "bare-stage", using all sorts of lamps and angles – quite an inventive production – and the only thing that marred it was the guy playing Tommy Traddles came on and tripped over his feet and fell over on his first entrance. And apart from that, it was all fine. And then Stephen – I said "how did you enjoy it?" – and he said he thought that "the bit where he fell over was the only spontaneous moment in the entire production". And I said, "Oh, thank you." And, yes, bang, straight in the face, you know, straight after the show. I said, "Oh gee – thanks Stephen" (Ibid.).

Perhaps Joseph's provocations – throwing out playful but wounding remarks, scheduling unnecessarily exhausting overnight drives – were part of his planning towards succession: he could assess potential heirs' stamina and team skills, test their ability to handle criticism, measure their ability to manage difficult people: Peter Cheeseman was apparently warned early on that, along with securing finance, any Joseph successor's biggest challenge would be to cope with 'the dogma arising from my own personal vision of what I want the company to be' (Lane 2006: 168). If so, the scale and adventurousness of the respective subsequent careers of twin protégés Ayckbourn and Cheeseman suggests that another risky strategy succeeded.

Joseph's decision to step back from the daily running of his theatre company may then have had a range of personal motivations: a wish to direct drama in a different medium; fear of his own instinct to control, which had soured his relations with critics and others; a lack of belief in his ability to provide sustained leadership for a major new theatre project, coupled with an ongoing need for time and space away from company management; a yearning to publish his ideas; and an intermittent but energy-sapping internal struggle that could leave him feeling 'empty and depressed' (Joseph 1958d). It's possible that the nihilism expressed in Joseph's May 1958 letter to Mary David had roots in his physical health. It's difficult to pinpoint the emergence of the cancer that would kill him in 1967; he seems to have kept its progress mostly hidden. But there were early signs that his physical health was suffering. Faynia Williams completed her last work with Studio Theatre in 1960; yet she remembers that while travelling on tour with Joseph she 'was always feeding him these tablets for his indigestion, which was a sign of the illness he was to have later on' (Williams 2008). *Reculer pour mieux sauter.* There are at least two English translations for this: to step back in order to jump further; to postpone the inevitable. In accepting a Fellowship at Manchester, Joseph may have done both. Just as he lost his footing in professional theatre in the Potteries, he found the time and resources for reflection, research, writing, planning. The University of Manchester, like Central years previously, granted him time and freedom to experiment. A step backwards, perhaps – but then a big leap forward. And then there was 'The Vic' in Stoke – now run by Peter Cheeseman but still, fundamentally, a Joseph experiment. Located less than 50 miles from Manchester, Britain's first permanent theatre-in-the-round could become a year-round laboratory – a living experiment for Peter Brook and others to come and see bare-stage, (relatively) poor theatre in action. There would be new skirmishes too: one of Joseph's 'biggest battles with the authorities' (Lane 2006: 186) took place within the University of Manchester when Joseph pushed through the wholesale conversion of a former church; Joseph's favouring of a windowless, black-walled interior – in contrast to the management-preferred 'light, airy atmosphere' (Ibid.) – would create one of Britain's first adaptable theatre spaces. Joseph also advised on the building of the university's new main-house theatre. While employed as a lecturer, he also found time to design the radical adaptable Nuffield Theatre in Lancaster – some 60 miles from Manchester – which would make real his 'vision of a purposeful work space' (Thomson 2008). All in all, there would be much in the north for visitors to examine and discuss.

Conclusion

Nearly 60 years on from Stephen Joseph's founding of Studio Theatre, there are aspects of life in England that he might recognize. As I write this a Judy Garland hit from *The Wizard of Oz* is in the popular music charts; in and around North Korea, there is strong talk of the threat of war. Meanwhile a new proposal to socially re-categorize Britons seems to steer theatregoers upwards towards the 'Elite', and non-theatregoers down towards the 'Precariat'. The class gap continues backstage too: Joseph's 1967 complaint about leadership within English theatre – that 'artistic endeavour . . . can only escape the scorn of the upper classes . . . by being rigorously unpractical' (Joseph 1968: 76) – finds an angry echo in Hull Truck founder Mike Bradwell's 2013 sideswipe at the 'floppy-haired [Oxbridge] men [who] know what theatre is, as they have read about it' (Bradwell 2013). *Plus ça change, plus c'est la même chose.*

Just before he died, Stephen Joseph unveiled his most radical design, the socially inclusive 'Fish and Chip Theatre' (Joseph 1967: 117) – a space which, in Alan Ayckbourn's view, moved Joseph 'very much into the realm of Joan Littlewood' (Ayckbourn 1997). The in-the-round Fish and Chip Theatre would facilitate almost total freedom of audience movement around an auditorium *during live performance*. Features include a 'viewing bar' (Joseph 1967: 117) to allow audience members to 'sit for a drink and snack and watch the play at the same time' (Ibid.); a 'low standing room pit' (Ibid.) on one side of the rectangular stage; and a 'dining room level' (Ibid.) on another side. Within this space 'All sections of the auditorium should be organically connected to encourage free flow of audience from one place to another, even during performance'. (Ibid.) Joseph asserted that 'the science of acoustics' (Ibid.) would combine with careful choice of materials to prevent noise problems; however he conceded that because the viewing bar would be 'a good rowdy place' (Ibid.) it would need to be 'acoustically separated from the main auditorium' (Ibid.), with speakers and headphones available for audience members who wish to follow the performance. Joseph's plan promises his performers 'showers and divans for resting' (Ibid.): 'the actors will need them' (Ibid.), he quips. Characteristically, Joseph's idea for this radical theatre space – clearly aimed at a potential new working-class audience – reached the stage of informal drawings; aerial and cross-section plans can be seen in Joseph's book *Theatre in the Round* (Ibid.: 118). Not that Joseph's proposal was met with much enthusiasm – including from his ever-practical heirs: Alan Ayckbourn remembers thinking, '"Hey – hey! A great plate of chips while we're trying to do our little Art?"' (Ayckbourn 2007).

Despite its working title, Joseph's design for a socially inclusive theatre is intriguingly non-English. This is not a space for subtle naturalism or a comedy of manners. Dario Fo's Commedia dell'Arte-inspired madcap political comedies would find a home here; likewise, competitive improvisation and the high-energy, clog-dance-peppered classics toured by Yorkshire's Northern Broadsides company. Stylistically John Godber's earlier, caricature-driven pieces such as *Bouncers* (1977) and *Up'n'Under* (1984) might well suit such a space – providing theatre directors can let go of the flat, chorus-line staging so favoured by English champions of non-naturalism. Boal-style Forum Theatre work could succeed here too, because tentative 'spectactors' on all sides would be spared the formality and the long seat-to-raised-stage journey inherent within most proscenium or thrust spaces.

In fact a few professional theatres are now making space for a Joseph-style inclusive space. Initiatives include the creation (mainly in the United States) of 'tweet seats' – seating areas within which audience members are allowed to share their thoughts in writing via mobile platforms during a performance. The debate continues: a March 2012 poll in the *Guardian* newspaper (*Guardian* 2012) reported that 10 per cent of respondents favoured allowing 'tweet seats' in British theatres; comments ranged from a proposal to introduce phone jamming, to the suggestion that 'Shakespeare would have approved' (Ibid.).

The book featuring the design for Joseph's Fish and Chip Theatre is long out of print. No such dedicated theatre space has yet been built in Britain, and, broadly, working class audiences still stay away. Meanwhile only the most 'experimental' theatre allows audience members to (even discreetly) eat, drink, text, tweet or speak during performance. Thus in the theatre, behaviour that is accepted at almost all popular audience events – sporting tournaments, circus performance, visitor attractions, live music gigs, even within some cinemas – remains taboo.

Yet there has been progress in the decades since Joseph died. Peter Cheeseman and Alan Ayckbourn provide surely the most visible evidence of Stephen Joseph's legacy: both travelled a great distance following their first-time exposure to the collaborative opportunities offered by the round theatre form; both were to become lifelong experimentalists after abandoning the 'bourgeois... thin, uninteresting and irrelevant' (Cheeseman 2008) theatre world they had encountered previously. Both would remain responsive to Stephen Joseph's broad mission to provide theatre that is both entertaining and accessible; and both would bequeath to British theatre a permanent theatre-in-the-round complex in which their individual responses to Joseph's work and ideas (continuing, in Ayckbourn's case) would inspire current and future theatre makers. In 2011 Olivier Award-winning playwright Simon Stephens – born 4 years after Stephen Joseph had died – stated that 'there's no theatrical architecture that challenges or interrogates what it is to be a human being more than theatre in-the-round' (Gardner 2011).

Ayckbourn and Cheeseman may have been among the first English theatre managers to run main-house theatre buildings with auditoria that featured open stages; but numerous such spaces now exist across the United Kingdom. In particular there is now a wide band of open stage theatres that traverses the north of England from coast to coast. Beginning on the Yorkshire coast with the SJT in Scarborough, and moving south to the old and new thrust-stage Hull Truck theatres, the band spreads through Sheffield (thrust-stage at the Crucible), Leeds (thrust-stage at the West Yorkshire Playhouse), Bolton (adaptable auditorium, including to in-the-round, at the Octagon), Manchester (in-the-round, at the Royal Exchange), Lancaster (in-the-round at the Dukes Theatre, plus the giant adaptable auditorium at the Nuffield Theatre), Bowness-on-Windemere (adaptable auditorium, including to in-the-round, at the Old Laundry), on to Liverpool (thrust-stage at the Everyman), and south to the Potteries. All these theatres have been, and remain, associated with the commissioning and staging of new work for the stage; all were built after Stephen Joseph's death in 1967. And all continue to offer year-round, or close-to-year-round professional work to actors, directors, designers, crew and audiences. Meanwhile, beyond the geographical sphere of Joseph's greatest influence, dozens of repertory theatres have either permanently gone dark, or are under current threat of closure.

Several of the northern theatres in my list (in addition to those in Scarborough and the Potteries) have an identifiable link to Joseph. Studio Theatre playwright Alan Plater was involved with the longstanding Humberside Theatre, renamed Spring Street Theatre when the Hull Truck company moved in. Bolton's Octagon theatre – founded by Robin Pemberton-Billing, the son of 'PB', Stephen Joseph's long-time housekeeper – sprang from 'the Book of Stephen' (Watson 1998: 9): Pemberton-Billing has recorded how 'The feeling behind the Octagon was to get everyone interested in the theatre and not just make it a middle class and middle-aged prerogative' (Pemberton Billing n.d.). Early Joseph plans for the Bolton theatre are held in the John Rylands archive. Manchester's Royal Exchange Theatre was founded by a group based at the University of Manchester during Joseph's tenure in the university's drama department, while Lancaster's Nuffield Theatre – named by Forced Entertainment's Tim Etchells as the best place in England to see innovative new work (Iqbal 2010) – was designed by Joseph. Joseph's influence was felt too at other post-1955 theatres – perhaps most notably at Edinburgh's Traverse Theatre Club (transverse), co-founded by former Studio Theatre company member Terry Lane (Lane n.d.).

Some five decades after James Roose-Evans consulted Joseph over new designs for the Hampstead Theatre Club (Joseph 1960g), there are fresh signs of a Joseph influence in central London. Kevin Spacey's radical 2008–09 temporary in-the-round conversion of the Old Vic hosted a sympathetic and critically acclaimed restaging of Alan Ayckbourn's *Norman Conquests* trilogy: advising architect Andrew Todd described the conversion as taking a 'corseted Victorian lady [who] wasn't living life to the full' (Todd 2008) and releasing 'new levels of excitement and intimacy' (Ibid.). But perhaps most striking of all is the work of London-based touring company Paines Plough.

Paines Plough is currently embracing intimate theatre-in-the-round with a Joseph-like fervour. In November 2012 the group completed their Roundabout Season at London's Shoreditch Town Hall: echoing Studio Theatre's work decades earlier, seats were unallocated within a wooden pop-up structure. Curiously, almost all the attending national critics felt compelled to comment on the in-the-round staging –favourably, this time: for The *Guardian*'s Lyn Gardner, the 'enticingly intimate space . . . [served] to magnify the plays' themes rather than cramp them' (Gardner 2012); for the *Stage* critic, the space's 'enforced intimacy ensures a laser-like focus from the rapt 138 strong audience' (Lovett 2012). The company has now raised funds for a 111-seat 'fully self-contained portable, demountable Roundabout auditorium' (Paines Plough 2012), which will allow the company to tour.

Paines Plough's company website provides an interesting historical summary, which locates the first theatre-in-the-round as the Odeon of Pericles, dated to 440BC. Sidestepping developments in the United States, the piece highlights advances in Britain – including, in London, the spread of mainly thrust-format pop-up structures. Much of the text of the piece reads as if written by Joseph: sports arenas are called on to exemplify the success of in-the-round spectatorship; and there is much discussion of the energy generated by in-the-round staging. There's also a neat modern contextualization –almost a slogan for theatre-in-the-round – which would surely have impressed Joseph:

> Forget the IMAX. Theatre-in-the-round is the best 3D experience, no silly glasses required (Ibid.).

One or two aspects of the company's work and planning might win a little less enthusiasm from Joseph. The design proposal for the new touring structure features a circular stage, rather than the rectangular format that gives actors playful access to irregular corners and diagonals. The company is currently exploring a restlessly physical acting dynamic that is 'like boxing' (Ibid.): the company quotes advice from the current director of Stoke's New Vic Theatre that directors working in-the-round must 'keep things moving; the round loves action, words are action and the pause is the enemy' (Ibid.). A similar view is held close to Joseph's other historic base in Scarborough: a University of York publication aimed at school and college groups mistakenly asserts that 'As a rule of thumb, [in-the-round] audiences can take twenty seconds or so of not being able to see the face of at least one of the major players in a scene before getting annoyed' (Wright 2013: 40). Such an approach, too liberally applied, risks a return to the sort of 'meaningless gyration, restless movement and irrelevant trickery' (Joseph 1968: 44) witnessed by Joseph in Chichester half a century earlier. This is a real risk: an online critic visiting Shoreditch wrote that she 'began to feel dizzy' (Roughan 2012) watching two actors circle restlessly.

Paines Plough's exciting in-the-round initiative would seem to be part of a growing enthusiasm for a greater degree of actor-audience intimacy within theatre in England's capital. Former Royal Court Theatre director Simon Curtis recently reflected that, in his view,

> the Almeida, the Donmar, the Court and the Cottesloe are doing well because audiences like to be close to their actors now . . . People don't want to sit at the back of the upper circle watching a show, so naturalistic, filmic performances are the ones (Curtis 2010: 29).

This move towards a heightened sense of actor-audience intimacy has also shaped the design of the main auditorium of the Royal Shakespeare Company (RSC), one of England's 'flagship' main-house spaces. Recent Artistic Director Michael Boyd wrote in 2008 of 'a tremendous fragmentation of culture' (Boyd 2008: 6) that provokes a 'need to grasp the nettle of how to behave more like a community' (Ibid.); both Boyd's words and his proposed solution are highly evocative of Stephen Joseph's earlier solution, proposed and delivered more than half a century earlier:

> . . . [we] need a new theatre architecture that reflects this [community] role, that makes the event of going to the theatre a communal event rather than what the proscenium arch offers: people sat in one room looking at people in another room (Boyd 2008: 7).

Former Joseph mentee and theatre internationalist Faynia Williams – still working as a theatre director and BBC producer – notes, in this context, that among a wide range of art forms British theatre 'is the most backward, the least able to react quickly to the changing times' (Williams 2008); but that on the international stage 'it's people like Stephen Joseph, it's people like Pina

Bausch, it's people like Kantor who [were] able to react quickly to the changing times' (Ibid.). Williams, concluding my interview with her, observed:

> It's a rare talent that does that, and these are the people that make up the history of our theatre. And I think [Stephen Joseph]'s up there with them (Ibid.).

Looking ahead, the need to evolve – in particular, the responsibility to popularize and repopulate something that has for so long been a minority entertainment – remains a huge challenge, as Western theatre makers move forward through the twenty-first century. Yet Joseph's posthumous demand for equal access to the best of live theatre seems to be in real jeopardy. Funding cuts are the most visible threat to live theatre; but threat comes too from well-meant solutions with their own missionary bent. One recent yet curiously reactionary innovation is the Arts Council-backed National Theatre initiative, which beams star-driven theatre performances staged live before metropolitan audiences, to distant cinemagoers. An intriguing opportunity for cross-media collaboration thus starts to resemble a cultural exercise in educating distant 'provincial' theatregoers ('cinematheatregoers'? – surely we need a new term) – who, while kept at a distance, must still pay high tickets prices for their reported fare, and must also have access to a cinema belonging to the chain which holds exclusive broadcast rights.

I'm not suggesting here that the idea of live theatre beamed elsewhere is intrinsically poor. Nor is it new: Stephen Joseph proposed it more than half a century ago. However, he sought a different dynamic – live work, filmed discreetly in 360 degrees within intimate theatres-in-the-round, beamed live and free-of-charge to domestic television screens. Back then, no broadcaster would invest. Now, technologically, we are in a new era: we have cheap, discreet, remotely operable and super-light-sensitive digital cameras, allowing theatre makers to even explore head-mounted broadcasting from micro-cameras attached to performers' heads (and by association to their thoughts and feelings); while binaural recording and replay techniques are producing astonishing aural fidelity when played back via suitable headphones. We also have cheap or free online access, enabling live streaming of sound and vision; and, as a result of Stephen Joseph's in-the-round examination of organic projection, we have authentically naturalistic stage acting. All in all, there's a real opportunity now to remotely disseminate the highest-quality live culture in a more egalitarian way. Where, though, could such live 3-D experimentation be based? Only one purpose-built, permanent theatre-in-the-round exists in the whole of Greater London. There are several in northern England, one in Australia, and dozens in the

United States. Might there actually be a missionary role for those in the provinces and former colonies? Perhaps the BBC, now part-based in Salford, Greater Manchester, might link up with one or more of several permanent or adaptable theatres-in-the-round that exist within a 50-mile radius. Doubtless audiences outside the actual theatre auditorium would miss the breath-by-breath liveness that adds so much to one-room live theatre; but with perhaps skilful integration of technology within some of the emerging cheap-to-rent venues, we could be providing a sensorally and intellectually thrilling fresh take on immersive live performance. Such an adventure could even help to heal the curious ongoing low-level war of attrition between Britain's broadly conservative, resolutely proscenium- or thrust-based traditional theatre, and an innovative yet separatist Performance Art culture which is currently, at least in Britain, mostly stewing discontentedly within academia. To quote the title of a relevant innovative theatrical event hosted annually in York by Pilot Theatre: *Shift Happens*. To paraphrase Professor Stephen Hawkins: we really do need to keep talking.

Afterword

By the summer of 1967, England could still boast only one permanent life-sized version of Stephen Joseph's model Penny Theatre: a Penniless Theatre, perhaps, because 'The Vic' in Stoke, an in-the-round small cinema conversion, had been built entirely without public funding. Prospects for that other, earlier theatre space – the temporary one in Scarborough Library's Concert Room, just half a mile from the house where Joseph now lay dying – appeared gloomy. Back in 1963 Joseph – suddenly exiled from the Potteries, but hoping to make a fresh start with summer theatre in Scarborough – had been refused Arts Council funding on the grounds, as he understood it, that York – an 85-mile round trip from Scarborough – 'is providing enough drama for this area, [so] York gets the grants' (Joseph 1963c). Joseph had added: 'There is more to it than that, of course, but at present there is no sign of further help from this source' (Ibid.).

Over time Joseph – increasingly lacking time, money, good health and patience – slowly withdrew from his beloved Scarborough Library base. The 1966 summer season was entirely amateur. The brief 1967 summer season poignantly reunited the talents of Rodney Wood, David Campton and Alan Ayckbourn, all former cast members of Joseph's Pinter-rescuing 1959 *The Birthday Party* production. However only Wood, snatching time out from his own teaching post to lead the company, was in residence; Campton and Ayckbourn – the latter now established as a BBC radio producer – were supplying new plays. Stephen Joseph declined to lend support the 1967 Scarborough season, blaming both ill-health – characterized as 'weariness from a [lecturing] job which is very taxing' (Ibid.) – and also 'certain details between myself and the [Scarborough] Corporation' (Ibid.). That summer Faynia Williams, another cast member from Pinter's Studio Theatre production, was also close by, nursing Joseph; she recalls a scarf, a gift of thanks from a fleetingly present Hermione Gingold. Alan Ayckbourn visited too; Joseph told him that he was 'fucking terrified [and] having the most ghastly nightmares' (Ayckbourn 2007). Ayckbourn remembers thinking 'I can't cope with this' (Ibid.) and stayed away. We know that before long he was back – this time for good.

Peter Cheeseman – to his deep regret, never reconciled with his former mentor – stayed on in the Potteries and built up the Vic Theatre in the image of his local community. Here was a space where, in Peter Brook's words, 'The audience participated fully' (Brook 1968: 144). Cheeseman reasoned smartly that the human need to share and hear stories – including stories about their own lives – would tempt new locals into the auditorium; support continued, and in August 1986, his New Vic – Europe's first purpose-built theatre-in-the-round – opened its doors for the first time.

After Joseph's death, Alan Ayckbourn found himself tied into another Scarborough reunion – this time with local theatre amateur Ken Boden, a well-connected 'Mr. Fixit' who had helped the young Acting ASM on his arrival in the town in 1957. Boden's Stephen Joseph Memorial Appeal – now drawing support from many of the great names in British theatre – provoked a search for a new in-the-round base in Scarborough. The search was timely: immediately after Joseph's death the Scarborough Corporation had announced, apparently without irony, that it needed to take back the Concert Room for 'cultural purposes' (Williams 2005).

In due course a new base was found and Ayckbourn was tempted back to the seaside; half a century on he still lives and writes in Scarborough, provoking audiences with his witty and skilfully disguised morality plays. Like his late mentor, Ayckbourn would go on to nurture much new work by company members: for example, actor Stephen Mallatratt's 1987 adaptation of locally born author Susan Hill's novel *Woman in Black* – now a worldwide hit – premiered in the tiny endstage theatre, just along the corridor from the Stephen Joseph Theatre-in-the-Round. Ayckbourn's supporters continue to travel long distances to Scarborough to see premieres of his latest work; visiting fans include acclaimed French film director Alain Resnais, currently adapting his third Ayckbourn play for the cinema screen.

A number of aspects of Joseph's work and legacy remain, at least for now, at the level of assertion. What is the significance of Joseph's interest in the teachings of Jiddu Krishnamurti? Krishnamurti's enthusiasm for learning; his rejection of his own privileged status and 'the nonsense of temples, rituals' (Krishnamurti n.d.: 1'15"); and his commitment to there being 'no outside authority . . . including me' (Krishnamurti n.d.: 3'15"), suggest a powerful influence on a director for whom rehearsal was simply a chance 'to meet his actors [with] some notion of how to help them' (Joseph 1967: 124). Professor Peter Thomson has identified Krishnamurti as a figure of importance to Joseph; however further research is needed. And what of Joseph's influence on the work of Sir Peter Brook, whose 1965 visit to the

University of Manchester (which produced a chapter in *The Empty Space*) was co-hosted by university faculty member Joseph? There could even be a link between Joseph's interest in Krishnamurti, and Brook's own interest in spiritual matters; but this has yet to be examined. What, too, of Joseph's status as the child of mixed Christian and Jewish parents? I have found no concrete evidence that matters of religion or ethnicity impacted on his working life, or indeed on the memorializing of his work; however, further research may well be warranted.

What did the knights and dames of post-war British theatre think of Joseph's revolution? Joseph pondered this too. Poignantly, he wrote down what he hoped they might say when he began a novel (Joseph n.d., g), unfinished and now tucked away in an archive in Manchester. It's the story of a traditional proscenium theatre destroyed by fire, and a group of friends who replace it with 'The Ring' – an experimental new theatre-in-the-round. Fictional director Michael Strutt is heard enjoying the reviews:

> I saw them printed in the Times, and the Express and a big spread in the magazine section of the Observer. Quotes from famous actors. Sir John: "The most exciting experiment I have witnessed." Sir Ralph: "It puts new blood into the living theatre." Sir Laurence: "I can't wait to act in this thrilling new medium" (Ibid.).

Of course Gielgud, Richardson and Olivier said no such thing. Strutt, like Joseph before him, drew only negativity from the big names in British theatre:

> Thirty-odd letters written to well known theatre people, four were answered so far and in each case the response was cool, or offensive, or lavishly uncomprehending, or simply inane (Ibid.).

Would such a coolly damning response be repeated half a century on? Or might today's British theatrical aristocracy offer something of real substance, to sustain the momentum of Stephen Joseph's still-incomplete egalitarian revolution? In fact, in one area at least, the signs are promising: Paines Plough's wooden 'O' will be built, largely thanks to funding from the Andrew Lloyd-Webber Foundation. A successful campaign of touring to the now-many theatreless towns outside London and the north of England might well ignite fresh interest in intimate, open-stage theatre. And brave men and women of the theatre might respond by bringing forward radical local theatre plans of their own.

Fish and chips, anyone?

Figure 6 Peter Cheeseman's minimalist staging of Shaw's *'O'Flaherty VC'*, Stoke-on-Trent 1962. Courtesy of Scarborough Theatre Trust

Appendices

Appendix 1: Opinions on Joseph's legacy

The following unpublished quotations are offered as supplementary material recording insights into Stephen Joseph's legacy. A number of the individuals interviewed for this book were asked what they personally considered Stephen Joseph's legacy to be. Answers included the following:

Sir Alan Ayckbourn: . . . his involvement with the ABTT [Association of British Theatre Technicians] with Percy Corry and all that crowd was quite important . . . there was no formal organization then for archiving and chronicling essential ideas in theatre building. . . . People just come [to Scarborough] and say, you know, within the limits of the building – 'This is a remarkable place. Just so easy to work in. So nice to play in'. And it's all the Stephen principles . . . [also] the practical experience – Stephen was always very anxious to break those barriers [between jobs in the theatre] down. Why not have your chief electrician writing a play? Why not have your lead actor working the lights? . . . Stephen would just say, 'Let's do it. Let's put it in front of an audience' – not workshop it – you know, 'we'll all stare at it and, you know, it'll disappear up our bloody anuses' . . . I think that's what his legacy was for me. . . . Another Stephen legacy is being interested in what other people are doing, without telling them their job, but at least appreciating their problems. But I think he was very helpful in at least passing on a bit of Renaissance Man to me, because he made sure I knew enough about lighting to light, enough about sound to do it – which I carry on doing – enough about scene painting.

Peter Cheeseman: Stephen was very active on the political side. He wrote a stack of books. He took the – put it on the map, the whole issue – and he was instrumental in setting up [the ABTT]. . . . He was a champion of creating – he worked and worked, lectured, wrote books and newspaper articles, for a long time – he had a real effect on people who were concerned with making theatre live. . . . It's very important, what he did. It's not spectacular, and it never had – he did a lot of things in the theatre outside the spotlight, that were terribly important – they just get overlooked, they don't happen. I mean I'm fighting like the devil [to archive] recordings of the [Stoke] documentaries – and most of it is still on reel-to-reel – what we achieved because of Stephen and his firm foundations I think was – I'm going to write the book, but it enabled me to do things that people told me have been amazing . . . . And it was Stephen . . . I don't know what I'd have done if I hadn't worked with Stephen, I'll never know – but he was responsible for that. But clearing the rubbish, he put a very big building block into the art. . . . I'm a great gardener. You've got to keep that soil going and nourish it, and that's what I've been trying to do. And I think so much of that comes from Stephen, and Alan – I mean Alan comes from Stephen. Alan's work has probably done as much as for the British theatre as the Arts Council Drama has.

Sir Ben Kingsley: He pioneered theatre-in-the-round. . . . So although I never met Stephen Joseph face-to-face, I knew that under his ethos, his guidance, his principle of 'No Hiding Place', of accessible theatre for communities, of the arena, – all these wonderful things contributed to my first two jobs. My first two jobs were in the round, thanks to – thanks to Stephen and his insistence that this was a great way to, for young actors particularly, to move forward.

Professor Peter Thomson: It must have been in late 1964 that he suggested to me that it was much less important to KNOW than to know how to FIND OUT. I've lived my teaching life on the excitement of realizing that ignorance is the great incentive – always provided that that ignorance generates curiosity rather than inertia – and that's probably the biggest single impact that Stephen had on me. He lived life as an adventure into the unknown . . .

Faynia Williams: What [Stephen Joseph] did was show that you could have theatre in non-theatre spaces, that you could – you didn't have to play safe and do the 'classics', that you could really promote new writers, that you could look to Europe, that you could do it cheaply – you didn't have to spend thousands of pounds, you know – that if people worked together as an ensemble it's much more efficient, very often. That everybody who works in theatre should be aware of what makes – you should know how to budget. You shouldn't just be an actor, you know. And I think he changed the aspirations of theatre. . . . I really don't understand why people don't realize how important he was in the development of British theatre. . . . I just think [Studio Theatre] is one of the most important theatres in the history of British theatre.

Appendix 2: The Joseph-designed Nuffield Theatre in Lancaster, England

Steph Sims, Technical Manager at the Lancaster Institute for the Contemporary Arts, offers the following summary of the character, development and updating of the Nuffield Theatre:

Steph Sims: The Nuffield in Lancaster is a black box studio design of 75ft × 75ft. Where it differs from traditional studios is that it has a removable floor in the centre of the space. The removable section is approximately 50ft × 50ft and reveals a 'pit' 5ft deep. Originally this pit area was filled with removable sections that could be configured to create a pit of any size and position; however one section that measured 25ft × 25ft was a single piece that contained an electric powered revolving stage, approximately 23ft diameter. This revolve section could be positioned anywhere within the pit area by removing other sections and pushing the revolve (rather like one of those tile games where you have to put numbered tiles in the correct order by sliding them around). Unfortunately, although the revolve turned by the magic of electricity, it had to be positioned using brute force and took 10 crew to move. The seating system also consisted of modular frames and blocks which could be configured and placed in various set ups to produce the desired effect.

However over the years, due to wear and tear, usage of the venue changing and licensing regulations limiting some configurations, we altered some things. First to go, about 24 years ago, was the framework that created the seating bank, although it was light it started to lose its strength and failing parts were difficult to repair. We replaced the seating units with aluminium frame sections that still maintained a lot of the flexibility of the original system but gave us a more traditional seating 'bank' look. Several years later we decided that the stage itself was needing replacing and that we should say goodbye to the, no longer used, revolve section. In order to keep the flexibility of the original design the 50ft pit section of the Nuffield is now filled in with Topdeck sections on 5ft legs. This means that we can still create lowered sections and trap doors etc. wherever we need them (within reason). Finally, a few years ago we replaced the seating frames with Steeldeck units, which gives us greater flexibility of seating layouts.

The lighting grid consists of five catwalks that cover the width of the theatre. These catwalks are great for rigging and focusing, even though bumped heads can be a hazard for first-time users. Now because the theatre is flexible the lighting had to be flexible too. Since the catwalks are fixed structures, [Joseph] designed 'bridges' that span between the catwalks. These are mounted on wheels running in girder tracks on each catwalk, two bridges between each catwalk pair so eight bridges in total.

Theatre makers like . . . the flexibility, the size, the convenience, and the accessibility. Assuming time and budget are available, we can create a multitude of layouts and set-ups. We have a level access from the loading bay, through the very large workshop, directly into the space. The dressing room is next to the stage and the foyer also has level access to the space: the performance doesn't have to be restricted to the studio itself, it can expand and spread out taking in the whole complex. We are able to offer a venue 75ft × 75ft or reduce it in size to a space suitable for a 'one-to-one' performance. We've even set up seven performance spaces each, with their own seating and control areas – perfect for promenade performance or workshops. The accessibility and flexibility of the lighting grid means that companies can experiment with lighting during production weeks and rehearsals.

However we have no flying facilities; and if a company wants to hang scenery we are restricted to the lighting bars, or we have to rig hanging points using ladders or scaffolding. The lighting grid also adds to the limitations – while the moving bridges are useful, they can't replace the flexibility you would find in a traditional pros arch theatre. As productions have got bigger and more demanding, the lighting requirements have reached a point where a fixed grid just can't handle it: a typical lighting plan will now require a dozen or so lighting bars in specific locations, when we can supply only eight in fixed positions. The catwalks themselves also get in the way, they make it extremely difficult to focus lighting straight down, and can cause a lot of grief for some lighting designers. But, taking everything into account, it's a great space and I really enjoy creating, and helping others create, all types of theatre and performance in the Nuffield.

Bibliography

Section 1: Published works

Allen, P. (2001), *Alan Ayckbourn – Grinning at the Edge* (London: Methuen).

Ayckbourn, A. (1991), quoted in ed. Dukore, B. (1991), *Alan Ayckbourn: A Casebook* (New York: Garland Publishing).

— (2002), *The Crafty Art of Playmaking* (London: Faber).

— (2012), Foreword to this book.

Baker, W. (2008), *The Harold Pinter Society Newsletter, October 30 2008 at* http://www.pintersociety.org/publications/publications-about-harold-pinter/.

Billington, M. (1983), *Alan Ayckbourn* (London: Macmillan).

— (2007a), *State of the Nation: British Theatre Since 1945* (London: Faber).

— (2007b), *Harold Pinter*, revised ed. (London: Faber).

Brook, P. (1968), *The Empty Space* (New York: Touchstone).

Campton, D. (1960), *The Lunatic View* (Scarborough: Studio Theatre Limited).

— (1967), *Incident: A Play for Women* (Malvern: J. Garnett Miller).

Chambers, C. (ed.) (2002), *Continuum Companion to Twentieth Century Theatre* (London: Continuum).

Cheeseman, P. (1970), [Introduction and Notes] in *The Knotty* (London: Methuen).

Cotes, P. (1949), *No Star Nonsense: A Challenging Declaration of Faith in the Essentials of Tomorrow's Theatre* (London: Rockliff).

Courtney, R. (1967), *The Drama Studio* (London: Pitman).

Debrett's, n.d., entry in Debrett's *People of Today online* at http://www.debretts.com/people/biographies/month/november/18613/Faynia%20Roberta+WILLIAMS.aspx.

Elsam, P. (2010), Harold Pinter's *The Birthday Party*: The 'lost' second production in *Studies in Theatre and Performance* 30:3 (Intellect).

Elvgren, G. and Favorini, A. (1992), *Steel/City* (Pittsburgh: University of Pittsburgh Press).

Fisher Dawson, G. (1999), *Documentary Theatre in the United States: An Historical Survey and Analysis* (Santa Barbara: Greenwood Press).

Gaskill, W. (1988), *A Sense of Direction* (London: Faber).

Giannachi, G. and Luckhurst, M. (eds) (1999), *On Directing: Interviews with Directors* (London: Marshall).

Gingold, H. (1988), *How To Grow Old Disgracefully* (London: Victor Gollancz).

Harris, K. (2008), 'Evolutionary Stages'. in Shellard, D. (ed.), *The Golden Generation: New Light on Post-war British Theatre* (London: British Library).

Hartnoll and Found (ed.) (1992), *The Concise Oxford Companion to the Theatre*, 2nd edn (Oxford: Oxford University Press).

Hunter, A. (2002a), 'Stephen Joseph': encyclopedia entry, in *The Continuum Companion to Twentieth Century Theatre* (London: Continuum).

— (2002b), 'Kenny, Sean [Noel]' encyclopedia entry, in Chambers, C. (ed.), *The Continuum Guide to Twentieth Century Theatre* (London: Continuum).

Jackson, A. and Rowell, G. (1984), *The Repertory Movement: A History of Regional Theatre in Britain* (Cambridge: Cambridge University Press).

Johnstone, K. (1981), *Impro: Improvisation and the Theatre* (London: Methuen).

Jones, C. (1961), in Joseph, S. 1962, *Adaptable Theatres* – conference notes from the third biennial congress of the Association internationale de techniciens de theatre (AITT), 25–30 June 1961 (ABTT).

Joseph, S. (1955a), Programme for *Turn Right at the Crossroads* located at: Bob Watson archive at the Stephen Joseph Theatre, Scarborough.

— (1955b), Programme for *Dragons Are Dangerous* located at: Bob Watson archive at the Stephen Joseph Theatre, Scarborough.

— (1956a), Programme for *Wuthering Heights* located at: Bob Watson archive at the Stephen Joseph Theatre, Scarborough.

— (1956b), Programme for *Call the Selkie Home* located at: Bob Watson archive at the Stephen Joseph Theatre, Scarborough.

— (1957), Programme for *The Lunatic View* located at: Bob Watson archive at the Stephen Joseph Theatre, Scarborough.

— (1958), Programme note for *Captain Carvallo* located at Bob Watson archive at the Stephen Joseph Theatre, Scarborough.

— (1959a), [Programme note for *The Birthday Party*, Leicester] Located at: Stephen Joseph Theatre archive, Scarborough.

— (1959b), Programme for *Love After All* located at: Bob Watson archive at the Stephen Joseph Theatre, Scarborough.

— (1959c), March 1959 article for *Theatre World*.

— (1961a), *Adaptable Theatres* – conference notes from the third biennial congress of the Association internationale de techniciens de theatre (AITT), 25–30 June 1961. Published by ABTT Feb 1962, ed. Stephen Joseph.

— (1961b), [programme note for *Bed Life of a Mad Boy*] located at: Stephen Joseph Theatre archive, Scarborough.

— (1963), *The Story of the Playhouse in England* (London: Barrie and Rockliffe).

— (1964a), *Scene Painting and Design* (London: Pitman).

— (1964b), *Letter to a Ratepayer in New Theatre Magazine*, October-December 1964.

— (ed.) (1964c), *Actor and Architect* (Manchester: Manchester University Press).

— (1967), *Theatre in the Round* (London: Barrie and Rockliffe).

— (1968), *New Theatre Forms* (London: Pitman).

— n.d., a, programme for *The Ark* located at: Bob Watson archive at the Stephen Joseph Theatre, Scarborough.

— n.d., b, programme for *Barnstable* located at: Bob Watson archive at the Stephen Joseph Theatre, Scarborough.

— n.d., c, programme for *The Pedagogue* located at: Bob Watson archive at the Stephen Joseph Theatre, Scarborough.

— n.d., d, programme for *Who Was Hilary Maconochie?* located at: Bob Watson archive at the Stephen Joseph Theatre, Scarborough.

— n.d., e, programme for *Halfway to Heaven/Alas Poor Fred* located at: Bob Watson archive at the Stephen Joseph Theatre, Scarborough.

Kennedy, D. (2003), 'Confessions of an Encyclopedist', in Worthen, W. B and Holland, P. (eds), *Theorizing Practice: Redefining Theatre History* (London: Palgrave).

Lacey, S. (1995), *British Realist Theatre – The New Wave in Its Context 1956–1965* (London: Routledge).

Lane, T. (2006), *The Full Round – The Several Lives and Theatrical Legacy of Stephen Joseph* (Rome: Duca della Corgna).

Law, J. and Helfer, R. (eds) (2001), *New Penguin Dictionary of the Theatre* (London: Penguin).

Lewis, P. (1978), *The Fifties* (London: Book Club Associates).

Littlewood, J. (1994), *Joan's Book: Joan Littlewood's Peculiar History As She Tells It* (London: Methuen).

McGrath, J. (1981), *A Good Night Out – Popular Theatre: Audience, Class and Form* (London: Nick Hern Books).

— (2002), *Naked Thoughts that Roam About* (London: Nick Hern Books).

Oxford Dictionary and Thesaurus (2007), 2nd edition (London: Oxford University Press).

Paget, D. (1990), *True Stories? Documentary Drama on Radio, Screen and Stage* (Manchester: Manchester University Press).

Pinter, n.d., *Trouble in the Works* – typescript located at Elsam archive.

Pinter, H. (1995), [interview with Kate Saunders for *The Sunday Times*, 9 July 1995] quoted *in* Batty, M. 2005, *About Pinter* (London: Faber).

Plater, A. (1969), *Close the Coalhouse Door* (London: Methuen).

Postlewait, T. (2009), *The Cambridge Introduction to Theatre Historiography* (Cambridge: Cambridge University Press).

Priestley, J. B. (1947), *Theatre Outlook* (London: Nicholson & Watson).

Rebellato, D. (1999), *1956 And All That* (London: Routledge).

Russell Taylor, J. (1962), *Anger and After* (London: Methuen).

— (1969), *Anger and After* (revised edition) (London: Methuen).

— (1993), *ThePenguin Dictionary of the Theatre,* 3rd ed. (London: Penguin)

Shellard, D. (1999), *British Theatre Since The War* (London: Yale University Press).

Shepherd, S. (2009), *The Cambridge Introduction to Modern British Theatre* (Cambridge: Cambridge University Press).

Stokes, J. (2001), *Pinter and the 1950's,* in Raby, P. (ed.), *The Cambridge Companion to Harold Pinter* (Cambridge: Cambridge University Press).

Walter, H. (2003), *Other People's Shoes: Thoughts on Acting* (London: Nick Hern).

Watson, I. (1981), *Conversations with Ayckbourn* (London: Macdonald).

Watt, D. (2007), New Theatre Quarterly review of *The Full Round – The Several Lives and Theatrical Legacy of Stephen Joseph* (Cambridge: Cambridge University Press).

White, L. (2008), 'Smashing open the French windows', in Shellard, D. (ed.), *The Golden Generation: New Light on Post-war British Theatre* (London: British Library).

Williams, F. (2005), *Surrounded* – BBC Radio documentary (prod. Faynia Williams).

— (2009), *Equity Committee Elections 2009 Candidate's Election Statements* booklet (Equity).

Wilson, C. (2007), *The Angry Years* (London: Robson).

Yaldren, R. (2005), *A Profile of Stephen Joseph 1921–1967* (Scarborough: Farthings Design).

Section 2: Correspondence

Arts Council (1959), [22 July 1959 Letter from the Drama Department of the Arts Council of Great Britain] located at: Stephen Joseph Papers, Rylands Library, University of Manchester.

Associated Television Ltd (1959), [31 March 1959 letter to Stephen Joseph] located at: Stephen Joseph Papers, Rylands Library, University of Manchester.

Ayckbourn, A. (1961a), [13 September 1961 letter to Stephen Joseph] located at: Stephen Joseph Papers, Rylands Library, University of Manchester.

— (1961b), [15 April 1961 letter to Stephen Joseph] located at: Stephen Joseph Papers, Rylands Library, University of Manchester.

Barry, M. (1956a), [28 August 1956 letter to Stephen Joseph] located at: Stephen Joseph Papers, Rylands Library, University of Manchester.

— (1956b), [28 December 1956 letter to Stephen Joseph] located at: Stephen Joseph Papers, Rylands Library, University of Manchester.

Beaumont, H. (1956a), [21 October 1956 letter to Stephen Joseph] located at: Stephen Joseph Papers, Rylands Library, University of Manchester.

— (1956b), [5 October 1956 letter to Stephen Joseph] located at: Stephen Joseph Papers, Rylands Library, University of Manchester.

Berry, C. (1978), [9 February 1978 letter to Rodney Wood] located at: Rodney Wood archive.

Boden, K. n.d., [Stephen Joseph Memorial appeal letter] located at: Scarborough Library Archive.

Borneman, E. (1957a), [24 July 1957 letter to Stephen Joseph] located at: Stephen Joseph Papers, Rylands Library, University of Manchester.

— (1957b), [29 July 1957 letter to Stephen Joseph] located at: Stephen Joseph Papers, Rylands Library, University of Manchester.

Campbell, D. (1958), [18 June 1958 letter to Stephen Joseph] located at: Stephen Joseph Papers, Rylands Library, University of Manchester.

— (1962), 1 February 1962 letter to the Editor of the *Stage*.

Cheeseman, P. (1959), [5 November 1959 letter to Stephen Joseph] located at: Stephen Joseph Papers, Rylands Library, University of Manchester.

— (1976), [30 July 1976 letter to Rodney Wood] located in Rodney
Wood archive.

Codron, M. (1962a), [20 November 1962 letter to Margaret Ramsay] located at:
Alan Plater Papers, Brynmor Jones Library, University of Hull.

— (1962b), [14 December 1962 letter to Margaret Ramsay] located at: Alan
Plater Papers, Brynmor Jones Library, University of Hull.

Daily Telegraph (1957), [22 August 1957 letter to Stephen Joseph] located at:
Stephen Joseph Papers, Rylands Library, University of Manchester.

Darlington, W. A. (1959a), [18 February 1959 letter to Stephen Joseph] located
at: Stephen Joseph Papers, Rylands Library, University of Manchester.

— (1959b), [8 March 1959 letter to Stephen Joseph as 'Stephen Savage'] located
at: Stephen Joseph Papers, Rylands Library, University of Manchester.

— (1957), [8 April 1957 letter to Stephen Joseph] located at: Stephen Joseph
Papers, Rylands Library, University of Manchester.

David, L. (2004), [15 September 2004 letter to Alan Ayckbourn] located at:
Ayckbourn Archive in Scarborough.

Day-Lewis, S. (2008), [10 May 2008 letter to the Editor] *in* the *Guardian*.

Dench, J. (1979), [18 January 1979 letter to Rodney Wood] located at Rodney
Wood archive.

Devine, G. (1958), [31 January 1958 letter to Stephen Joseph] located at: Stephen
Joseph Papers, Rylands Library, University of Manchester.

Foster, R. (1962), [8 November 1962 letter to Peggy Ramsay from the Theatre
Guild in New York] located *at* Alan Plater Archive, University of Hull.

Garrett, S. (1977), [7 November 1977 letter to Rodney Wood] located at Rodney
Wood archive.

Goff, L. (1977), [27 July 1977 letter to Rodney Wood] located at Rodney Wood
archive.

Guardian (1957), [18 July 1957 Letter from the Editor of the Manchester
Guardian] Located at: Stephen Joseph Papers, Rylands Library, University of
Manchester.

Guthrie, T. (1954), [30 November 1954 letter to Stephen Joseph] located at:
Stephen Joseph Papers, Rylands Library, University of Manchester.

Harland, R. (2008), [13 May 2008 email to Paul Elsam] Located at Elsam
archive.

Hobson, H. (1957a), [24 October 1957 letter to Stephen Joseph] located at:
Stephen Joseph Papers, Rylands Library, University of Manchester.

— (1957b), [17 October 1957 letter to Stephen Joseph] located at: Stephen
Joseph Papers, Rylands Library, University of Manchester.

— (1957c), [25 September 1957 letter to Stephen Joseph] located at: Stephen
Joseph Papers, Rylands Library, University of Manchester.

Hodgkinson, J. (1962), [4 July 1962 letter to Stephen Joseph] quoted *in* Lane, T.
2006: *The Full Round – The Several Lives and Theatrical Legacy of Stephen
Joseph*: 170 (Rome: Duca della Corgna)

Jones, D. (1959a), [10 July 1959 letter to Stephen Joseph] located at: Stephen
Joseph Papers, Rylands Library, University of Manchester.

— (1959b), [3 August 1959 letter to Stephen Joseph] located at: Stephen Joseph Papers, Rylands Library, University of Manchester.

Jones, P. (2009a), [18 December 2009 email to Paul Elsam] at Elsam archive.

Joseph (1955b), [24 June 1955 letter to Harold Hobson] located at: Stephen Joseph Papers, Rylands Library, University of Manchester.

Joseph, S. (1955d), [17 February 1955 letter to Mr Smettem at the Scarborough Corporation Libraries Committee] located at Scarborough Library Archive.

— (1955e), [17 February 1955 letter to Mervyn Edwards, Director of the Scarborough Corporation Libraries Committee] located at Scarborough Library Archive.

— (1956b), [23 October 1956 Letter to Literary Editor of *Observer*] located at: Stephen Joseph Papers, Rylands Library, University of Manchester.

— (1957a), [20 April 1957 Letter to George Devine] located at: Stephen Joseph Papers, Rylands Library, University of Manchester.

— (1957b), [11 May 1957 letter to Mrs Layton] located at Rodney Wood archive.

— (1957b), [17 May 1957 Letter to Editor of The *Guardian*] located at: Stephen Joseph Papers, Rylands Library, University of Manchester

— (1957c), [25 April 1957 letter to George Devine] located at: Stephen Joseph Papers, Rylands Library, University of Manchester.

— (1957d), [30 September 1957 letter to Mr Edwards] located at: Stephen Joseph Papers, Scarborough Library.

— (1957f), [3 December 1957 letter to unknown person] located at: Stephen Joseph Papers, Rylands Library, University of Manchester.

— (1957g), [14 May 1957 letter to 'Mervyn'] located at: Stephen Joseph Papers, Scarborough Library.

— (1957h), [24 September 1957 letter to Mr Edwards] located at: Stephen Joseph Papers, Scarborough Library.

— (1957j), [6 August 1957 letter to J. W. ('Jimmy') James] located at: Bob Watson Archive, Stephen Joseph Theatre, Scarborough.

— (1957k), [12 October 1957 letter to Mr Edwards] located at: Stephen Joseph Papers, Scarborough Library.

— (1958a), [6 December 1958 letter to Harold Pinter] located at: Stephen Joseph Papers, Rylands Library, University of Manchester.

— (1958b), [4 May 1958 letter to Colin Wilson] located at: Stephen Joseph Papers, Rylands Library, University of Manchester.

— (1958c), [17 April 1958 letter to Margaret Rawlings] located at: Stephen Joseph Papers, Rylands Library, University of Manchester.

— (1958d), [24 May 1958 letter to 'Mary'] located at: Stephen Joseph Papers, Rylands Library, University of Manchester.

— (1958e), [9 April 1958 letter to George Devine] located at: Stephen Joseph Papers, Rylands Library, University of Manchester.

— (1958f), [24 December 1958 letter to Jo Hodgkinson] located at: Stephen Joseph Papers, Rylands Library, University of Manchester.

— (1958g), [8 February 1958 letter to Michael Barry] located at: Stephen Joseph Papers, Rylands Library, University of Manchester.

— (1958i), [19 February 1958 letter to Harold Hobson] located at: Stephen Joseph Papers, Rylands Library, University of Manchester.

— (1958j), [30 April 1958 letter to 'Uncle Lionel'] located at: Stephen Joseph Papers, Rylands Library, University of Manchester.

— (1958k), [19 February 1958 letter to Harold Hobson] located at: Stephen Joseph Papers, Rylands Library, University of Manchester.

— (1958m), [30 January 1958 letter to Professor Dobree] located at: Stephen Joseph Papers, Rylands Library, University of Manchester.

— (1958n), [13 February 1958 letter to Editor of the *Observer*] located at: Stephen Joseph Papers, Rylands Library, University of Manchester.

— (1958o), [26 January 1958 letter to Mr Dobie] located at: Stephen Joseph Papers, Rylands Library, University of Manchester.

— (1958p), [8 February 1958 letter to Michael Barry] located at: Stephen Joseph Papers, Rylands Library, University of Manchester.

— (1958q), [23 April 1958 letter to 'Elma'] located at: Stephen Joseph Papers, Rylands Library, University of Manchester.

— (1958r), [30 January 1958 letter to Campbell Allen] located at: Stephen Joseph Papers, Rylands Library, University of Manchester.

— (1958s), [6 May 1958 letter to 'Jimmy' James] located at: Bob Watson Archive at the Stephen Joseph Theatre, Scarborough.

— (1958t), [28 October 1958 letter to 'Jimmy' James] located at: Bob Watson Archive at the Stephen Joseph Theatre, Scarborough.

— (1958u), [11 November 1958 letter to 'Jimmy' James] located at: Bob Watson Archive at the Stephen Joseph Theatre, Scarborough.

— (1958v), [26 April 1958 letter offered for publication] located at: Bob Watson Archive at the Stephen Joseph Theatre, Scarborough.

— (1959a), [19 March 1959 letter to ABC Television] located at: Stephen Joseph Papers, Rylands Library, University of Manchester.

— (1959b), [16 February 1959 letter to W. A. Darlington] located at: Stephen Joseph Papers, Rylands Library, University of Manchester.

— (1959c), [22 February 1959 letter to W. A. Darlington] located at: Stephen Joseph Papers, Rylands Library, University of Manchester.

— (1959e), [12 February 1959 letter to Mervyn Edwards] located at: Stephen Joseph Papers, Scarborough Library.

— (1959h), [31 March 1959 letter to Mervyn Edwards] located at: Stephen Joseph Papers, Scarborough Library.

— (1959i), [19 March 1959 letter to SJ to Howard Thomas] located at: Stephen Joseph Papers, Rylands Library, University of Manchester.

— (1959j), [3 August 1959 letter to David Jones] located at: Stephen Joseph Papers, Rylands Library, University of Manchester.

— (1959k), [24 September 1959 letter to Bernard Miles] located at: Stephen Joseph Papers, Rylands Library, University of Manchester.

— (1959m), [8 July 1959 letter to 'Dick' at the Arts Council of Great Britain] located at: Stephen Joseph Papers, Rylands Library, University of Manchester.

— (1959o), [16 January 1959 letter to the Lord Chamberlain's Office] located at: Stephen Joseph Papers, Rylands Library, University of Manchester.

— (1960a), [19 December 1960 letter to Phyllis Kramer] located at: Stephen Joseph Papers, Rylands Library, University of Manchester.

— (1960b), [25 April 1960 letter to editor of *New Theatre* magazine] located at: Stephen Joseph Papers, Rylands Library, University of Manchester.

— (1960d), [15 October 1960 letter to Maurice Plows] located at: Stephen Joseph Papers, Rylands Library, University of Manchester.

— (1960e), [25 October 1960 letter] located at: Stephen Joseph Papers, Rylands Library, University of Manchester.

— (1960f), [12 December 1960 letter to Richard Southern] located at: Stephen Joseph Papers, Rylands Library, University of Manchester.

— (1960g), [20 December 1960 letter to James Roose-Evans] located at: Stephen Joseph Papers, Rylands Library, University of Manchester,

— (1960h), [29 December 1960 letter to Tyrone Guthrie] located at: Stephen Joseph Papers, Rylands Library, University of Manchester.

— (1960i), [25 August 1960 letter to Dona Martyn] located at: Stephen Joseph Papers, Rylands Library, University of Manchester.

— (1961b), [1 May 1961 letter to Alan Stockwell] located at: Stephen Joseph Papers, Rylands Library, University of Manchester.

— (1961c), [26 July 1961 letter to Alan Stockwell] located at: Stephen Joseph Papers, Rylands Library, University of Manchester.

— (1961d), [13 April 1961 letter to Alan Ayckbourn] located at: Stephen Joseph Papers, Rylands Library, University of Manchester.

— (1961j), [13 April 1961 letter to Alan Ayckbourn] located at: Stephen Joseph Papers, Rylands Library, University of Manchester.

— (1961f), [10 April 1961 letter to Alan Stockwell] located at: Stephen Joseph Papers, Rylands Library, University of Manchester.

— (1961g), [4 April 1961 letter to Editor of *The Sunday Times*] located at: Stephen Joseph Papers, Rylands Library, University of Manchester.

— (1961h), 20 July 1961 letter to the Editor of the *Stage*.

— (1961i), [24 August 1961 letter to Alan Stockwell] located at: Stephen Joseph Papers, Rylands Library, University of Manchester.

— (1962), 1 February 1962 letter to the Editor of the *Stage*.

— (1963b), [25 November 1963 letter to Ian Watson] located at Rodney Wood archive.

— (1964b), 15 October 1964 letter to the Editor of the *Stage*.

— (1964d), 12 November 1964 letter to the Editor of the *Stage*.

— (1966), [11 March 1966 letter to Rodney Wood] located at Rodney Wood archive.

Lewsen, C. (1978), [20 August 1978 letter to Rodney Wood] located at Rodney Wood archive.

Lintlaker, N. V. (1958), [3 October 1958 letter to Stephen Joseph] located at:
Stephen Joseph Papers, Rylands Library, University of Manchester.
— (1977), [8 March 1977 letter to Rodney Wood] located at Rodney Wood archive.
Lord Chamberlain (1959), [21 January 1959 letter to Stephen Joseph] located at:
Stephen Joseph Papers, Rylands Library, University of Manchester.
Loveland, A. (2008), [30 January 2009 email from CSSD Librarian to Paul
Elsam] located at Elsam archive.
Marshall, S. (1979), [19 January 1979 letter to Rodney Wood] located at Rodney
Wood archive.
McAlpine, J. (1960), [28 July 1960 letter to drama critic at *Punch*] located at:
Stephen Joseph Papers, Rylands Library, University of Manchester.
Mitchley, J. (1976), [28 July 1977 letter to Rodney Wood] located at Rodney Wood
archive.
Morley, S. (1998b), [15 March 1998 letter to Peter Cheeseman] located at:
Stephen Joseph Theatre archive, Scarborough.
Observer (1955), [12 May 1955 letter to Stephen Joseph from the Arts Editor of
the *Observer*] located at: Stephen Joseph Papers, Rylands Library, University
of Manchester.
Perry, J. (1955), [23 May 1955 letter to Stephen Joseph] located at: Stephen
Joseph Papers, Rylands Library, University of Manchester.
Pinter, H. (1958a), [letter to editor of *The Play's The Thing*' October 1958] quoted
in Pinter, H. (2005, 2nd ed.): *Various Voices: Prose, Poetry, Politics 1948–2005*
(Faber).
— (1958b), [2 October 1958 letter to Stephen Joseph] located at: Stephen Joseph
Papers, Rylands Library, University of Manchester.
— (1958c), [12 October 1958 letter to Stephen Joseph] located at: Stephen
Joseph Papers, Rylands Library, University of Manchester.
— (1959), [9 August 1959 letter to Stephen Joseph] located at: Stephen Joseph
Papers, Rylands Library, University of Manchester.
— (1979), [15 February 1979 letter to Rodney Wood] located at Rodney Wood
archive.
Priestley, J. B. (1955a), [19 April 1955 letter to Stephen Joseph] located at:
Stephen Joseph Papers, Rylands Library, University of Manchester.
— (1959), [10 June 1959 letter to Stephen Joseph] located at: Stephen Joseph
Papers, Rylands Library, University of Manchester.
Ramsay, M. (1960), [15 February 1960 letter to Stephen Joseph] located at:
Stephen Joseph Papers, Rylands Library, University of Manchester.
— (1962), [3 December 1962 letter to Alan Plater] located at: Alan Plater Papers,
Brynmor Jones Library, University of Hull.
— (1963), [1 October 1963 letter to Reg Colin at ABC-TV] located at: Stephen
Joseph Papers, Rylands Library, University of Manchester.
— (1963a), [29 January 1963 letter to Alan Plater] located at: Alan Plater Papers,
Brynmor Jones Library, University of Hull.
— (1963b), [1 October 1963 letter to Reg Colin at ABC-TV] located at: Alan
Plater Papers, Brynmor Jones Library, University of Hull.

— (1964), [31 March 1964 letter to Reg Colin at ABC-TV] located at: Alan Plater Papers, Brynmor Jones Library, University of Hull.

Saunders, J. (1958), [8 December 1958 letter to Stephen Joseph] located at: Stephen Joseph Papers, Rylands Library, University of Manchester.

Sims, S. (2013), [17 April 2013 email to Paul Elsam] located at Elsam archive.

Southern, R. (1960), [10 December 1960 letter to Stephen Joseph] located at: Stephen Joseph Papers, Rylands Library, University of Manchester.

Stockwell, A. (1961a), [6 April 1961 letter to Stephen Joseph] located at: Stephen Joseph Papers, Rylands Library, University of Manchester.

— (1964), 22 October 1964 letter to The *Stage*.

Stott, M. (1979), [22 October 1979 letter to Rodney Wood] located at: Rodney Wood archive.

The Stage (1959), [March 1959 letter from M. Plows to the *Stage*] located at Bob Watson archive at the Stephen Joseph Theatre, Scarborough.

Thomas, H. (1959a), [6 April 1959 letter to Stephen Joseph] located at: Stephen Joseph Papers, Rylands Library, University of Manchester.

— (1959b), [21 April 1959 letter to Stephen Joseph] located at: Stephen Joseph Papers, Rylands Library, University of Manchester.

Thomson, P. (1977), [11 April 1977 letter to Rodney Wood] located at the Rodney Wood archive.

— (1998), [24 July 1998 letter to Stacey Morley] located at Elsam archive.

— (2008), [29 January 2008 email to Paul Elsam] located at Elsam archive.

— (2008b), [29 January 2008 email to Paul Elsam] located at Elsam archive.

— (2008c), [3 December 2008 email to Paul Elsam] located at Elsam archive.

— (2010), [28 April 2010 email to Paul Elsam] located at Elsam archive.

Tynan, K. n. d., letter to Stephen Joseph located at: Stephen Joseph Papers, Rylands Library, University of Manchester.

Vincent Wallis, H. (1977), [15 August 1977 letter to Rodney Wood] located at Rodney Wood archive.

Watson, I. (1962), 1 February 1962 letter to the Editor of the *Stage*.

Weller, M. (2009a), [19 May 2009 email to Paul Elsam] located at Elsam archive.

— (2009b), [13 September 2009 email to Paul Elsam] located at Elsam archive.

Wilson, C. (1957), [29 September 1957 letter to Stephen Joseph] located at: Stephen Joseph Papers, Rylands Library, University of Manchester.

— (1957b), [14 October 1957 letter to Stephen Joseph] located at: Stephen Joseph Papers, Rylands Library, University of Manchester.

— (1957c), [29 September 1957 letter to Stephen Joseph] located at: Stephen Joseph Papers, Rylands Library, University of Manchester.

— (1958), [6 May 1958 letter to Stephen Joseph] located at: Stephen Joseph Papers, Rylands Library, University of Manchester.

Winch, J. (1956a), [13 August 1956 letter to Stephen Joseph] located at: Stephen Joseph Papers, Rylands Library, University of Manchester.

— (1956b), [21 October 1956 letter to Stephen Joseph] located at: Stephen Joseph Papers, Rylands Library, University of Manchester.

— (1957), [11 January 1957 letter to Stephen Joseph] located at: Stephen Joseph Papers, Rylands Library, University of Manchester.

— (1958), [16 July 1958 letter to Stephen Joseph] located at: Stephen Joseph Papers, Rylands Library, University of Manchester.

Witts, N. (2012), 20 April 2012 email response to Paul Elsam.

Wood, R. (1959), [15 January 1959 letter] located at: Stephen Joseph Papers, Scarborough Library.

— (2009a), [21 December 2009 email to Paul Elsam] located at Elsam archive.

— (2009b), [26 October 2009 letter to Paul Elsam] located at Elsam archive.

Section 3: Printed and online reviews and articles

Ayckbourn, A. (1974), quoted in *Daily Mail,* 26 August 1974.

— (1996), quoted in *The Times,* 10 April 1996, *n.p.*

Benedick, A. (1998), [12 November 1998 obituary of Peter Cotes] in *TheIndependent* located at http://www.independent.co.uk/arts-entertainment/obituary-peter-cotes-1184306.html.

Billington, M. (2006), http://arts.guardian.co.uk/features/story/0,1836056,00.html.

— (2007a), The *Guardian,* G2 section, 24 October 2007.

— (2008), *Fighting Talk in* The *Guardian,* 03.05.08 *at* http://www.guardian.co.uk/books/2008/may/03/theatre.stage.

Birmingham Post (1959), [13 January 1959 article] located at: Stephen Joseph Theatre archive, Scarborough.

Birmingham Weekly Post (1959), [16 January 1959 article] located at: Stephen Joseph Theatre archive, Scarborough.

Boyd, M. (2008), Review section in *The Observer,* 25 January 2008.

Campton (1970), [talk at the 1970 Drama Festivals Conference] quoted in *Amateur Stage* Vol XXV No 4, April 1970.

Campton, D. (1970), *[lecture for the 1970 Drama Festivals Conference] reported in Amateur Stage volume XXV No 4, April 1970.*

Chaillet, N. (2008), The *Stage,* 31 December 2008.

Curtis, S. (2010), *The Stage,* 11 February 2010.

'D. G.' (1959), 11 January 1959 article in *Manchester Guardian.* located at: The Bob Watson Archive, Stephen Joseph Theatre, Scarborough.

Darlington, W. A. (1958), [May 1958 review of *The Birthday Party*] in *The Daily Telegraph.*

Daily Mail (1960), 8 March 1960 review.

Ellis, S. (2003), The *Guardian at* http://www.guardian.co.uk/stage/2003/apr/23/theatre.samanthaellis.

Elsam, P. (2010), 20 April 2010 lecture. Stephen Joseph versus the Establishment at http://str.org.uk/events/lectures/archive/index.html.

Encore (2007), 15.05.07 article *at* http://www.encoretheatremagazine.co.uk/?p=76.

— (2008), 06.01.08 article at http://www.encoretheatremagazine.
co.uk/?p=90#more-90.

Evening Sentinel (1963), 1 January 1963 review located at http://
christmasvmastermind.alanayckbourn.net/CVM_Reviews.htm.

Gardner, L. (2011), [19 October 2011 Theatre Blog *in* The *Guardian*] at http://
www.guardian.co.uk/stage/theatreblog/2011/oct/19/flatpack-touring-
theatre-paines-plough.

Gascoigne (1959), [10 January 1959 article *in Birmingham Post*] located at:
Stephen Joseph Theatre archive, Scarborough.

Gazette and Herald (1960), [2 September 1960 article] located at: Bob Watson
archive at the Stephen Joseph Theatre, Scarborough.

Gomm, T. (1956), [4 August 1956 review in the *Socialist Leader*] located at: Bob
Watson archive at the Stephen Joseph Theatre, Scarborough.

Guardian (1956a), 20 September 1956 article.

— (1956b), 24 November 1956 article.

— (1961a), [16 January 1961 article] located at: Bob Watson archive at the
Stephen Joseph Theatre, Scarborough.

— (1961b), [4 February 1961 review] located at: Bob Watson archive at the
Stephen Joseph Theatre, Scarborough.

— (2006a), 12 August 2006 article.

— (2006b), [quotation from Daniel Farson in the Daily Mail in 1956, reported
in *Guardian*] 12.08.06, *n.p.*

Haydon, A. (2008), 4 June 2008 article in the *Guardian* at http://www.guardian.
co.uk/stage/theatreblog/2008/jun/04/onceinawhilea.

Hobson, H. (1958a), *The Sunday Times*, 25 May 1958.

— (1958b), *The Sunday Times*, January 1958.

Joseph, S. (1957e), *No New Playwrights?* Article *in Encore*, June/July 1957.

— (1960c), article in *New Theatre Magazine*, July 1960 located at: Elsam
archive.

Krishnamurti, J. n.d., at http://www.awaresilence.com/Page-9.html.

Leigh, M. (2010), Peter Cheeseman obituary by Robin Thornber *in* the
Guardian at http://www.guardian.co.uk/stage/2010/apr/29/peter-cheeseman-
obituary.

Marowitz, C. (2006), *The Coronation of Harold Pinter at* http://www.swans.com/
library/art12/cmarow61.html.

Marriott, R. B. (1961), *Theatre World*, September 1961.

Max, T. (2006), David Campton obituary *in* The *Stage*, 2 October 2006 located
at http://www.thestage.co.uk/features/obituaries/feature.php/14327/david-
campton.

Murgatroyd, S. (2009), Stephen Joseph located *at* http://www.sjt.uk.com/
stephen-joseph.asp.

— n.d., (a) http://mrwhatnot.alanayckbourn.net/MW_Productions.htm.

— n.d., (b) http://actors.alanayckbourn.net/.

— n.d.: (d) http://biography.alanayckbourn.net/styled-22/page41/index.html.

New School (2009), biographical summary, located *at* http://www.newschool.
edu/drama/faculty.aspx?id=9468.

New Vic Theatre, n.d., http://www.newvictheatre.org.uk/history-2.

O'Mahoney, J. (2005), 12 February 2005 article on Peter Hall *in* The *Guardian*
located *at* http://www.guardian.co.uk/stage/2005/feb/12/rsc.theatre.

Paines Plough (2012), 9 November entry on company website *at* http://www.
painesplough.com/blog/roundabout/roundabout-throughout-history/.

Pinter, H. (1980), *Daily Telegraph*, 2 June 1980.

Plays and Players (1955), article located *at* Bob Watson archive at the Stephen
Joseph Theatre, Scarborough.

Pratt, D. (1956), [review in the *Yorkshire Post*, 24 August 1956] located at: Bob
Watson archive at the Stephen Joseph Theatre, Scarborough.

Ritchie, H. (2006), 12 August 2006 article in The *Guardian*.

Robinson, D. (2005), [23 June 2005 obituary of Disley Jones in the *Guardian*]
located *at* http://www.guardian.co.uk/news/2005/jun/23/guardianobituaries.
artsobituaries.

Scarborough Evening News (1955), [12 August 1955 review] located at: Bob
Watson archive at the Stephen Joseph Theatre, Scarborough.

— (1956a), [20 July 1956 review] located at: Bob Watson archive at the Stephen
Joseph Theatre, Scarborough.

— (1956b), [21 July 1956 article] located at: Bob Watson archive at the Stephen
Joseph Theatre, Scarborough.

Sheffield Star (1960), [15 August 1960 article] located at: Bob Watson archive at
the Stephen Joseph Theatre, Scarborough.

Shorter, E. (2005), [22 August 2005 obituary of Clifford Williams in The
Guardian] located at http://www.guardian.co.uk/news/2005/aug/22/
guardianobituaries.artsobituaries.

Shrapnel, N. (1955), [15 July 1955 review in the *Manchester Guardian*] located at:
Bob Watson archive at the Stephen Joseph Theatre, Scarborough.

The Stage (1956), 30 August 1956 review.

— (1955), [18 August 1955 review] located at: Bob Watson archive at the
Stephen Joseph Theatre, Scarborough.

— (1956), [30 August 1956 review] located at: Bob Watson archive at the
Stephen Joseph Theatre, Scarborough.

— (1961a), 13 July 1961 review.

— (1961b), 16 July 1961 article.

— (1962), 16 August 1962 article.

— (1963), 1 August 1963 advertisement.

— n.d., electronic copy held in Elsam archive.

— (1960), 10 March 1960 review.

Strachan, A. (2005), [23 August 2005 obituary of Clifford Williams *in* The
Independent] located *at* http://www.independent.co.uk/news/obituaries/
clifford-williams-503961.html.

Sutherland, J. (2006), *The Daily Telegraph* (n.p., n.d.) located at: The Bob Watson Archive, Stephen Joseph Theatre, Scarborough.

The *Daily Telegraph* (1960), 8 March 1960 review.

— (2005), [9 March 2005 obituary of Clifford Williams] located at http://www.telegraph.co.uk/news/obituaries/1496742/Clifford-Williams.html.

— (1961), [31 January 1961 article] held electronically in Elsam archive.

Theatre World (1960), [April 1960 review] located at: Bob Watson archive at the Stephen Joseph Theatre, Scarborough.

Thornber, R. (2010), [29 April 2010 obituary on Peter Cheeseman] *at* http://www.guardian.co.uk/stage/2010/apr/29/peter-cheeseman-obituary.

The Times (1957), [26 November 1957 theatre review] held electronically in Elsam archive.

— (1960a), 22 July 1960 article *Mr Pinter's Concession.*

— (1960b), [14 March 1960 theatre review] held electronically in Elsam archive.

— (1961), [6 February 1961 theatre review] held electronically in Elsam archive.

— (1967), [7 October 1967 obituary article] reported in Wood, R, 1979, *Stephen Joseph: His Work and Ideas,* unpaginated third page (Cardiff: University College, *n.p.*).

— (2006), [21 September 2006 obituary on David Campton] located at http://www.timesonline.co.uk/tol/comment/obituaries/article645713.ece.

— (2010), 3 May 2010 obituary on Peter Cheeseman located at http://www.timesonline.co.uk/tol/comment/obituaries/article7114452.ece.

Toynbee, P. (1956), *Unlucky Jims* – 27 May 1956 article in *The Observer.*

Trewin, J. C. n.d., [review of Stephen Joseph's *The Story of the Playhouse in England*] – on rear dust sheet of Joseph's *Theatre in the Round.*

Tynan, K. (1955), [11 September 1955 article in the *Observer*] located at *Guardian/Observer* online archive *at* http://guardian.chadwyck.co.uk/password.

— (1956), *Oxford as a Start For a Career On StageinPretoria News* January 1956.

Wardle, I. (1958), [September 1958 article *Comedy of Menace*] *in Encore Magazine.*

Watson, I. (2002), *An American (Back) in London* located *at* http://www.whatsonstage.com/index.php?pg=207&story=E8821036332859.

Williams, F. (2008), 6 May 2008 letter to Editor, The *Guardian.*

Wolverhampton Express and Star, (1959), [16 January 1959 article] located at: The Bob Watson Archive, Stephen Joseph Theatre, Scarborough.

Wood, R. (2008), [4 January 2008 article *A Man of Influence*] in The *Stage.*

Yorkshire Post, (1955), [12 August 1955 review] located at: Bob Watson archive at the Stephen Joseph Theatre, Scarborough.

Section 4: Interviews

Ayckbourn, A. (1972), interview in Wood, R. Davies, 1979: *Stephen Joseph: His Work and Ideas* (Cardiff: University College, *n.p.*).

— (1983), March 1983 edition of *Marxism Today.*

— (1997), 29 July 1997 interview by Stacey Morley located at http://www. playwrites.net/playwrights/1999/f_june/AlanAyckbourn1.html (accessed on 10 January 2008).

— (1998), 2 April 1998 interview by Stacey Morley located at Elsam archive.

— (2001), interview by D. Lefkowitz *in Playbill,* 6 February 2001 *at* http://www. playbill.com/features/article/65051.html.

— (2002), interview by C. Coulson posted on 25 January 2002 *at* http://www. durham21.co.uk/index.php/2002/01/an-hour-with-sir-alan-ayckbourn.

— (2005), 19 July 2005 interview for American Theatre Wing, at http://itunes. apple.com/podcast/atw-downstage-center/id74195482.

— (2007), 26 July 2007 interview by Paul Elsam located at Elsam archive.

— (2009), 16 October 2009 interview by Jan Bee Brown located at Elsam archive.

— (2010), 6 February 2010 interview by Nick Utechin *in The Oxford Times.*

— (2012), 29 June 2012 interview by Liz Green located at http://www.bbc.co.uk/ radio/player/p00tdn8v.

Cheeseman, P. (1998), 18 May 1998 interview by Stacey Morley located at Elsam archive.

— (2004), 11 November 2004 interview by Kate Dorney located at http://www. bl.uk/projects/theatrearchive/cheeseman.html.

— (2008), 24 April 2008 interview by Paul Elsam located at Elsam archive.

Goodhead, C. (2008), 10 December 2008 interview by Paul Elsam located at Elsam archive.

Griffiths, T. (2008), 8 July 2008 interview by Paul Elsam located at Elsam archive.

Grotowski, J. (1969), interview by Prof Margaret Croyden at Creative Arts Television.

Hall, P. (2010), 1 November 2010 interview by Michael Billington in *The Guardian* at http://www.guardian.co.uk/stage/2010/nov/01/sir-peter-hall-at-80.

Hall, W. (2007), 13 July 2007 interview by Paul Elsam located at Elsam archive.

Harris, D. (2007), 23 July 2007 interview with Paul Elsam located at Elsam archive.

Hogg (2008), 10 July 2008 interview with Paul Elsam located at Elsam archive.

Hunnings, N. (2010), 20 April 2010 interview by Paul Elsam located at Elsam archive.

Jaffe, S. (2007), 24 July 2007 interview with Paul Elsam located at Elsam archive.

Kingsley, B. (2008), 18 July 2008 interview by Paul Elsam located at Elsam archive.

Landis, H. (2007), 5 December 2007 interview by D. Meehan for Theatre Archive Project, at http://www.bl.uk/projects/theatrearchive/landis.html.

— (2008), 8 September 2008 interview by Paul Elsam located at Elsam archive.

Mason, M. (2003), [26 September 2003, interview by Rachel Baxter] located at http://www.bl.uk/projects/theatrearchive/mason.html.

Petherbridge, J. (2010), 23 April 2010 interview by Paul Elsam located at Elsam archive.

Pinter, H. (2008), interview by Harry Burton for The British Library, 8 September 2008 located *at* http://www.bl.uk/onlinegallery/whatson/downloads/files/pinter.mp3.

Plater, A. (2007), 7 September 2007 interview by K. Harris at http://www.bl.uk/projects/theatrearchive/plater4.html.

— (2007), interview *at* http://www.bl.uk/projects/theatrearchive/plater4.html.

— (2008), 8 September 2008 interview with Paul Elsam located at Elsam archive.

Ravenhill, M. (2010), 1 April 2010 interview by Paul Elsam located at Elsam archive.

Stoney, H. (2007), 26 July 2007 interview by Paul Elsam located *at* Elsam archive.

Taylor, G. (1998), 30 June 1998 interview by Stacey Morley located at: Elsam archive.

Watson, I. (1998), 20 April 1998, interview by Stacey Morley located at Bob Watson archive at the Stephen Joseph Theatre, Scarborough.

Williams, F. (2008), 7 September 2008 interview by Paul Elsam located at Elsam archive.

Wilson, C. (2006), phone interview by Guy Leigh: 'Colin Wilson, Part One' located *at* http://www.astraeamagazine.com.

Section 5: Unpublished works

Allen, R. (1959), *Love After All* [playscript].

— (1960), *Dad's Tale* [playscript].

Baker, C. F. (1961), *Report of the Auditor to the Members of Studio Theatre Limited*, 4 April 1961. Located *at* Stephen Joseph Papers, Scarborough Library.

Campton, D. (1955), *Dragons Are Dangerous* [playscript].

Cheeseman, P. (2005), *Summary of Published Books with References* located at Cheeseman archive (ref. Romy Cheeseman).

Elsam, P. (2008), video image of artefact recorded prior to interview with Faynia Williams, 7 September 2008.

Goodhead, C. (2007), [*Stephen Joseph's Theatre in the Round in 1965* (memoir, unpub.)] located at: Bob Watson archive at the Stephen Joseph Theatre, Scarborough.

Joseph, S. (1953), playscript of *The Key* located at Elsam manuscript archive, Scarborough.

— (1956a), playscript *Professor Taranne* located at Elsam Archive, Scarborough.

— (1959g), [30 June 1959 Studio Theatre Ltd Year End Report] located at: Stephen Joseph Papers, Scarborough Library.

— (1963c), [confidential 1963 Studio Theatre Ltd Report] located at: Stephen Joseph Papers, Scarborough Library.

— (1965), [design for University of Lancaster Drama Centre] located at: Stephen Joseph Papers, Rylands Library, University of Manchester.

— n.d., f, image file for *The Bed Life of a Mad Boy* located at: Bob Watson archive at the Stephen Joseph Theatre, Scarborough.

— n.d., g, unfinished novel located at: Stephen Joseph Papers, Rylands Library, University of Manchester.

Morley, S. (1998a), *Stephen Joseph – Lunatic or Visionary Pioneer?* (Arden School of Theatre, *n.p.*).

Murgatroyd, n.d., List of new plays at the Library Theatre & Victoria Theatre (1955–67) located at Bob Watson archive at the Stephen Joseph Theatre, Scarborough.

Murgatroyd, S. (2008), *Stephen Joseph Theatre List of Plays 1955 – Present Day* located at The Bob Watson Archive, Stephen Joseph Theatre, Scarborough.

Note 1, n.d., note on cover of Joseph, n.d. *Professor Tarranne*, located at: Stephen Joseph Papers, Rylands Library, University of Manchester.

Saunders, J. (1959), *Alas Poor Fred* manuscript located at Elsam manuscript archive, Scarborough.

Stockwell, A. (1961b), [typescript for *Bed Life of a Mad Boy*] located at Elsam archive.

Thomson, P. (2008a), [*Sixty Years of University Drama Departments* – 20 February 2008 lecture at the Society for Theatre Research] STR Archive recording made by Norman Tozer – copy held at Elsam archive.

Williams, C. n.d., [typescript for *The Disguises of Arlecchino*] located at Elsam archive.

Wood, R. (1979), *Stephen Joseph: His Work and Ideas* (Cardiff: University College, *n.p.*)

Section 6: Online resources

Campton, D. n.d, *http://www.samuelfrench-london.co.uk/sf/Pages/feature/campton.html.*

doollee.com, n.d., (a): http://www.doollee.com/PlaywrightsS/saunders-james-a.html.

— n.d., (b): *http://www.doollee.com/PlaywrightsW/williams-clifford.html#37181.*

— n.d., (c): http://doollee.com/PlaywrightsC/campton-david.html.

Florance, J. n.d., at http://www.samuelfrench-london.co.uk/sf/Pages/feature/campton.html.

Gardner, L. (2012), theatre review at http://www.guardian.co.uk/stage/2012/sep/26/roundabout-lungs-review.

Guardian, 6 May 2012 at http://www.guardian.co.uk/stage/poll/2012/mar/06/tweet-seats-in-theatres-poll?INTCMP=ILCNETTXT3487.

Harry Ransom Centre, University of Texas, n.d., at http://research.hrc.utexas.edu:8080/hrcxtf/view?docId=ead/00171.xml.

Iqbal, N., [listings in The *Guardian* newspaper] at http://www.guardian.co.uk/culture/2010/oct/17/insider-guide-to-arts.

Jamesaunders.org, n.d., (a): http://www.jamessaunders.org/jsobtg.htm.

— n.d., (b): http://www.jamessaunders.org/jsobtr.htm.

— n.d., (c): http://www.jamessaunders.org/jsobtt.htm.

Lane, n.d., at http://terrylane.it.

Lane, T. (2006b), 'The Full Round – what they said' at http://www.terrylane.it/
  pag.htm.

— n.d., profile at http://terrylane.it/index.htm.

Lovett, J. (2012), theatre review at http://www.thestage.co.uk/reviews/review.
  php/37460/the-roundabout-season-one-day-when-we-were.

Murgatroyd, S. (2008), interview with Alan Ayckbourn at http://
  standingroomonly.alanayckbourn.net/SRO_AAQuotes.htm.

Pemberton-Billing, R. n.d., at http://www.octagonbolton.co.uk/1967–1977.

Roughan, R. H. (2012), theatre review at http://oxfordstudent.com/2012/10/18/
  lungs-leaves-us-breathless-the-paines-plough/

Spacey, K. (2009), http://www.wnyc.org/shows/lopate/2009/apr/07/the-norman-
  conquests/.

Todd, A. (2008), at http://news.bbc.co.uk/1/hi/entertainment/7636220.stm.

University of Glasgow, n.d., introduction to archives at http://special.lib.gla.
  ac.uk/sta/search/detaild.cfm?DID=46944.

University of Kent, n.d., [archival record identiying production pogramme] *at*
  http://library.kent.ac.uk/library/special/html/specoll/BOUCSHA4.HTM.

Wright, T. (2013), at http://www.york.ac.uk/media/library/documents/
  borthwick/Alan%20Ayckbourn%20Resource%20Pack%20final.pdf.

Index